In Search of a Moral Foundation for Capitalism

The search for a moral foundation for capitalism has a long history that continues to unfold, yet many are unaware of this search or its implications for the future of capitalism. The recent pandemic has uncovered cracks in the foundation of capitalism and raised doubts regarding its ability to meet the broader needs of society. *In Search of a Moral Foundation for Capitalism* explains the continuing demand for a moral foundation from the perspective of business leaders, business educators, and policymakers and tells the story of the search for that moral foundation through its leading characters. By presenting the life stories and writings of these leading characters – from Adam Smith to Amartya Sen – this book reveals the rich moral critique provided by these great thinkers and explains how that rich critique was lost through the influence of the Chicago School and its emphasis on self-interest.

Douglas E. Stevens is Professor and Copeland-Deloitte Chair in Accountancy at Georgia State University. His research extends traditional economic theory by incorporating social and moral norms and appears in top academic journals and a book entitled, *Social Norms and the Theory of the Firm* (Stevens 2019, Cambridge University Press).

In Search of a Moral Foundation for Capitalism

From Adam Smith to Amartya Sen

DOUGLAS E. STEVENS

Georgia State University

CAMBRIDGE UNIVERSITY PRESS

Shaftesbury Road, Cambridge CB2 8EA, United Kingdom

One Liberty Plaza, 20th Floor, New York, NY 10006, USA

477 Williamstown Road, Port Melbourne, VIC 3207, Australia

314–321, 3rd Floor, Plot 3, Splendor Forum, Jasola District Centre,
New Delhi – 110025, India

103 Penang Road, #05–06/07, Visioncrest Commercial, Singapore 238467

Cambridge University Press is part of Cambridge University Press & Assessment,
a department of the University of Cambridge.

We share the University's mission to contribute to society through the pursuit of
education, learning and research at the highest international levels of excellence.

www.cambridge.org
Information on this title: www.cambridge.org/9781009434393

DOI: 10.1017/9781009434423

First published 2024

Printed in the United Kingdom by TJ Books Limited, Padstow, Cornwall

A catalogue record for this publication is available from the British Library

*A Cataloging-in-Publication data record for this book is available from the
Library of Congress*

ISBN 978-1-009-43439-3 Hardback

To my parents Edwin and Priscilla,
two pastor's kids whose romance survived being apart during
the Korean War
and whose moral values are imprinted on my heart and mind

Contents

Preface

In this book, I tell the story of the search for a moral foundation for capitalism. Despite its long history, many are unaware of this search and its implications for the future of capitalism. Something has gone wrong in capitalist societies across the world, and renewing this search may be the critical challenge of our age. As commonly happens during times of social and economic upheaval, the recent global pandemic has raised doubts regarding the ability of capitalism to meet the broader needs of society. This has led to a resurgence of Marxist ideology in the West, but Marxist socialism has produced tepid economic growth and harsh authoritarian regimes wherever it has been tried. The political economists highlighted in this book viewed Marxism as a utopian idea that threatened a free society. Yet, they also viewed unregulated capitalism as a utopian idea that threatened capitalist society. Their attempt to address the vulnerabilities and excesses of unregulated markets helped save capitalism from Marxism in their time, yet their insightful moral critique has largely been lost. This book seeks to resurrect that moral critique.

I witnessed first-hand the social and economic upheaval brought on by the global pandemic as the Director of the School of Accountancy at Georgia State University from 2018 to 2021. Within months of the COVID lockdowns in the spring of 2020, demonstrators filled Atlanta's streets smashing windows, looting, and burning businesses. Instead of supporting law enforcement and the rule of law, city leaders seemed paralyzed and gave the rioters free reign as large corporations and foundations funneled millions of dollars to their progressive causes. The administrators at GSU dealt with the lockdown the best they could. As with other departments heads, I was called upon to quickly shift from taking courses fully online, to planning for deep budget cuts and layoffs, to addressing renewed concerns regarding diversity, equity, and inclusion (DEI). While I joined my faculty and staff in setting up an office in my home and conducting meetings and classes online, I also made weekly trips to my downtown office amid boarded-up buildings and the wandering homeless.

I had always emphasized the importance of social and moral norms in my MBA and graduate accounting courses. My strongest pedagogical tool was my own research demonstrating how the economic theory of the firm could be enhanced by incorporating such norms. I had just published a book on the topic and was beginning to use it in my classes and in workshops for accounting and business groups. During the pandemic, however, I found myself being asked to discuss the challenges of directing a highly diverse accounting program at an urban university. I was placed on discussion panels with speakers who used critical race theory and social Marxism in their efforts to promote new DEI initiatives. My own experience had convinced me that we could not survive as an academic institution by pitting one race or ethnicity against another. In my leadership role, I also participated in AACSB accreditation visits at other business schools to assess their programs designed to address the new social realities brought about by the pandemic. Far too often, I found that these programs lacked a theoretical framework that could support capitalism and yet address the new social challenges facing capitalist society.

My three-year term as Director in the middle of the pandemic left me exhausted and disillusioned. Fortunately, my contract included two years of summer funding to "restart" my research agenda. The first summer I purchased airline tickets to the United Kingdom and arranged housing at Glasgow and Oxford to continue my research on Adam Smith, the father of modern economic theory. When the day of my departure arrived, however, the United Kingdom had imposed a two-week quarantine for travelers arriving from the United States. Given the uncertainty of travel and shifting COVID mandates, I spent my first research summer in Atlanta finishing up neglected research projects and beginning new ones. I also spent time alone at a family lake house in northern Georgia pondering my future. I had planned to develop a follow-up book on the general topic of Adam Smith's moral theory and its ability to support capitalist society. After realizing how much the Chicago School had distorted his writings, however, I decided to shift my research focus to the dominant paradigm in economics. As a result of that shift in focus, I spent my second research summer at Stanford University combing through the Hoover Institution Archives for new insights on Milton Friedman and the other main characters in the formation of the Chicago School.

In my first book (Stevens 2019), I had presented Adam Smith's moral theory based on social norms and discussed how that moral foundation had been lost due to the influence of a group of neoclassical economists associated with the University of Chicago. Although Smith maintained his moral foundation for capitalism throughout his writings, the Chicago School reinvented him as the originator of their neoclassical theory based on narrow self-interest and highly efficient markets. To provide further motivation for the book's topic, I had included a chapter describing the importance of social norms in the development of capitalism. After struggling with the social upheaval of the pandemic, however, I had become sensitized to the critical challenge of our age – *the ability of capitalism to meet the broader needs of society.* In attempting to explain the content of my first book to friends and colleagues, I would jokingly say it was about "the moral foundation for capitalism." That now became the topic of my second book.

My first book begins by confronting Milton Friedman's (1953) methodological argument against the need for realistic assumptions in economic theory. Thus, it begins with the narrow neoclassical theory out of Chicago and uses historical insights and the latest theoretical and empirical research to show how adding social norms enhances that theory. I have begun to call this approach, which has been endorsed by Nobel Prize–winning economists such as Vernon Smith and Amartya Sen, the "New Chicago School." By contrast, this second book begins by addressing the continuing demand for a moral foundation for capitalism. In particular, this book begins from the perspective of business leaders, business educators, and policymakers and maintains that perspective as I tell the story of the historical search for a moral foundation for capitalism. As such, this book is targeted for those who are tired of the "straightjacket of self-interest" and are eager to unleash the promise of capitalism to all members of capitalist society.

This book continues many of the major themes of my first book. For example, I continue the theme of revealing the real Adam Smith to the reader, including his rich moral theory based on social norms. I also continue the theme that social norms can readily be incorporated within the rigorous theory of the firm developed by the Chicago School. In this book, however, I introduce extended historical context to emphasize new themes of importance to modern-day capitalism. For example, I discuss the lives and writings of economists who attempted to address the social challenges of early capitalism during the industrial revolution, including Max Weber, R. H. Tawney, and Karl Polanyi. The moral critiques of capitalism provided by these political economists helped fight back the Marxist threat during the social upheaval of two world wars and the Great Depression, yet they also attempted to explain how early industrial capitalism contributed to that upheaval. I also discuss the life and writings of John Maynard Keynes, who played a significant role in saving capitalism from Marxist socialism and fascism in the West.

I also highlight the writings of leading neoclassical economists associated with the Chicago School to show how they left capitalism with a moral foundation based on narrow self-interest. In particular, I present the writings of Milton Friedman, George Stigler, and Michael Jensen during the peak of their influence to demonstrate how they purposefully rejected any motivation in economics other than narrow self-interest. I also present Ayn Rand's moral theory based on the glorification of self-interest and demonstrate how it represents a natural extension of the Chicago School's straitjacket of self-interest. Further, I discuss how leading neoclassical economists such as Vernon Smith and Michael Jensen have joined the search for a moral foundation for capitalism after emerging evidence in experimental economics and the near collapse of the global financial system in 2007–08. Finally, I discuss Amartya Sen's search for a moral foundation from India and how it led him back to the real Adam Smith. I conclude the unfolding story of the search for a moral foundation by summarizing its insights, including some from my own search, and discussing the implications for business leaders, business educators, and policymakers.

While I was completing the final editing for this book in the fall of 2022, the story broke regarding the sudden bankruptcy of cryptocurrency exchange FTX and the investor fraud perpetuated by its founder and CEO, Sam Bankman-Fried (SBF). The FTX case represents all that has gone wrong with modern capitalism in the wake of the COVID pandemic. SBF had become a media darling by promoting business ethics and a unique moral theory that encouraged amassing great wealth to promote progressive causes. Evidence revealed in bankruptcy court, however, suggested that SBF had used FTX customer assets to bail out his hedge fund Alameda Research, lend himself $1 billion, purchase vacation homes for his family and friends, and become the second largest contributor to the democratic party after George Soros. In the chaos of poor record-keeping and nonexistent corporate governance, a substantial amount of FTX's customer assets were reported missing. The bankruptcy of FTX and related companies ensnared millions of individual and institutional investors. The fifty largest creditors alone were owed more than $3 billion. In the end, up to $10 billion in funds may have evaporated in an investor fraud that has been described as rivaling Enron, Lehman Brothers, and Bernie Madoff.

The FTX investor fraud was precisely what Milton Friedman warned about in his famous 1970 article arguing that the only purpose of the corporation was to earn profits for its shareholders. SBF was heavily influenced by a unique moral theory called "effective altruism." That moral theory apparently supported his lavish lifestyle featuring constant computer gaming, rampant drug use, and polyamorous sexual relations. As this book reveals, the utopian hedonism of SBF and his small group of friends raises similarities with a young John Maynard Keynes and his elite friends at Cambridge and Bloomsbury. After two world wars and the Great Depression, however, an older and wiser Keynes rejected the utopian hedonism of his youth and embraced a more traditional moral system based on responsibility and duty. That moral system led him to reject both the individualism of unregulated capitalism and the collectivism of Marxist socialism. In their war against Keynesianism, however, the Chicago School of Economics emphasized self-interest and left little room for social or moral responsibility. The FTX case illustrates the ongoing demand for a moral foundation for capitalism. Unfortunately, Milton Friedman never gave that much thought.

Readers will notice that my brief foray into economic history in my first book has become a full-blown obsession. That is attributable to several factors. First, I have taught from that book in my accounting and MBA courses and my students have repeatedly asked me to explain how the Chicago School could get so much wrong about Adam Smith and his view of political economy. Second, I have felt compelled to address tired, old Marxist arguments against capitalism that have been recycled during the recent pandemic. These arguments come from a unique period of history in the late nineteenth and early twentieth centuries that led a group of "moral economists" to develop a rich critique of capitalism. In telling the story of those moral economists, therefore, I identify the source of the Chicago School's misinterpretation of Adam Smith and address the Marxist ideology attempting to make a comeback in the West. Nevertheless, I do not attempt a systematic critique of Marx's illiberal system and provide only a limited description of the path to restoring Adam Smith's moral foundation. The first topic has received ample coverage elsewhere for the interested reader (e.g., Schumpeter 1942/1950) and the second topic awaits a third book by the author.

After the global market crash of 2007–08, Richard Posner (2009) admitted that the causes and cures of economic depressions had not progressed to the point at which ideology no longer influences analysis. The same can be said of most all economic analysis, including the analysis of pandemics or global warming. It would serve us well to retain a healthy humility regarding the uncertainties of science and the ever-present threat of ideological bias. Unfortunately, the current discussion of economics and public policy is too often dominated by the latter. It is my hope that by presenting the unfolding story of the search for a moral foundation for capitalism, this book will help heal the deep social divisions that have emerged in the wake of the global pandemic. It is also my hope that this book will help return the field of economics to its historical roots in moral philosophy and the social sciences. Finally, readers will notice that this book describes my own search for a moral foundation for capitalism. This autobiographical approach serves a particular purpose. In addition to disclosing my own limited conclusions and potential ideological bias, I hope to encourage readers to join me in this important search and reach their own conclusions.

Acknowledgments

As a Ph.D. student at Indiana University in the early 1990s, I was fortunate to study accounting and economics under a group of talented researchers who were trained in the dominant paradigm out of Chicago yet open to alternative theoretical perspectives. This included a group of behavioral researchers who applied theory in psychology and sociology in their experimental research. When I learned that Indiana had a group of economists who used experimental methods to test the assumptions and predictions of that dominant paradigm, however, I was hooked. I became an experimental economist in the tradition of Vernon Smith, Mark Isaac, Jim Cox, Shyam Sunder, and Glenn Harrison. I owe a special debt of gratitude to my behavioral dissertation co-chairs, Joe Fisher and Mike Tiller. I am also deeply indebted to Arlie Williams, one of Vernon Smith's former Ph.D. students who taught me the value of experimental economics and became a friend, mentor, and coauthor. I have also benefitted greatly from the broad liberal arts education I received at Spring Arbor College and the rigorous MBA program I endured with the engineering students at the Krannert School of Management at Purdue University. My MBA program at Purdue turned me into a "quant," but I have retained the "poet" from my undergraduate days.

Research attempting to extend the powerful economic theory out of Chicago has a long history in accounting. I stand on the shoulders of many talented researchers in my own discipline who have developed powerful experiments to test the robustness of the assumptions and predictions of the dominant paradigm. Pathbreaking experimental economists in accounting who have come before me include Joyce Berg at Iowa, John Dickhaut at Minnesota and Chapman, Harry Evans and Don Moser at Pittsburgh, Steve Kachelmeier at Texas, Ron King at Washington University, Shyam Sunder at Yale, Mark Young at USC, and Rick Young at Ohio State. I also have benefitted greatly from economic theorists in accounting who have incorporated social norms into their models, including Paul Fischer at Pennsylvania (Wharton), Brian Mittendorf at Ohio State, and Mark Penno at Iowa. Daniel Arce at UT Dallas has also incorporated social and moral norms into traditional economic models. Accounting researchers have also led the way in providing archival evidence that social norms affect financial reporting and corporate governance including Linda Bamber at Georgia, David Larcker at Stanford, and Bill Mayew at Duke. As an associate editor at *Behavioral Research in Accounting*, I have benefitted from working with two excellent senior editors who have helped me advance experimental economics research in accounting: Steve Salterio at Queens and Charlie Bailey at James Madison.

I am deeply indebted to the many biographers I relied upon to tell the life stories of my leading characters. For *Adam Smith*, I relied on Nicholas Phillipson as well as my mentor at the University of Glasgow, Christopher Berry. For *Max Weber*, I relied on his biographer Lawrence Scaff as well as his wife, Marianne Weber. Tim Rogan's book on the moral economists was an invaluable resource for the life stories of *R. H. Tawney* and *Karl Polanyi*. I also benefitted greatly from Lawrence Goldman's biography of Tawney and Kari Polanyi Levitt's writings on her father. Of course, I relied heavily on Robert Skidelsky's three-volume biography for *John Maynard Keynes*. For the story of the *Chicago School*, I relied on the memoirs of Milton and Rose Friedman and George Stigler as well as the archives at the Hoover Institution. In addition to her invaluable help accessing the archives at Hoover, I relied on Jennifer Burns for the life story of *Ayn Rand*. I turned to the two-volume memoirs of *Vernon Smith* for his story and for *Michael Jensen* I relied on Rakesh Khurana's detailed account of his role in the development of the university-based business school. Finally, for *Amartya Sen*, I relied on his recently completed memoir that arrived just in time for me to add important details regarding his life story. While the life stories in this book are heavily documented and historically accurate to the greatest extent possible, I have taken some creative liberties to make the characters "come alive" to the reader. Any errors in fact or interpretation, of course, are entirely the fault of the author.

I owe a special debt to the J. Mack Robinson College of Business at Georgia State University for generous financial support during the writing of this book. This includes financial support I received as the James E. & Patricia W. Copeland Deloitte Chair in Accountancy. Jim Copeland had a particular interest in my research as the former CEO of Deloitte's global firm and a leader in his church, and his untimely death in 2018 has left me without a major source of inspiration. I also lost a major source of inspiration from the passing of Bill Mulcahy who, along with Richard Chambers, has been an example of consistent moral leadership at the Institute for Internal Auditors. I also have been inspired by the many talented CFOs and controllers I have met during my time on the advisory board of the Deloitte Center for Controllership, directed by Beth Kaplan and Vijay Pinto. My research has benefitted from the generous funding of the Center for the Economic Analysis of Risk (CEAR) at the Robinson College of Business, directed by Glenn Harrison. Joint funding by CEAR and the School of Accountancy have allowed me to organize research conferences on the topics of social norms, formal and informal controls, and the Chicago School. I also have benefitted from conferences organized by the finance department at Robinson, including Financial Leadership Network conferences cosponsored by the McCracken Alliance.

My three years as an administrator at a major business school have given me a deep appreciation for the heavy responsibility of leadership in academia, business, and government. As such, I would like to thank Dean Richard Phillips at Robinson and former Dean of Florida State University's College of Business, Caryn Beck-Dudley, for their strong leadership and for promoting professional ethics at their home institutions as well as in business schools across the globe through the AACSB. I would also like to thank the accounting partners and other dedicated members of my advisory board at the School of Accountancy during my time as Director. I would also like to acknowledge the support I have received over the years from the faith community, including colleagues and friends in the Protestant, Catholic, Mormon, Jewish, Muslim, and Hindu faiths. While my own Christian faith tradition played a major role in the development of capitalism and continues to dominate capitalist societies in the West, the largest capitalist country in the world is now India where Hindu and Muslim faiths dominate. Thus, I find Amartya Sen's rediscovery of Adam Smith's moral foundation particularly encouraging for the future of capitalism.

I want to thank the editorial staff at Cambridge University Press, especially publishing editor of economics and political science Robert Dreesen, editorial assistant Sable Gravesandy, content manager Jessica Norman, project manager Snadha Suresh Babu, and copyeditor Shamili

Rajan. Two outside reviewers provided especially useful insights and pushed me to discuss more of my own search and conclusions, which I was hesitant to do at first. In particular, one reviewer challenged me to provide the reader with suggestions for restoring the moral perspective of Adam Smith that has been removed by the Chicago School. While I leave a fuller treatment of that challenge to a future book, I have added suggestions to Chapter 8 inspired by a recent global research conference I attended in Melbourne, Australia. As such, I would like to thank the organizers of that conference, especially Christo Karuna of Monash University and Wim Van der Stede of the London School of Economics. I also thank graphic artist Christian Coppoletti for his art and design work on the book cover and my agent D. J. Snell at the Legacy Agency for his continued encouragement and valuable legal advice. I have also benefitted greatly from the social media advice of Marco Ciavolino, a former MBA student of mine at GSU who has become a valued advisor and friend.

Finally, I would like to thank my wife Carol for her endless patience and flexibility during my extended writing periods and research travels. This book required that I focus deeply on my leading characters, including their backgrounds, countries, times, and personalities. I have walked in their shoes and feel like I know them intimately. Carol had to endure my excursions into their worlds and the frequent absence from her world. Now that she has met my characters through my writing and research, she fears that my deep focus resembles the Asperger's of Adam Smith and Vernon Smith. I look forward to returning to normal life, however, including the occasional round of golf with my wife and friends at the Georgia Club. I also thank my daughter and two stepsons and their families for enduring my absence or distracted presence during the writing of this book. I especially look forward to being a better "bumpa" to my grandkids. As I was writing this book, I never stopped thinking about them and the world we are leaving for future generations.

Introduction

The Continuing Demand for a Moral Foundation

There are obviously many economists who still believe that self-interest is the dominant human motive. There's no doubt that it's a very important human motive ... but I think most people who aren't in that narrow tradition realize that other motives are important, too. We try to get ahead of our rivals, but we also care about other people and wish them well. We don't take advantage of every conceivable opportunity to gain at the expense of others. Students exposed to the narrow self-interest model often don't like it; they often feel alienated by it.

Robert H. Frank
An Interview with Robert H. Frank

A Harvard Business School professor has recently written about "the economist's straightjacket" or "the unquestioning and universal acceptance by economists of self-interest – of shareholders, managers, and employees – as the conceptual foundation for business design and management" (Simons 2019, 2). The inability to think beyond narrow self-interest can be attributed to the rising influence of a group of prominent economists associated with the University of Chicago after the 1970s. Nobel Prize winners in economics have questioned the commitment to narrow self-interest within their field, including Amartya Sen (awarded in 1998) and Vernon Smith (awarded in 2002). Yet, the powerful influence of the "Chicago School" ensures that the straightjacket of self-interest remains in place in economics as well as the sister disciplines of finance and accounting. Through its continuing influence on business education in general, the economist's straightjacket also impacts business practice, public policy, and public opinion regarding capitalism itself. In this introductory chapter, I address the continuing demand for a moral foundation for capitalism from the perspective of business leaders, business educators, and policymakers.[1]

1.1 THE DEMAND FROM BUSINESS LEADERS

On August 19, 2019, the Business Roundtable announced the release of a new Statement on the Purpose of a Corporation. Signed by 181 CEOs of America's leading corporations, the Statement represented a significant departure from previous statements issued by the Business Roundtable for over twenty years (since 1997). While expressing continued support for free-market capitalism, the new Statement challenged business leaders to ensure "that the benefits of capitalism flow to every American." In particular, it extended corporate responsibility beyond the interests of shareholders to other stakeholders of the firm including employees, customers, suppliers, creditors, and the communities where the corporation resides and does business. According to a lead author, "It was time to reflect more accurately how our CEOs operate their companies and to challenge each other to do more" (Business Roundtable 2019).

After releasing its new Statement on the Purpose of a Corporation, the Business Roundtable welcomed public comments on its website. As expected, critics on the left expressed deep skepticism regarding the ability of corporations to reform themselves after decades of corporate scandals and related market crashes including the dotcom crash of 2000 and the mortgage market crash of 2007–08. Surprisingly, however, critics on the right expressed equally deep skepticism because they viewed the new statement as a veiled descent into socialism. As I read through the comments, it became clear to me that the discussion was dominated by the powerful influence of the Chicago School. Milton Friedman and George Stigler cited the eighteenth-century Scottish philosopher Adam Smith as the poster child for their economic theory based on narrow self-interest. As Friedman made clear in a 1970 article in *The New York Times*, their theory left the corporation with no direct social responsibility other than to increase profits for its shareholders.[2]

---

[1] As the epigraph to this chapter states (Schmotter 1998), students exposed to the assumption of narrow self-interest in economics often don't like it. It typically takes years of training and indoctrination for students to set aside their own moral beliefs and accept this behavioral assumption as an inevitable aspect of capitalism.

[2] In his strongly worded article, Friedman (1970) stated that business leaders who believed the firm should take seriously "its responsibilities for providing employment, eliminating discrimination, avoiding pollution and whatever else may be the catchwords of the contemporary reformers ... (were) preaching pure and unadulterated socialism."

The new Statement on the Purpose of a Corporation by the Business Roundtable reflected the continuing search for moral legitimacy among business leaders in capitalist society. In his book, *From Higher Aims to Hired Hands: The Social Transformation of American Business Schools and the Unfulfilled Promise of Management as a Profession*, Rakesh Khurana (2007, 14) characterized legitimacy as the currency of capitalist institutions: "For organizations in general, legitimacy is an important aspect of the social fitness that enables them to secure advantages in economic and political markets and improve their chances of survival." Written immediately before the great market crash that threatened capitalism in 2007–08, Khurana (2007, 366) emphasized the need for corporate managers to look beyond the narrow self-interest of shareholders:

In a world increasingly characterized by collaborative systems rather than rigid hierarchies, where public attention to the consequences of corporate activity now focuses on issues such as global labor standards and environmental degradation, and where a vacuum in global political leadership has left the world rudderless in a period of enormous economic and social upheaval, the purpose of management and corporate leadership necessarily goes beyond "maximizing shareholder value." It is not hyperbole to suggest that business is at a unique inflection point calling for a fundamental reconsideration of the meaning of corporate leadership.

Prior to the powerful influence of the Chicago School, the Business Roundtable emphasized the corporation's responsibility to other stakeholders of the firm besides shareholders. The new Statement on the Purpose of the Corporation, therefore, represented a delayed response to what Khurana saw as an urgent need for business leaders to return to the social and moral concerns of an earlier era. The COVID pandemic in 2020 led to further soul-searching among business leaders due to the unevenness of the economic hardship and the social unrest it unleashed. The shareholder primacy view promoted by the Chicago School, however, left corporate leaders with little moral legitimacy on which to fall back on. Consistent with Khurana's (2007) thesis, these leaders often caved to the progressive agenda of the far left to signal moral legitimacy and secure advantages in economic and political markets. The backlash from their more moderate stakeholders was as rapid as it was predictable.

Privately funded initiatives by business corporations provide further evidence of the continuing demand for a moral foundation for capitalism. I witnessed such a funding initiative while a member of the accounting faculty at Florida State University. In the summer of 2008, FSU received a $1,500,000 grant from BB&T Bank "to encourage a thorough discussion of the moral foundations of capitalism." The agreement letter between BB&T and the University, however, made clear that the bank supported a moral foundation built on narrow self-interest. The BB&T grant required the Economics Department at FSU to establish a new course on "Morals and Ethics in Economic Systems" featuring Ayn Rand's novel, *Atlas Shrugged* (Rand 1957). Even when providing valuable funds to support the search for a moral foundation for capitalism, therefore, BB&T was unable to escape the straightjacket of self-interest.

Fortunately, economists at FSU did not limit their discussion of the moral foundations of capitalism to Rand's novel glorifying self-interest or the Chicago School's narrow interpretation of Adam Smith's *Wealth of Nations*. To explain emerging evidence from their own experimental research, these economists applied insights from Adam Smith's other major work, *The Theory of Moral Sentiments*. As an accounting professor who conducted experimental economics research, I attended weekly workshops with the experimental economics faculty and joined the monthly workshop series funded by BB&T entitled, "Economics and Moral Sentiments" (EMS). I later learned that BB&T funded similar programs at over sixty colleges and universities across the United States including Chapman, Charleston, Duke, George Mason, North Carolina Chapel Hill, Virginia, and Wake Forest. Similar to FSU, many of the faculty at these schools found narrow self-interest an insufficient moral foundation for capitalism.[3]

Business leaders also communicate the need for a moral foundation for capitalism through conferences and workshops. For example, I was invited to attend a three-day conference sponsored by Koch Industries at their world headquarters in Wichita, KS, in July 2010. I was an associate professor at the time, and it was not unusual for me to attend conferences during the summer to present my research. At this conference, however, we listened to top executives at Koch and participated in group discussions among faculty who had been hand-picked and flown-in from across the country. This included faculty in accounting, economics, engineering, ethics, entrepreneurship, finance, law, marketing, and philosophy.

[3] Other researchers have questioned BB&T's private funding of a moral foundation for capitalism based on the Chicago School's straightjacket of narrow self-interest (see Beets 2015). Although I share their general concerns and have never received any direct funding from BB&T, I have personally benefitted from the valuable contributions made to the field through their funding initiative. BB&T merged with SunTrust Bank to form Truist Bank in 2022.

The purpose of the conference was to promote an innovative management system developed by Koch called "Market-Based Management" (MBM). Koch had recently established a new business unit called MBM University to teach its management system to faculty at colleges and universities across the country. The conference included presentations from leaders at the newly formed MBM University.

Surprisingly, much of the discussion at the conference involved the need to encourage virtue and integrity in business. In the opening session, the VP of Academic Programs warmed up the crowd by stating that the pursuit of profit was a moral pursuit. This statement was met by enthusiastic nods and noises of agreement from the audience. He continued by asserting that a lack of free-market thinking at colleges and universities was destroying *economics*. This assertion was met with more nods and noises of agreement. He also asserted that free-market thinking without virtue and integrity was destroying *business*. This assertion was also met with general agreement, but I sensed a noticeable reduction in enthusiasm. I could tell that the mere mention of virtue and integrity made many in the audience uncomfortable. Although capitalism had arisen in the West under a set of moral norms supported by religion (Weber 1905/2002; Tawney 1926/2017), most business school faculty had removed all discussion of such norms from their research and teaching.

At the end of the opening session, I took advantage of a short break to scroll through incoming emails on my laptop computer. I sighed as I observed the high volume of emails from MBA students complaining about their final grade in my recently completed summer course on financial reporting and managerial control. It seemed that students expected better grades for less work each passing year. As the faculty director of our MBA program, I was always attempting to hold the line on our academic rigor. More concerning, I noticed a growing lack of appreciation for topics related to professional ethics and corporate social responsibility. This should not have surprised me, however, since business schools as a rule rarely emphasized such topics. As with other leading business schools, FSU's finance and accounting departments relied heavily on the modern finance theory out of the Chicago School. That theory was based on narrow self-interest and provided little support for professional ethics. I wondered if business schools were contributing to the lack of virtue and integrity that the speaker said was destroying business. Perhaps that is why Koch had begun inviting business faculty to their MBM conferences instead of just economics faculty.

An important email caught my eye. One of my Ph.D. students had forwarded me a new draft of a paper we currently had on the third round at *The Accounting Review*. The paper presented the results of an experimental study we had conducted examining the effect of a code of ethics on manager trustworthiness and investor trust using the investment game in Berg, Dickhaut, and McCabe (1995). On the first two rounds at the journal, two reviewers had asked us to make relatively minor changes to our motivation and statistical analysis. After satisfying the two reviewers, however, the editor insisted that we develop a comprehensive theory that was able to explain our key result that the code of ethics only improved manager trustworthiness and investor trust when the manager signed off on the code. The stakes were very high on this round. My Ph.D. student needed the publication for a good placement upon graduation, and I needed it for any hope of promotion to full professor at FSU.[4]

The second presenter at the MBM conference was CEO Charles Koch. A tall, trim man who conveyed considerable authority camouflaged by midwestern charm, he welcomed us to the firm he had taken over from his father in 1967 at the age of thirty-two. Along with his younger brother David, he had built Koch Industries into a large industrial conglomerate that included holdings in petroleum, chemicals, energy, paper, and ranching. After graduating from MIT with a bachelor's degree and two master's degrees in engineering, he spent his spare time studying history, economics, and philosophy. This had left him with a strong belief in science, rationality, and free-market capitalism. As background reading we had each received a copy of his best-selling book, *The Science of Success: How Market-Based Management Built the World's Largest Private Company* (Koch 2007), as well as a list of readings from such free-market thinkers as F. A. Hayek and Michael Polanyi. Koch and the other conference speakers quoted freely from these sources, which emphasized the power of markets to achieve superior outcomes in the economy.

During the discussion sessions, it became clear that many faculty at the conference shared Charles Koch's unshakable belief in free-market capitalism based on scientific rationality and narrow self-interest. It appeared to be a sign of intellectual purity to claim to be a libertarian or

---

[4] Fortunately, we found the ideal comprehensive theory in Bicchieri's (2006) model of social norm activation. After being assigned to another senior editor, that editor not only accepted our paper at *TAR* but asked us to include Bicchieri's formal model in the paper (Davidson and Stevens 2013).

follower of Ayn Rand. While at FSU, I had been exposed to the use of Rand's "Objectivist Ethics" as a moral foundation for capitalism through BB&T's funding initiative. I felt uncomfortable with Rand's rationalist, anti-religious views and her glorification of narrow self-interest. Further, my theoretical and experimental research demonstrated that narrow self-interest was a poor behavioral assumption and that adding preferences for norm-based behavior made the theory of the firm more descriptive, prescriptive, and pedagogically useful. While I shared Koch's support for free-market capitalism, I was beginning to think that Chicago's neoclassical theory and Ayn Rand's moral philosophy were destroying *both* economics and business.

At one of the group sessions, I met a professor who was Distinguished Chair in Business Ethics from a Catholic university. He also was uncomfortable with Rand's moral foundation for capitalism because of its glorification of narrow self-interest and its anti-religion bias. He agreed with me that Koch Industries had no real theoretical support for their emphasis on values and integrity. He told me he used insights from classical moral philosophy and the Catholic religion to build a moral foundation for capitalism. I told him about the norm-based behavior emerging in experimental economics and how many of my colleagues at FSU had rediscovered Adam Smith's first book on moral sentiments. I also told him that my interactions with the experimental economists at FSU had motivated me to study Smith's life and writings in more depth. He told me he had not considered using Adam Smith's writings in his own quest to form a moral foundation for capitalism, but he thought it could be a fruitful area.

Charles Koch and the speakers at the MBM conference clearly supported free-market capitalism and rejected the Marxist ideology arising at American universities. By restricting their discussion to the self-interested view out of Chicago, however, they left capitalism vulnerable to its detractors in academia. Although I was well trained in the neoclassical theory out of Chicago, I knew that it could not explain emerging evidence of norm-based behavior in the lab or reliance on norm-based organizational controls such as a code of ethics. I had just published a formal model with a coauthor showing that the traditional theory of the firm was better able to explain contracting behavior with the assumption of a promise-keeping norm (Stevens and Thevaranjan 2010). Thus, I knew well that the neoclassical theory out of Chicago was unable to support Koch's emphasis on values and integrity in their MBM system. The MBM conference, however, represented a watershed event in my own search for a moral foundation for capitalism as it confirmed the continuing demand for such a moral foundation among business leaders.[5]

I.2 THE DEMAND FROM BUSINESS EDUCATORS

The founding of the university-based business school was a product of the search for moral legitimacy among business executives. There was a grave concern during the Second Industrial Revolution in America (1870–1920) that the emerging business corporations generated by early capitalism would use their great wealth and power to lord it over all of society. This concern was heightened by the opportunism displayed by "Robber Barons" in banking and industry and the failure of many corporate leaders to acknowledge any responsibility for the broader social good.[6] This crisis of moral legitimacy represented a threat to American democracy that generated two responses in the population. Populist sentiment sought to dismantle large corporations altogether while progressive reformers sought to use such corporations to address the vexing social problems that had arisen in capitalist society. In this environment, an influential group of business educators leveraged their social and economic resources to create a unique legitimizing institution for business management: the university-based business school (Khurana 2007).

University-based professional schools can be traced back to the original founding of colleges and universities in medieval Europe. Church-funded institutions of higher learning were founded primarily for the training of clergy through the teaching of theology and the liberal arts. State-funded institutions, on the other hand, were founded for the training of civil servants through the teaching of professions such as law, medicine, and later, accounting (Soll 2014). Similar to the first English universities at Oxford (1096) and Cambridge (1209), the first American universities were sectarian institutions of higher learning that focused on theology and the liberal arts. This included Harvard (1636), William and Mary (1693), and Yale (1701). By contrast, Benjamin Franklin encouraged the

---

[5] Other researchers have questioned Koch's previous funding of republican campaigns and efforts to stall climate change legislation (see Leonard 2019). Although I share their general concerns and have never received any direct funding from Koch, I have personally benefitted from Charles Koch's books and efforts to support responsible capitalism in America. I discuss Koch's recent contributions to this important effort in Chapter 8 (Koch and Hooks 2020).

[6] The opportunism of business leaders during the second industrial revolution is epitomized by J. P. Morgan's quip in 1901, "I owe the public nothing" (Marchand 1998).

founding of an institution of higher learning that, while based on the Protestant religion, was nonsectarian and included instruction in practical skills such as grammar, arithmetic, accounting, and other business skills. The new institution opened in his home state in 1751 and became known as the University of Pennsylvania by 1791 (Isaacson 2003).[7]

The first university-based business school was founded at the University of Pennsylvania in 1881 through a large donation by Joseph Wharton, a devout Quaker who had made a fortune in the steel and nickel industries. Wharton was motivated by what he perceived as the need for moral training and character formation in business education. In particular, he envisioned a business education that would elevate not only technical competence but also social consciousness and moral character worthy of a profession. Wharton's professionalism project took over the role formerly played by private business schools that had proliferated across the young nation and became the model for all university-based business schools founded over the next forty years (Khurana 2007). Similar to the professions of law and medicine, the founders of the university-based business school sought to transmit norms of business conduct from one generation to the next. These professional norms included integrity, honesty, and trustworthiness as well as transparency and accountability. A particularly important professional norm in the eyes of the founders was *disinterestedness* or the ability of the business professional to place the interests of those whom they worked for above their own (Stevens 2019).

The professionalism project of the founders of the university-based business school was granted greater urgency during the Great Depression. Upon becoming dean of the Wharton School in 1933, economist Joseph Willits portrayed the Great Depression as a summons to the newly formed business schools to direct their gaze beyond the problems of business to the broader needs of the nation (Sass 1982). In a meeting of the American Association of Collegiate Schools of Business that same year (AACSB 1933, 255–256), Harvard professor Clyde Ruggles emphasized the need for business schools to study and teach professional standards of business conduct:

---

[7] The oldest institution of higher learning has been traced back to the Buddhist university at Nalanda in modern day Patna, India. The university at Nalanda educated thousands of students each year from many countries in the world from the fifth century to the end of the twelfth century and was reestablished as Nalanda University in 2014 (Sen 2022, 105). Under the Frankish kingdom of Charlemagne in medieval Western Europe, there was a substantial cultivation of the liberal arts, Roman history, and early Christian history as far back as the late eighth and early ninth centuries (McKitterick 2008, 369).

The business schools have a clear challenge to study standards of business conduct, and to furnish instruction which will give a clear perspective of the social responsibility of business men... (U)niversity education in business will be incomplete in a vital respect if our studies of the field of business do not recognize the obligations of these schools to aid in raising the standards of business conduct. If the business schools do not accept this challenge, they will not only fail to justify their existence as part of modern university education but they will also fail to make the greatest possible contribution to business itself.

The university-based business school was founded by institutional economists at a time when their own departments were becoming increasingly dominated by neoclassical economists. Institutional economists used primarily case studies and plant visits in their research and emphasized the role of power, values, belief systems, and historical contingency. Neoclassical economists, in contrast, used primarily mathematical models and large data sets in their research and emphasized the role of markets, contracts, trade, and property rights. Given the large difference in emphasis and methodology, the founders of the university-based business school rooted their curriculum in institutional economics and made deliberate decisions to maintain independence from economics departments within their universities. Similar to the mother discipline, however, the influence of neoclassical economists soon swamped the influence of institutional economists in the newer business disciplines.

The demand for a moral foundation for capitalism continues to inspire and motivate business educators. While at FSU, for example, I was heavily involved in a special dean's committee to encourage discussions of business ethics at the business school. The committee was called the "Business Ethics Roundtable" and was funded by alumni and corporate organizations including the Cecil B. Day Foundation. I was a member of the Business Ethics Roundtable from 2006 to 2008 and was its chair from 2009 to 2011 before becoming faculty director of the MBA program from 2011 to 2013. Over this time, I recruited speakers from academia and practice to discuss business ethics at faculty and student workshops. I found that academic speakers applied abstract theory from moral philosophy with little direct application to business practice. Practitioners, in contrast, presented practical insights from their work experience or involvement in large fraud cases such as Enron and WorldCom but provided few insights that could be applied to business theory.

During this time, I was attending weekly research workshops with the experimental economics faculty at FSU. Thus, I was being exposed to the latest experimental research revealing preferences for social norms such as reciprocity and fairness. Further, my own experimental research examining predictions from the theory of the firm was revealing preferences for social norms such as honesty, responsibility, reciprocity, and fairness. I was also working on a principal-agent model with an agency theorist at Syracuse University demonstrating how the model could be enhanced by incorporating a norm for promise-keeping. Our model, which was eventually published in *Accounting, Organizations, and Society* (Stevens and Thevaranjan 2010), demonstrated that adding social norms made the theory of the firm more descriptive, prescriptive, and pedagogically useful. I began to use my theoretical and experimental research in my graduate courses and in presentations to business groups to encourage professional ethics in business.[8]

The ongoing effort by business educators to promote professional ethics has been supported by the Association to Advance Collegiate Schools of Business (AACSB). The AACSB was established in 1916 by an elite group of business deans committed to supporting the professionalism project of the founders of the university-based business school.[9] This group included Edwin Gay of Harvard University, Leon Marshall of the University of Chicago, and A. E. Swanson of Northwestern University. These business deans were all progressive reformers who sought to legitimize management education by attaching it to the high-status institutions of science, the professions, and the university. In particular, they viewed the establishment of the university-based business school as consistent with the general goal of the university to use social science and research as the means to a better society (Khurana 2007).

The demand for a moral foundation for capitalism is particularly strong in my own discipline of accounting, which includes the specialties of auditing, financial accounting, managerial accounting, and tax accounting. As an independent profession within the business school, accounting programs across the globe have their own AACSB accreditation standards. Because of its importance to the profession, accounting programs must demonstrate instruction in professional ethics to achieve AACSB accreditation. The theoretical frameworks commonly used to teach professional ethics, however, are incompatible with the underlying economic theory used by accountants in their research. As the Director of the School of Accountancy at GSU from 2018 to 2021, I helped design a program to teach professional ethics in our undergraduate and graduate

[8] I present further details of the principal-agent model in Stevens and Thevaranjan (2010) in Chapter 2 on Adam Smith and his moral foundation for capitalism.

[9] Because of its original focus on American business schools, the organization was initially named the "American Association of Collegiate Schools of Business."

accounting programs based on Adam Smith's moral foundation for capitalism (see Chapter 2). That program includes important historical context and the latest theoretical, experimental, and archival research incorporating social norms into the traditional theory of the firm (Stevens 2019).

1.3 THE DEMAND FROM POLICYMAKERS

The societal effects of capitalism have always posed a challenge for public policy. This was especially true during the two industrial revolutions spawned by early capitalism. The first industrial revolution occurred primarily in Great Britain from 1760 to 1840, and the Second Industrial Revolution occurred primarily in the United States from 1870 to 1920. As the result of the Second Industrial Revolution, the United States surpassed Britain as the world's strongest economic power and New York surpassed London as the world's center of banking and international trade (Burk 2007). Both industrial revolutions brought in their wake profound social and psychological dislocations due to rapid technological change and the urbanization of society. The resulting societal challenges included the breakdown of traditional communities, the decline of traditional religious belief, economic depression, immigration, and labor violence. These challenges required the implementation of a more active public policy than had previously existed in the West.

The great wealth and power concentrated in large corporations during the Second Industrial Revolution, along with the opportunistic behavior demonstrated by key business leaders, was seen as a threat to Western democracy. This led to a general mistrust of big business in America. As the excesses of the 1920s gave way to the economic hardships of the 1930s, this distrust was magnified, and business regulation became a major theme of public policy. Leon Marshall, one of the business school deans who helped found the AACSB, would play an important role in shaping New Deal policies as a member of the National Industrial Recovery Board. In 1933, the US Congress enacted the Glass-Steagall Act, which separated the activities of investment and commercial banking to prevent investment banks from putting depositors' funds at risk. In 1934, the Roosevelt administration established the Securities and Exchange Commission (SEC) to standardize accounting and reporting for publicly traded companies. These regulations were added to prior business regulations including the establishment of the Interstate Commerce Commission in 1887 to regulate the railroad industry and the Sherman

Antitrust Act in 1890 designed to break up the great monopolies and trusts that had put too much power into too few hands. The importance of high professional standards in business as an antidote for overly active public policy can be seen in the comments of Wharton's Dean Joseph Willits at the 18th meeting of the AACSB (AACSB 1936, 12–13):

It may not be unfair to say that the chances of obtaining a wise and rational policy by government ... are increased in direct proportion to the extent to which the ethical standards and social mindedness of business men are of a kind that society can approve. In the long run, short-sightedness and unsocial practice by business will lead to political reprisals of a not very discriminating kind by those who have little understanding of business activity. All of business will continue to suffer for the conduct of a few until business learns specifically to condemn and control the practices that do not measure up.

Many policymakers at the time blamed the economic hardships of the Great Depression on an uncritical embrace of laissez-faire economics. This led to a new philosophy of public policy determined to curb the excesses of unbridled capitalism. In response to this new philosophy, Harvard modified its required courses to acknowledge the legitimate role of government in capitalist economies. Wharton also instituted the new "Wharton Assembly" to gather together the entire Wharton community to hear prominent public officials speak about the economic and social challenges facing the nation and the role of business in solving those challenges. During this time, the shift in business and government relations occasioned by the New Deal became a major theme of policymaking debates. These policy debates soon shifted to the role of industry and business management should the United States enter the war breaking out across Europe and Asia (Khurana 2007).

The scientific rigor of neoclassical economics would soon prove its worth during World War II and the postwar period. A vigorous economy was needed to meet the growing demands of the war effort as well as to demonstrate the virtues of American capitalism to the world. The war effort not only demonstrated the ability of science and industry to meet the defense needs of a rising superpower, but it also lifted the United States out of the Great Depression. Unlike other major industrial nations, the United States entered the postwar period with its economy intact and its technological assets preserved. Thus, its domestic production was buoyed by foreign demand. Further, the United States stood as the world's defender against communist aggression as well as its main creditor and currency provider, as the dollar had become the world's currency by default and by the multilateral agreements at Bretton Woods. These strong economic tailwinds assured that the United States would enter a period of unparalleled economic growth that lasted throughout the 1950s and 1960s.

The new social contract between business and government was so successful that it became fashionable by the early 1960s for economists to speak on "the end of the business cycle" (Bernstein 2001). In addition to the policy experience derived from the war, the growing confidence in the ability of policymakers to advance effective public policy was buoyed by a revolution in macroeconomics brought about by British economist John Maynard Keynes. Most of the increase in status and legitimacy earned by economists during this period, however, accrued to neoclassical economists and not institutional economists. In the increasing pursuit of scientific rigor, graduate instruction in economics became increasingly dominated by advances in mathematical modeling and statistics (econometrics). As a result, literacy in economic history and the classic texts began to wane, and the social, institutional, and cultural insights of institutional economists were largely removed from consciousness (Stevens 2019).[10]

At the same time neoclassical economists were rising in status, however, the university-based business school came under increasing scrutiny. In 1959, the Carnegie and Ford Foundations issued book-long reports that were highly critical of business school education (Pierson 1959 and Gordon and Howell 1959, respectively). The Carnegie and Ford Foundations believed that strengthening the management of business organizations was integral to their postwar missions. Both of their reports were unanimous in their condemnation of the quality of the business schools that had been established at research universities. Less than half of business school faculty held Ph.D. degrees, and there was a glaring lack of research and scholarly activities. Teaching loads were heavy with approximately forty percent of courses taught by part-time instructors. While both foundations sought the continuance of the professionalism project of institutional economists through multidisciplinary research based in the social sciences, the end result of their two reports was the further promotion of the narrow research paradigm of neoclassical economists (Khurana 2007).

[10] As discussed in Chapter 5, this growing lack of consciousness regarding economic history and the classic texts would enable neoclassical economists associated with the Chicago School to distort Adam Smith's legacy in defense of their economic theory based on narrow self-interest.

Economic trends in the United States would soon be used by neoclassical economists associated with the University of Chicago to discredit the role of public policy in the economy. The economic tailwinds that fueled the postwar prosperity of American capitalism in the 1950s and 1960s became strong headwinds during the 1970s and 1980s. Recovering industrial nations began to meet their own production needs and, in turn, became formidable competitors in the new global economy. Further, the Bretton Woods international monetary agreements expired, and many nations began to rely on their own financing and currency. When combined with other socio-economic shocks, such as the 1973 oil embargo by the Organization of the Petroleum Exporting Countries (OPEC), these trends led to an extended period of economic stagnation in the United States. The previous confidence in an active public policy inspired by Keynesian economics was severely shaken as the economic stagnation and accelerated inflation of the late 1960s and 1970s, named "stagflation," were blamed on fiscal interventionism and big government programs (Bernstein 2001).

Given the neoclassical assumptions of narrow self-interest and highly efficient markets, the logical solution to the economic stagnation in the United States was to subject self-interested managers to the discipline of the financial markets. Further, neoclassical economists associated with the Chicago School increasingly viewed the government as just another self-interested group focused on expanding its power through increased taxes and regulation (Stigler 1971b). From this view, "most government policies (even those prohibiting insider trading, as some of the more extreme members of this group argued) typically destroyed incentives for sound economic and social behavior. Thus, the solution to the problems of American competitiveness entailed minimizing the government's role in the national economy" (Khurana 2007, 301). In the hands of these economists, public policy was too often reduced to a choice between free-market capitalism and socialism. This truncation of the public policy debate concealed the ongoing demand for a moral foundation for capitalism, which became clear during the crisis of capitalism in 2007–08.

In their book, *Good Capitalism, Bad Capitalism, and the Economics of Growth and Prosperity*, Baumol, Litan, and Schramm (2007) analyze various forms of capitalism found around the world. They define an economic system as capitalist if most of its means of production are in private hands rather than being owned and operated by the government. Their detailed economic analysis highlights the following basic facts regarding capitalist economic systems. First, all capitalist systems require some form of government support.[11] Second, capitalist systems have provided significantly more economic growth and prosperity than socialist systems that place the means of production fully in the hands of the government. Third, the economic growth provided by capitalist systems differs by the form of capitalism and the time period examined. In contrast to the truncated view of public policy out of the Chicago School, Baumol, Litan, and Schramm conclude that government plays an essential role in the successful functioning of capitalist economies.

Baumol, Litan, and Schramm (2007, 60–61) identify four forms of capitalism based on the power and influence of big business versus the size and scope of government:

1. *State-guided capitalism*, in which government tries to guide the market, most often by supporting particular industries that it expects to become "winners." (Examples include economies in India, Japan, and South Korea.)
2. *Oligarchic capitalism*, in which the bulk of the power and wealth is held by a small group of individuals and families. (Examples include many economies in Latin America, in the former states of the Soviet Union, in the Arabic Middle East, and in Africa.)
3. *Big-firm capitalism*, in which the most significant economic activities are carried out by established giant enterprises. (Examples include the United States, the United Kingdom, Australia, and many economies in Continental Europe.)
4. *Entrepreneurial capitalism*, in which a significant role is played by small, innovative firms. (Examples include periods of technological innovation in the United States – such as the automobile industry in the late nineteenth century and the computer industry in the late twentieth century – and periods of deregulation in Ireland, Israel, and the United Kingdom.)

Baumol, Litan, and Schramm devote an entire chapter to defending their use of economic growth as a key measure of success in their analysis of capitalist systems. They argue that economic growth is essential because humans want an opportunity to better their lives. They also cite studies documenting that economic growth leads to reduced poverty. While evidence does not support a direct link between economic growth and happiness,

---

[11] In the US economy, for example, critical utilities are provided by a combination of municipal governments and the federal government and previous attempts to privatize utility markets have often resulted in disaster (e.g., Enron).

that is likely due to confounding effects such as increased expectations and social comparisons.[12] Critics on the Left have argued that economic growth depletes natural resources, but such growth has led to technological innovations and efficiencies that have served to preserve the world's resources. Further, strong economic growth leads people to demand the preservation of natural resources. Baumol, Litan, and Schramm (2007, 33–34) conclude: "Economic growth is and continues to be important, indeed, morally necessary if individuals and society care about improving the living standards of peoples around the world."

Baumol, Litan, and Schramm analyze the economic performance of each of the four capitalist systems, using economic growth and other economic performance measures such as disparities in wealth and income. They conclude that the optimal form of capitalism ("Good Capitalism") is a blend of entrepreneurial and big-firm capitalism. In particular, optimal economic performance occurs at the efficiency frontier where there are incentives for entrepreneurs to innovate and yet the opportunity for large corporations to form and profit from such innovation. Yet, each form of capitalism requires sound public policy and high moral standards to maintain its benefits while minimalizing its shortcomings. For example, big firm capitalism can lead to bloated corporations that use their wealth and power to reduce competition and seek beneficial public policy from government ("crony capitalism"). Big firm capitalism also leads to the classic principal-agent problem where professional managers act in their own self-interest rather than the interest of the owners of the firms they manage. Finally, a lack of transparency and accountability can lead to opportunistic behavior that threatens capitalist institutions and increases government regulation.

According to Baumol, Litan, and Schramm, state-guided capitalism shares many of the key weaknesses of oligarchic capitalism. Thus, the Chicago School's suspicion of government involvement in the economy remains valid. When government picks the winners and losers, or subsidizes certain companies and industries, it inevitably leads to inefficiency and corruption. This susceptibility to corruption helps explain why both state-guided and oligarchic capitalism are often characterized by lackluster economic growth and greater income inequality. The shutdown of world economies due to the

---

[12] Baumol, Litan, and Schramm point out that relative income appears to be more important to happiness than income. Scitovsky (1976/1992) was one of the first economists to question the central tenet that higher income leads to greater happiness. He applied theories of behavioral psychology and concluded that *increases* in income provided greater happiness rather than income levels per se.

COVID pandemic has led to a new era of debate over the role of government in the economy. This fiery debate has been stoked in the United States by recent evidence of big government colluding with big business and big media to silence opposing viewpoints and political speech. Thus, the role of government continues to be an important and contentious issue in capitalist economies.

The sudden collapse of FTX in November of 2022 uncovered widespread investor fraud at the cryptocurrency exchange. Although the details of this investor fraud continue to unfold in bankruptcy court, the FTX case represents the worst of crony capitalism. Sam-Bankman Fried (SBF) allegedly used investor funds at FTX to support president Biden's presidential campaign in 2020 and the midterm campaigns of many democrats in 2022, which bought him important access and political influence. At the same time SBF was using the unregulated cryptocurrency industry to bilk investors of billions of dollars, he was meeting privately with US politicians to help shape regulations for that industry. Recent revelations at Twitter after the takeover of the social media giant by Elon Musk also suggest a troubling alliance between big government, big tech, and big media. These troubling examples demonstrate the risk of crony capitalism arising in developed as well as developing economies. These examples also demonstrate the need for vigilant public policy to increase responsibility, transparency, and accountability in both business and politics.

1.4 CONCLUSION AND OUTLINE OF THE BOOK

As reflected in the recent actions of the Business Roundtable, top business leaders continue to promote initiatives to regain the "stakeholder view" of the corporation that existed before the influence of the Chicago School. Further, business educators continue to promote the professional norms that inspired institutional economists to establish the university-based business school. Finally, policymakers continue to seek sound public policy that maximizes the benefits of capitalism for all members of capitalist society. This behavior reflects the continuing demand for a moral foundation for capitalism. The search for such a foundation has a long history, going back to Adam Smith and the Scottish Enlightenment. Yet few are aware of this search or its importance for the future of capitalism. The purpose of this book is to tell the story of this search through the lives and writings of its leading characters.

Albert Hirschman (1977/1997, 59) argued that the triumph of capitalism in the West "owes much to the widespread refusal to take it seriously or to believe it capable of great design or achievement." The economists and philosophers in this book, however, took capitalism seriously by addressing its vulnerabilities and excesses. In Chapter 2, I discuss the moral foundation for capitalism provided by Adam Smith, the great philosopher of the Scottish Enlightenment. Although he is frequently invoked by economists as the father of their discipline, I show that Smith's life and writings have been widely distorted by both classical and neoclassical economists. In Chapter 3, I address religion as a moral foundation for capitalism by discussing the lives and writings of Max Weber and R. H. Tawney. Weber was a German political economist who is best known for his emphasis on the role of the Protestant Reformation in the founding of capitalism. Tawney was a British economist who is best known for his association with the Christian socialist movement that was popular in late nineteenth-century Britain. Both economists wrote major works addressing the importance of religion to the development of capitalism in the West.

In Chapter 4, I address humanism as a moral foundation for capitalism by discussing the lives and writings of Karl Polanyi and John Maynard Keynes. Polanyi shared Tawney's deep Christian faith, but he moved away from Tawney's moral foundation based on that faith and developed a moral foundation for capitalism based on the infinite value of humanity. Polanyi was initially attracted to the early arguments of Marx, but he ended up rejecting the narrow utilitarianism of both Marx and the classical economists. His search for a moral foundation for capitalism led him to rediscover Adam Smith's moral foundation based on social norms and culture. Keynes initially adopted the radical humanism of his elite friends at Cambridge University and the Bloomsbury group, but he shifted to a more traditional form of humanism later in life. Similar to Polanyi, Keynes rejected the narrow utilitarianism of both Marx and the classical economists and formed a moral foundation for capitalism based on responsibility and duty.

In Chapter 5, I address self-interest as the foundation for capitalism by discussing the Chicago School and Ayn Rand. Neoclassical economists after Alfred Marshall continued the narrowing of their discipline begun by classical economists. Whereas Polanyi and Keynes emphasized responsibility and duty in their moral foundation based on humanism, neoclassical economists associated with the Chicago School eschewed all social and moral responsibility and made narrow self-interest the dominant behavioral assumption in economics. I show how Rand's moral philosophy (rational egoism) represented a natural extension of the straightjacket of self-interest out of Chicago. Similar to the Chicago School, her moral foundation for capitalism provided no legitimate role for government involvement in the economy. In Chapter 6, I address how neoclassical economists have joined the search for a moral foundation for capitalism by discussing the lives and writings of Vernon Smith and Michael Jensen. In his attempt to explain norm-based behavior emerging in experimental tests of neoclassical theory, Vernon Smith rediscovered Adam Smith's moral foundation for capitalism. Jensen, one of the engineers of the neoclassical theory of the firm out of Chicago, abandoned the underlying behavioral assumption of narrow self-interest after the near collapse of the global financial system in 2007–08. He now promotes values and integrity as necessary components of business management and education.

In Chapter 7, I discuss the life and writings of another neoclassical economist who has played a major role in the search for a moral foundation for capitalism. In particular, I discuss Amartya Sen's childhood in colonial India and his rise to the top academic institutions of the West to rescue capitalism from the capitalists. Similar to Karl Polanyi and Vernon Smith, Sen's journey led him to discover Adam Smith's moral theory and incorporate that theory into neoclassical economic theory. In Chapter 8, I conclude by discussing the promise of capitalism revealed by those who have joined the search for a moral foundation. I first discuss how both classical and neoclassical economic theory have proven to be incomplete and in need of revision. Next, I summarize key insights from the nine leading characters discussed in this book. I also discuss three responses to the recent crisis of capitalism in 2007–08 and how they reflect the continuing influence of the Chicago School and yet leave the theoretical landscape ripe for theoretical development and innovation. After presenting insights from my own research, I discuss my recent experience at an international research conference in Australia to describe current efforts to recover Adam Smith's moral foundation for capitalism and establish a "New Chicago School."

2

The Moral Economist

Adam Smith

There is nothing surprising in Adam Smith's well known statement (in The Wealth of Nations): "It is not from the benevolence of the butcher, the brewer, or the baker, that we expect our dinner, but from their regard to their own interest." Who would suppose this to imply that Adam Smith had come to disbelieve in the very existence or the moral value of benevolence? Nobody with any sense. But this does not necessarily exclude scholars, some of whom have adopted ... the hypothesis that the moral philosopher who made sympathy the basis of social behaviour in TMS did an about-turn from altruistic to egoistic theory in WN owing to the influence of the French "materialist" thinkers whom he met in Paris in 1766.

David Raphael and Alec Macfie
Introduction, The Theory of Moral Sentiments

A deeper understanding of Adam Smith and his writings was greatly advanced by the publication in 1978 of the "Glasgow Edition of the Works and Correspondence of Adam Smith" (Teichgraeber 1981). In addition to shattering the myth that Smith attributed all human motivation to narrow self-interest, the publication of Smith's corpus uncovered the lack of support for *das Adam Smith Problem* perpetuated by German economists and philosophers in the nineteenth century. The full body of Smith's writings reveals no evidence that he altered his views or that he attributed human motivation to "altruism" in *The Theory of Moral Sentiments* and "egoism" (narrow self-interest) in *The Wealth of Nations*. The picture that emerges from Smith's writings has led scholars to associate his system of thought with the writings of the German econo-mist Max Weber (Haakonssen and Winch 2006). That system reflects an institutional individualism that emphasizes social norms and culture. Although his first major work has been diminished in the eyes of many economists due to the inconsistency debate (Reeder 1997), it provides a fully developed moral theory that is capable of explaining the moral conscience and norm-based behavior that arise in society. Thus, it is able to address the benefits, shortcomings, and social implications of capitalist economies. In this chapter, I present the moral foundation for capitalism provided by Adam Smith.[1]

2.1 EARLY ARGUMENTS FOR CAPITALISM PRIOR TO ITS TRIUMPH IN THE WEST

Early arguments for capitalism before its triumph in the West were based on political challenges related to the power of sovereigns and the uncertainties of medieval life. With the fall of Rome in 476 AD, the state became the fiefdom of emperors, kings, and lords. During the ensuing Middle Ages, the Catholic Church and its monastery system played a major role in administering land, goods, and payments. By the twelfth century, however, a new economic system evolved that offered increased freedom and prosperity to its citizens. As a result of this economic system, northern Italy emerged as the richest and most populous region of Europe dominated by merchant-run city republics such as Florence, Genoa, and Venice. Jacob Soll (2014, 9) describes the new merchant culture that arose to threaten the old monarchy culture in the West:

Without kings and with its nobles urbanized and recognizing the authority of city governments, northern Italy became something entirely new: a patchwork of rich city states, ruled by patrician merchants whose wealth came from trade. It was here that multipartner firms, banking, and long-distance trade developed, and with them the concepts of capitalistic profit and double-entry bookkeeping.

Albert Hirschman (1977/1997) has written the definitive history of the political arguments for capitalism before its triumph in the West. According to Hirschman, the Renaissance drive to see man "as he really is" raised doubt about whether moralizing philosophy and religious zeal could restrain the destructive worldly passions. Early supporters of capitalism focused on its ability to tame the passions without appealing

---

[1] As the epigraph to this chapter clearly conveys (Raphael and Macfie 1982, 20), the editors of the Glasgow edition of the works and correspondence of Adam Smith conclude *das Adam Smith problem* was a pseudo-problem based on ignorance and a fundamental misunderstanding of Smith's use of the terms "sympathy" and "self-interest."

to coercion and repression from princes, clerics, or lords. The passions were viewed as wild and dangerous, whereas looking after one's material interests was viewed as calm and innocent. Thus, seeking material gain achieved legitimacy as a gentle and non-violent means of restraining the destructive passions. This positive view of material gain provided a major breakthrough in the transition from feudalism to early capitalism in Europe.

By the beginning of the sixteenth century, however, early capitalism came under siege as the struggle for power intensified across Europe. Princes and Popes waged wars against the new city-states and against each other as France, Spain, and the Holy Roman Empire battled for control. It was during this tumultuous time that the Florentine Niccolò Machiavelli (1469–1527) wrote his political treatise, *The Prince*. Machiavelli took for granted that the passions of the prince were greater than those of the people and generally destructive. Thus, the task of a wise public policy was to control the passions of the prince which war against the dictates of duty and reason. Given Machiavelli's pessimism, the optimal solution was to align the interests of the prince with the interests of his realm. Thus, the concept of interest as a consistent and countervailing force took hold in politics long before it became a matter of doctrine in economics (Hirschman 1977/1997).

The two human motivations that had dominated Western philosophy since Plato were passion and reason. Once the idea of interest as a buffet for destructive passions appeared, however, it was only a short time before most of human behavior became explained by self-interest. As Hirschman (1977/1997, 43) states:

Once passion was deemed destructive and reason ineffectual, the view that human action could be exhaustively described by attribution to either one or the other meant an exceedingly somber outlook for humanity. A message of hope was therefore conveyed by the wedging of interest in between the two traditional categories of human motivation. Interest was seen to partake in effect of the better nature of each, as the passion of self-love upgraded and contained by reason, and as reason given direction and force by that passion. The resulting hybrid form of human action was considered exempt from both the destructiveness of passion and the ineffectuality of reason.

The emergence of interest as a third human motivation helped the West avoid the pessimistic political philosophy of Machiavelli. By the end of the seventeenth century, however, the meaning of interest as a motivational force had begun to narrow to encompass only wealth and material goods. Through the identification of interest as a human motivation, therefore, the lust for money eventually lost its position as one of the three deadly sins.[2]

Hirschman's (1977/1997) economic history suggests that the main argument for capitalism at its birth was its predictability and ability to establish stability in society. Given developments in the West, money-making gained a positive and curative connotation that overtook the negative connotation that had dominated it over most of the Middle Ages. The new economic system – with private property rights and increasingly global trade – became viewed as an improvement over the feudal economic systems based on the powers of the monarchy and the medieval church. This positive view of capitalism could not have persisted, however, had the new economic system not demonstrated its superiority over the previous economic systems. Early capitalism yielded unparalleled wealth and prosperity and allowed Europe to enter a new age characterized by advances in art, architecture, music, science, and literature called the Renaissance.

The merchant-run city states that emerged in northern Italy, however, continued to face threats of invasion from French and Spanish monarchies, power struggles with the Roman Catholic Church, and new power struggles with rising aristocrats. As a result, the spirit of capitalism migrated north. Supported by the Protestant Reformation, the Netherlands soon became the new center of banking and international trade in Europe. To Dutch Calvinists, wealth and success in commerce became signs of one's membership in God's elect (See Chapter 3). New political and economic freedoms, along with increasing religious tolerance, allowed the Netherlands to enter a Dutch Golden Age from about 1588 to 1672. Advances in trade, science, art, and naval power allowed the Netherlands to become the dominant economic power in the world at that time. The spirit of capitalism eventually migrated west to Britain, where it benefited from a new theory of natural law that affirmed private property rights and controlled the power of government.

2.2 ARGUMENTS FOR CAPITALISM FROM SCOTTISH ENLIGHTENMENT PHILOSOPHERS

The pessimistic political philosophy of Machiavelli and later the English philosopher Thomas Hobbes (1588–1679) gave way to more moderate views of human nature in the eighteenth century. Scottish

---

[2] To St. Augustine and the early Christian church, the main three passions worthy of condemnation (the three deadly sins) included lust for money, lust for power, and sexual lust (Hirschman 1977/1997).

Enlightenment philosophers looked increasingly to the passions to counterbalance selfish and violent tendencies in both princes and the general populace.[3] Thus, the passions were rehabilitated as the essence of life, and the proposition that human conduct is wholly shaped by the interests was rejected on the grounds that the passions still had a major role to play. The emerging view of human nature saw the passions as improving upon a world governed by interest alone. In the hands of Scottish Enlightenment philosophers and their emphasis on the passions, arguments for capitalism took on political, social, and moral dimensions.

The Scottish Enlightenment philosophers were heavily influenced by the political philosophy of John Locke (1632–1704). Locke not only provided a positive view of human nature, he also provided a state of nature that was supportive of the emerging capitalist institutions in Europe. This included the existence of private property, inheritance, commerce, and currency. Locke published his classic work of political philosophy in 1689, *Two Treatises of Government*. In his first treatise he challenged the divine right of kings, and in his second treatise he established a foundation for law and government based on the concept of natural law. Locke argued that humans were entirely free and equal in their natural state. Thus, the law of nature required that all humans be free, equal, and subject only to the will of the "infinitely wise maker." This enlightened political philosophy supported capitalism by controlling the power of the state and providing the average citizen with unparalleled economic, political, and religious freedoms (Stevens 2019).[4]

The political philosophy of John Locke supported the growing positive view of early capitalism in the West. This positive view is reflected in the writings of French philosopher Montesquieu (1689–1755), who wrote the following in Part One of *Esprit des lois*: "(T)he spirit of commerce brings with it the spirit of frugality, of economy, of moderation, of work, of wisdom, of tranquility, of order, and of regularity."

Scottish Enlightenment philosophers such as David Hume, Francis Hutcheson, and Adam Smith were heavily influenced by this positive

[3] In fact, Hume frequently used the term "passion of interest" to describe the love of gain. He describes this passion as perpetual and universal in contrast to other passions, such as envy and revenge, that operate only at intervals and are specific to the situation and people involved (Hume 1739/1975, III.2.2).

[4] Locke had been in self-imposed exile to the Netherlands prior to 1689, and his two treatises reflected the Dutch merchant culture that had migrated from northern Italy and established capitalist institutions and a republican government.

view of commerce.[5] In his account of the erosion of feudalism in *The Wealth of Nations* (Smith 1776/1791, WN III.iv.4), for example, Smith writes:

(C)ommerce and manufactures gradually introduced order and good government, and with them, the liberty and security of individuals, among the inhabitants of the country, who had before lived almost in a continual state of war with their neighbours, and of servile dependency upon their superiors. This, though it has been the least observed, is by far the most important of their effects.

The above quote reflects the conviction among Scottish Enlightenment philosophers that commerce was capable of taming the destructive passions and promoting a spirit of self-control, liberty, and peace. In sharp contrast to George Stigler's (1971a) characterization of *The Wealth of Nations*, Smith built his arguments for capitalism on the ability of commerce, religion, education, and government to maintain high moral character and advance the common good (Griswold 1999). Given the view of Smith promoted by the Chicago School, these arguments seem strange and idealistic. Yet, they help explain why early capitalism gripped the imagination of eighteenth-century philosophers throughout the West.

Leading philosophers of the period also addressed potential weaknesses of capitalism, including its tendency to generate disparities in wealth. Montesquieu, for example, argued that a democracy can ordinarily survive only when wealth is not too unequally distributed. He made an important exception to this rule, however, for a democracy based on the merchant culture of liberty and freedom (Hirschman 1977/1997). Similarly, Scottish Enlightenment philosophers did not view disparity of wealth as a critical weakness as long as the other benefits of capitalism were present. Adam Smith argued that such disparity feeds the inner desire to better one's condition under the economic system of perfect liberty (Rothschild and Sen 2006). Both Hume and Smith argued that the desire to better one's condition nourished commerce and industry, which provided the greatest opportunity for the poor and disadvantaged to achieve wealth and independence (Skinner 2003). Again, these arguments were based on the merchant culture of liberty and freedom.

---

[5] The term "capitalism" was not used by the Scottish Enlightenment philosophers. Marx also did not invent the term, as some have suggested, although he frequently referred to "capital" and the "capitalist mode of production" in *Das Kapital* (Marx 1867/1990). The term was coined by social critics in Germany and Britain who were apprehensive about the social change brought about by the first Industrial Revolution (Rogan 2017). By the time Weber began his seminal critique of capitalism in the summer of 1903, the term had been well established in political economy.

By the end of the eighteenth century, Montesquieu was proven correct in his own country as disparity of wealth based on the monarchy culture of privilege and entitlement led to the French Revolution.

In contrast to the Augustinians, who relied on reason and love of God to overcome the destructive passions, the Scottish Enlightenment philosophers gave the passions a prominent role in society. The pervasive influence of the passions is reflected in David Hume's famous proclamation, "Reason is, and ought only to be the slave of the passions." (Hume 1739/1975, II.3.3). In their extension of the Renaissance quest to see man as he really is, the Scottish Enlightenment philosophers incorporated the countervailing view of the passions. In particular, Adam Smith based his moral foundation for capitalism on countervailing passions rather than on reason or divine law. In *The Theory of Moral Sentiments*, Smith uses the terms "sentiment," "passion," and "emotion" interchangeably. Thus, the moral theory behind his corpus is a theory of passions, sentiments, and emotions (Griswold 1999).[6]

In addition to their focus on the passions, the Scottish Enlightenment philosophers were heavily influenced by the Stoic philosophy of the ancient Greeks and Romans.[7] In contrast to the Augustinians and Epicureans, who viewed pleasure as the ultimate good, the Stoics viewed the practice of virtue as the ultimate good. The Anglo-Dutch philosopher Bernard Mandeville (1670–1733) describes the Stoics in his satire on vanity and self-interest, *The Fable of the Bees* (Mandeville 1732, 150):

They (the Stoics) wisely considered the instability of fortune, and the favor of princes; the vanity of honor, and popular applause; the precariousness of riches, and all earthly possessions; and therefore placed true happiness in the calm serenity of a contented mind free from guilt and ambition; a mind, that, having subdued every sensual appetite, despises the smiles as well as frowns of fortune, and taking no delight but in contemplation, desires nothing but what everybody is able to give to himself.

Scottish Enlightenment philosophers were also heavily influenced by recent advances in mathematics and science, including Francis Bacon's scientific method and Isaac Newton's discovery of the laws of physics.[8]

---

[6] This countervailing view of the passions influenced the framers of the US Constitution, who incorporated important checks and balances throughout their founding document.

[7] Stoicism has gained popularity in recent times as a practical system of personal ethics that promotes resilience and virtue (Holiday and Hanselman 2020).

[8] Scottish Enlightenment philosophers referred to science as "natural philosophy" and to scientists as "philosophers." The labels "science" and "scientists" were not widely used prior to 1839 (Wightman 1982, 13).

David Hume sought to develop the laws of human behavior along similar lines. Adam Smith was exposed to Hume's "science of man" as a student at Oxford. According to reliable historical sources, a copy of Hume's (1739/1975) *A Treatise on Human Nature* was seized from Smith's dorm room, and he was severely reprimanded for being in possession of the heretical book (Phillipson 2010). That episode was but one of many slights that led the young Scottish philosopher to leave Oxford in disgust at the end of his sixth year. From his initial exposure at Oxford, however, Smith took up Hume's challenge to develop a science of man that would enlighten our understanding of morality, religion, and commerce (Berry 2006).

It was not unusual for Scottish students to be poorly treated at Oxford. King Henry VIII established the Anglican Church of England in 1534 after the Pope's refusal to grant him an annulment from his first wife, Catherine of Aragon. The strong influence of moderates and Catholic sympathizers at the time, however, caused church reforms in England to be relatively minor. In contrast, the Presbyterian Church of Scotland represented a radical break from the Roman Catholic Church. When Queen Elizabeth assumed the English throne in 1558, Scotland's Catholic Queen, Mary Stuart, was urged by her Catholic supporters to return to Scotland from the safety of the French Court. By the time Mary Stuart returned to Scotland in 1561, however, her Catholic regents had lost control of the country to Protestant lords who were more aligned with England than France. Further, John Knox and his radical reformers had established a new Protestant denomination and installed it as the official Church of Scotland. This explains the powerful influence of Presbyterianism in Scotland during the seventeenth and eighteenth centuries.

The emergence of capitalism in Britain occurred in an environment of intense religious and political conflict. The first half of the seventeenth century found England locked in a violent conflict between Parliament and two Stuart Kings, James I and Charles I. This conflict led to a bloody civil war and the eventual beheading of Charles in 1649. The Stuart Monarchy was replaced by the Commonwealth of England (1649–53) followed by the Protectorate under the rule of Oliver Cromwell (1653–58) and his son (1658–59). During the years of the Commonwealth and the Protectorate, England became increasingly influenced by the merchant culture of the Netherlands. Over this time period, unquestioned loyalty to the nobility faded, and public policy became increasingly influenced by Parliament, the courts, and public opinion. Further, public opinion became increasingly shaped by a people who made their living by buying and selling (Pincus 2009).

Charles II was king of England, Scotland, and Ireland from the restoration of the monarchy in 1660 until his death in 1685. Charles sided with France and his first cousin, Louis XIV, against the rising economic and military power of the Netherlands. This led to two Anglo-Dutch wars during Charles's reign (1652–54 and 1665–67). By the time of the reign of his brother James II from 1685 to 1688, however, the merchant culture of the English had developed to the point where its people preferred Dutch capitalism to French monarchy. After consolidating political and financial support, and under the invitation of Parliament, William III, Prince of Orange, invaded England in 1688 and took the English throne with Mary II in 1689. As Pincus (2009) argues, the Glorious Revolution was the result of the development of capitalist institutions in England that had begun at the beginning of the century and accelerated with the Commonwealth and Protectorate in the 1650s. This historical perspective explains why the Scottish Enlightenment philosophers were so exercised by the promise of capitalism with its unsurpassed liberty and freedom.

By the eighteenth century, therefore, the scene was set for a new philosophical movement incorporating the expanded freedoms provided by John Locke's natural rights theory, the Glorious Revolution, and the Act of Union in 1707. Major contributors to this philosophical movement in Scotland included Adam Ferguson, David Hume, Francis Hutcheson, Thomas Reid, Adam Smith, Sir James Steuart, and forty-seven other identifiable figures (McCosh 1875). Despite the view held by many economists today, Hume was generally rejected by his contemporaries as a renegade whose philosophical views were to be refuted (Graham 2003). Hutcheson warmly welcomed Smith to the faculty of Glasgow after his brief stint as a public lecturer at Edinburgh whereas he joined others in assuring that Hume never received an academic post in Scotland. For his part, Smith was uncomfortable enough with Hume's anti-religion views that he never cited them in his own writings and refused to use his reputation to assist Hume in acquiring a faculty position at any of the prominent Scottish universities of his day. Further, he refused Hume's request to publish a summary of his anti-religion views posthumously.

Recent scholarship suggests that Scottish Enlightenment philosophers "were generally sincere Christians who found it virtually unthinkable that there might be no God requiring duties of us" (Emerson 2003, 24). Even Hume, despite his deep criticism of religious belief, did not discount the influence of religion in his science of man. In particular, Hume joined Hutcheson and Smith as the main Scottish participants in the

British debate on the foundations of morals. While they had rival moral theories, their source of the ability to judge right from wrong had many similarities. For example, Hume, Hutcheson, and Smith attributed moral judgment to the ability of humans to "sympathize" with other humans. Thus, the source of moral judgment is our common social experiences "which enable us to establish general rules and to create a stable, common language of moral praise and blame" (Turco 2003, 145). All three philosophers also argued that these socially derived rules become operationalized in the "impartial spectator," which explains not only moral judgment but also the moral conscience. While the impartial spectator is assumed to be disinterested, it incorporates commitments to "self-love" and a person's unique social circle as well as various virtues or religious commitments (Griswold 1999).

2.3 ADAM SMITH'S MORAL FOUNDATION FOR CAPITALISM

Adam Smith's moral foundation for capitalism cannot be fully understood apart from his place and times. Smith's father passed away six months prior to his birth in 1723, leaving him to be raised by his beloved mother and a series of legal guardians. Perhaps because of his frailty – he barely survived to see his first birthday – Margaret Smith enrolled her only child in the local burgh school just a short walk from their home in the trading port of Kirkcaldy, Scotland. The school provided a rigorous classical education. Young Adam was so accomplished in Latin, Greek, and the classics by the time he entered the university at Glasgow in 1737 that he was exempted from the first two years of the curriculum. As a student at Glasgow, he studied mathematics, natural philosophy, and the Stoics under the tutelage of Francis Hutcheson and other Presbyterian clergy. Given the efforts of Hutcheson and William Smith, his older cousin and legal guardian, he was able to secure one of the coveted Snell Exhibitions to continue his studies at Balliol College in Oxford. As a Snell Exhibitioner, Smith's only obligation was to attend prayers twice a day and lectures twice a week. During his six years at Oxford, therefore, Smith largely engaged in private study, taught himself French, and attended Anglican worship services.[9]

---

[9] The Snell Exhibitions had been established for the express purpose of preparing young men from Glasgow to take holy orders in the Anglican Church of England in the hope that they would return to Presbyterian Scotland to disseminate the religion of the mother country (Addison 1901).

Smith published the first edition of *The Theory of Moral Sentiments* in 1759 during his tenure as Chair of Moral Philosophy at Glasgow. He published a second edition of his major work in 1761 in response to comments received after his first edition. This was followed by three more editions which differed little from edition 2: edition 3 in 1767, edition 4 in 1774, and edition 5 in 1781. Edition 6, however, which he published in the final year of his life in 1790, contained extensive additions including a new section devoted to the topic of moral virtue (Part VI). Coming as it did at the end of his life, this new material reflects Smith's lifelong reflections on commerce and society (Raphael and Macfie 1982). During his lifetime Smith had observed early capitalism as a young man growing up in the trading port of Kirkcaldy, as a lecturer in the metropolitan city of Edinburgh, and as a prominent professor of moral philosophy in the port city of Glasgow.[10] He had also traveled to London and continental Europe and discussed political economy with many dignitaries of his day including Benjamin Franklin, François Quesnay, and the circle of *économistes* in Paris (Phillipson 2010).

Rather than reflect a view that he would abandon in his later years, therefore, the moral theory in the sixth edition of *The Theory of Moral Sentiments* reflects Smith's final and most developed view of his science of man. Consistent with other philosophers of the Scottish Enlightenment, Smith viewed the topic of political economy as a branch of ethics. Student notes and correspondence regarding Smith's days at Glasgow confirm that political economy was included from the start in his lectures on moral philosophy. Thus, Smith's political economy in *The Wealth of Nations* is part of a larger system that is itself a branch of moral philosophy (Griswold 1999).

Each edition of *The Theory of Moral Sentiments* begins with the following passage (*TMS* I.i.1.1):

How selfish soever man may be supposed, there are evidently some principles in his nature, which interest him in the fortune of others, and render their happiness necessary to him, though he derives nothing from it except the pleasure of seeing it.

---

[10] The Act of Union in 1707 brought Scottish merchants under the protection of the Navigation Acts, which made Glasgow one of the most important ports for the increasing trade between the Americas and Europe. Glasgow merchants shipped tobacco and sugar as well as coffee, cheese, ginger, rum, canes, cotton, tar, canvas, and gunpowder bound for Europe in exchange for European goods bound for America. The rich Glasgow merchants who traded in tobacco became known as the *Tobacco Lords* (Phillipson 2010).

Thus, Smith begins his corpus by refuting the narrow self-interest view attributed to him by classical and neoclassical economists. In particular, he begins by rejecting the view that "we empathize with others only when we think it to our advantage to do so – that is, that we treat others as means to our self-interest, narrowly understood" (Griswold 1999, 78). Not only does Smith grant mankind the ability to empathize with others, which he calls *sympathy*, he makes it the major force behind all moral behavior. Smith devotes an entire section debunking the narrow self-interest view of human motivation which he would later be credited with authoring. Consistent with other Scottish Enlightenment philosophers, including Hume, Smith directly confronts Mandeville's political satire attributing all "so-called virtue" to vanity and self-interest (*TMS* VII.ii.4.7):

> Dr. Mandeville considers whatever is done from a sense of propriety, from a regard to what is commendable and praise-worthy, as being done from a love of praise and commendation, or as he calls it from vanity. Man, he observes, is naturally much more interested in his own happiness than in that of others, and it is impossible that in his heart he can ever really prefer their prosperity to his own. Whenever he appears to do so, we may be assured that he imposes upon us, and that he is then acting from the same selfish motives as at all other times.

Smith demonstrates the inconsistency in Mandeville's reasoning by emphasizing that there are two forms of self-interest, one honorable and one dishonorable. First, he points out that "self-love may frequently be a virtuous motive of action" (*TMS* VII.ii.4.8). Smith calls this honorable form of self-interest *prudence* and identifies it as one of the three main categories of virtues discussed in Part VI. Second, he calls the dishonorable form of self-interest *selfishness*, and identifies it as a vice that is to be strongly condemned. As discussed above, the attribution of all human behavior to narrow self-interest began with Machiavelli and Hobbes in the political sphere, but it was later applied in the economic sphere by classical and neoclassical economists.

Adam Smith maintains a unified view of human motivation in both the political and economic spheres throughout his writings. To Smith, the same human motivation applies to the aristocrat in court as the merchant in the course of commerce and trade. He attributes the whole of human motivation to "bettering our condition." That is, Smith attributes all the toil and bustle of this world, including "the pursuit of wealth, of power, and preeminence," to the human motivation to better our condition in a hierarchical society (*TMS* I.iii.2.1):

From whence, then, arises that emulation which runs through all the different ranks of men, and what are the advantages which we propose by that great purpose of human life which we call bettering our condition? To be observed, to be attended to, to be taken notice of with sympathy, complacency, and approbation, are all the advantages which we can propose to derive from it. It is the vanity, not the ease, or the pleasure, which interests us.

Two points from this passage bear emphasizing. First, bettering our condition is geared toward the symbolic gain of consideration and esteem from others rather than material gain *per se* (Force 2003). According to Smith, we never pursue wealth for its own sake, but because wealth buys us gains in social status. Second, securing and maintaining social status includes adopting social behavior that is highly esteemed by society. Smith makes this clear in the passage where he describes the young man who wishes to advance his station (*TMS* IV.I.8):

The poor man's son, whom heaven in its anger has visited with ambition, when he begins to look around him, admires the condition of the rich ... (In order to arrive at some superior rank), he devotes himself for ever to the pursuit of wealth and greatness.... He studies to distinguish himself in some laborious profession. With the most unrelenting industry he labours night and day to acquire talents superior to all his competitors. He endeavours next to bring those talents into public view, and with equal assiduity solicits every opportunity of employment. For this purpose he makes his court to all mankind; he serves those whom he hates, and is obsequious to those whom he despises.

This passage shows that the desire for consideration and esteem from others, when combined with opportunities for commerce and trade, supports behavior that is highly esteemed by capitalist society such as creativity, initiative, hard work, and industry. This suggests a circularity or interdependence between virtue and capitalist institutions. "In particular, a flourishing commercial society requires, and in turn may support, 'moral capital,' that is, virtue" (Griswold 1999, 359). The motivation to better our condition, however, is based on a fundamental "deception" of the imagination that is capable of reducing our quality of life. As Smith explains later (*TMS* IV.I.9), the perceived pleasures of wealth and greatness "strike the imagination as something grand and beautiful and noble, of which the attainment is well worth all the toil and anxiety which we are so apt to bestow upon it."

And it is well that nature imposes upon us in this manner. It is this deception which rouses and keeps in continual motion the industry of mankind. It is this which first prompted them to cultivate the ground, to build houses, to found cities and commonwealths, and to invest and improve all the sciences and arts, which ennoble and embellish human life.

Smith repeats and magnifies this argument in *The Wealth of Nations*, where he argues that "the desire of bettering our condition" is one that "comes with us from the womb, and never leaves us till we go into the grave." Smith argues that this motivation is the source from which both national and private wealth are derived, and even inefficient public policy is not able to stop it (*WN* II.iii.31): "The uniform, constant, and uninterrupted effort of every man to better his condition, the principle from which public and national, as well as private opulence is originally derived, is frequently powerful enough to maintain the natural progress of things towards improvement, in spite both of the extravagance of government and of the greatest errors of administration."

Here, we see the consistency of Smith's moral system across his two seminal works. The motivation of every person to "better their condition" causes them to work hard and adopt social behavior that is highly esteemed by capitalist society. This generates the social norms of the merchant culture, which include creativity, initiative, hard work, and industry as well as honesty, reciprocity, responsibility, fairness, and promise-keeping. The Scottish Enlightenment philosophers attributed the generation of these societal norms to the invisible hand of divine providence. By the means of commerce and the perfect system of liberty, society operates as if it were a republic of saints.[11]

While Adam Smith attributes the great wealth created by capitalism to the division of labor in *The Wealth of Nations*, it remains a product of the motivation of every person to better their condition and achieve higher esteem. Further, the desire to achieve higher esteem is ultimately grounded in the Stoic virtues and the desire to be praiseworthy. Therefore, when nineteenth-century classical economists adopted Hobbes's and Mandeville's "selfish hypothesis" as the first principle of their discipline, they adopted a principle that Smith, Hume, and the other Scottish Enlightenment philosophers had adamantly rejected in their own writings (Force 2003).

What about the passage in *The Wealth of Nations* that George Stigler and other neoclassical economists associated with the Chicago School used to attribute their first principle of narrow self-interest to Adam

---

[11] Adam Smith himself invokes the "invisible hand" three times in his corpus of writings: once in the *History of Astronomy*, once in *The Theory of Moral Sentiments*, and once in *The Wealth of Nations*. In the first occurrence, Smith refers to the invisible hand of Jupiter as contrasted with the visible hand of thunder and lightning. In the other two occurrences, Smith follows the common practice among English and French philosophers of referring to the invisible hand of divine providence (Force 2003).

Smith? It is instructive that Smith uses the term *self-love* rather than self-interest in the passage on the butcher, brewer, and baker. The commonly used attributional passage, therefore, refers to the form of self-interest that Smith associated with the virtue of prudence rather than the vice of selfishness. Charles Griswold Jr. (1999, 260) highlights the difficulty of the typical interpretation of this passage in his book, *Adam Smith and the Virtues of Enlightenment*:

(T)he "Adam Smith problem" depended on a misunderstanding of the terms "sympathy" and "self-interest," according to which the first was taken to mean "benevolence" and the other "selfishness." The "problem" then seemed to be that the book on ethics praised virtue whereas the book on political economy built a large edifice on vice. Smith's famous remark to the effect that in procuring our dinner we address ourselves not to the humanity or benevolence of the butcher, brewer, or baker but to their self-love (WN I.ii.2) seemed to underline the point and to encapsulate everything that is both necessary to and morally repulsive about market economies.

Griswold proposes a more likely interpretation of this passage based on Smith's delineated motivation of every person to better their condition and the propensity to barter and trade. Just before the passage in question, Smith argues that the division of labor and its resulting national wealth are "not originally the effect of any human wisdom," but are the unintended consequence of "the propensity to truck, barter, and exchange one thing for another" (WN I.ii.1). He then argues that this propensity, which "is common to all men, and to be found in no other race of animals," is "the necessary consequence of the faculties of reason and speech" (WN I.ii.2–3). Thus, the necessity of developing rhetorical skills is especially great in a commercial society. In this society, according to Smith, the division of labor makes each person highly dependent on exchange for their basic needs and yet, one's "whole life is scarce sufficient to gain the friendship of a few persons" (WN I.ii.2).

Rather than supporting the first principle of narrow self-interest in economics, therefore, the passage on the butcher, brewer, and baker is part of Smith's larger argument supporting the "civilizing" role of persuasion and the ability of commerce and trade to support moral virtue. The passage commonly used by neoclassical economists to establish their straightjacket of self-interest simply provides another example of Smith's invisible hand of divine providence, or the ability of commerce to generate the social norms of the merchant culture absent human wisdom. Griswold (1999, 297) provides the following interpretation of Smith's passage within its full context:

(I)n a "civilized" society, the arts of persuasion, communication, and noncoercive speech are essential. (Smith's) typically counterintuitive claim is thus that precisely in appealing to each other's self-interest, precisely in enacting what seems to be our fundamental separateness and indifference to one another, we "civilize" ourselves and each other by binding ourselves to one another through speech.... Paradoxically, in a "collection of strangers," ... civility is all the more important and likely. Although when we deal with the butcher, the baker, and brewer, we "address ourselves, not to their humanity but to their self-love," the unintended result is that their humanity and ours is enriched. Not only is our mutual dependence binding, but its accomplishment through language is civilizing.

Karl Marx applies the same narrow interpretation of *The Wealth of Nations* as neoclassical economists associated with the Chicago School. In contrast with the Chicago School, however, that narrow interpretation leads Marx to associate the selling of one's labor with manipulation and alienation. Adam Smith, in sharp contrast, associates the selling of one's labor with character development in capitalist society. Further, Smith does not view religion as an opiate of the people but rather as another source of character formation and moral norms. To Smith, "what people desire from religion is not power over others but comfort in the face of death, community as a context for the development of virtues, and assurance that there exists a standard of right (an 'impartial spectator') over and above the judgments of the moment" (Griswold 1999, 281). Smith's moral foundation for capitalism, therefore, shared the Scottish Enlightenment conviction that religion is and ought to be a permanent feature of society and that religious liberty is a central means to societal peace and prosperity.[12]

2.4 A FORMAL MODEL SUPPORTING SMITH'S MORAL FOUNDATION

There has always been a deep-seeded concern among researchers that the Chicago School's economic theory of the firm, called *agency theory*, left out social and moral issues of critical importance to capitalist society. Shortly after Watts and Zimmerman (1986) published their book applying agency theory to the discipline of accounting, for example, Eric Noreen (1988) published a paper challenging accountants to use the new

---

[12] The liberty and freedom provided by the liberal Enlightenment of the eighteenth century has proven to be irresistible to the world's inhabitants, and explains why "it has all but destroyed its fraternal enemy, the illiberal Enlightenment fathered by Marx" (Griswold 1999, 2).

theory to illustrate the adverse consequences of unethical behavior in the firm. Shortly after Pratt and Zeckhauser (1985) published their book of scholarly articles making agency theory accessible to managers, Bowie and Freeman (1992) published a book of scholarly articles emphasizing the moral implications of the theory. I add to this literature in my book, *Social Norms and the Theory of the Firm* (Stevens 2019). In that book, I present the latest theoretical, experimental, and archival research supporting Adam Smith's moral foundation for capitalism based on social norms.

Among my examples of theoretical research supporting Smith's moral foundation, I present the principal-agent model that I published with Alex Thevaranjan (Stevens and Thevaranjan 2010). Principal-agent theory is the highly mathematical version of the theory of the firm out of Chicago (Jensen 1983). Through its mathematical rigor and intuition, it has become one of the most important theoretical frameworks in economics, finance, and accounting (Lambert 2001).[13] The theory views the firm as a cascade of principal-agent relationships, where the principal hires the agent to perform some productive task that requires effort. Principal-agent relationships include the relationship between owners (investors) and management, upper management and division managers, division managers and supervisors, and between supervisors and laborers. The theory focuses on contract solutions to the agency conflicts that arise due to information asymmetry and self-interest and is consistent with a "nexus of contracts" view of the firm (Jensen and Meckling 1976).

Ken Arrow (1985, 38) explains the usefulness of principal-agent theory to prescribe and describe contracting behavior within the firm:

The principal-agent theory is in the standard economic tradition. Both principal and agent are assumed to be making their decision optimally in view of their constraints; intended transactions are realized. As is usual in economic theory, the theory functions both normatively and descriptively. It offers insights used in the construction of contracts to guide and influence principal-agent relations in the real world; at the same time it represents an attempt to explain observed phenomena in the empirical economic world, particularly exchange relations that are not explained by more standard economic theory.

In the classic single-period principal-agent model, the principal hires the agent to provide a productive effort and the level of effort provided by the agent effort is unobservable to the principal. As a result of this

---

[13] The development of agency theory has been credited to Stephen Ross (1973) in economics and Barry Mitnick (1974) in political science.

information asymmetry, a *moral hazard* arises whereby the agent has an opportunity to take advantage of the principal. The term *opportunistic* is commonly used to describe agents who take advantage of their private information at the expense of the principal (Williamson 1975). The firm's production requires the agent's effort but it is also affected by other factors outside of the agent's control. Under the economic assumption of narrow self-interest, the principal's only motivation is to achieve the most efficient contract (earn the highest return on her capital) and the agent's only motivation is to achieve the highest level of pay with the lowest amount of effort.

The first mover is the principal, who offers the agent a compensation contract. The second mover is the agent, who decides whether to accept or reject the contract and, if accepted, the level of effort to provide. At the end of the period, the output of the agent's effort is observed by both parties. For simplicity, it is commonly assumed that there are many potential agents in the labor market. Therefore, the principal must pay the agent his reservation wage on the open market to provide the desired effort. Because the agent privately provides the productive effort after accepting the contract, the contract must also induce the agent to voluntarily provide the principal's desired effort.[14] Given the assumption of narrow self-interest, the moral hazard for the principal is severe. In particular, the principal can never offer the agent a fixed wage and expect any effort in return. Thus, the agent can only receive an incentive contract that links pay to the production outcome (e.g., a piece rate contract) and shifts risk onto the agent. Further, the agent can only expect to receive the minimal level of pay he would receive from the competitive labor market.

The principal-agent model is rich with symbolism and labels that imply the presence of a moral dilemma. In addition to the labels "moral hazard" and "opportunism," providing less than an expected level of effort is labeled "shirking" by economists. Yet the traditional principal-agent model ignores all moral solutions to the moral hazard problem. For example, Adam Smith identifies sloth and laziness as common vices in both of his major works, and a work ethic is present in most religious traditions. Thus, a work ethic would be one moral solution to the moral hazard problem. Another moral solution would be to incorporate a simple reciprocity norm for both the principal and the agent based on Smith's human propensity to barter and trade. Despite the realism of

---

[14] These two constraints on the traditional contract solution are commonly called the *individual rationality constraint* and the *incentive compatibility constraint*, respectively.

such moral solutions, the traditional theory of the firm relies entirely on contract solutions based on narrow self-interest (Stevens 2019).

In the principal-agent model of Stevens and Thevaranjan (2010), we present a moral solution to the moral hazard problem based on a promise-keeping norm. We assume that the principal specifies a standard level of effort at the time of contracting. Any notion of a standard for effort is ignored in the traditional principal-agent model because it would be completely ignored by the agent. In our model, however, we assume that the agent suffers disutility if he chooses to violate the standard for effort after agreeing to the contact. We model the disutility for violating the agreed-upon standard for effort as increasing in the moral sensitivity of the agency and the level of violation. We defend our model's assumptions by observing that promise-keeping is widely viewed as a legitimate norm by practitioners and moral theorists alike (Bicchieri 2006). In relation to our previous discussion of Scottish Enlightenment philosophers, David Hume (1739/1975, III.2.5) argued that a promise-keeping norm made the formation of commerce and trade possible. We preserve all the other assumptions of the traditional principal-agent model.[15]

We examine the interplay between the agent's moral sensitivity and firm productivity in determining the optimal employment contract. When moral sensitivity is nonzero, our model yields new and interesting results. Our key result is that the agent would rather provide the standard level of effort than shirk as long as the standard is below a critical level and the principal pays the agent his reservation wage for the effort (his cost of effort). This allows the agent to receive a fixed-wage contract from the principal rather than an incentive contract that imposes significant risk on the agent. We also find that the principal can induce the agent to provide effort beyond his critical level by including a wage premium that more than compensates him for the extra effort. Finally, we find that the optimal contract for firms with high productivity relative to the agent's moral norm sensitivity involves a wage premium. In this special condition, it is optimal for the principal to induce higher effort from the agent. However, our model shows that the principal must share the incremental gain with the agent to induce the higher effort.

We conclude that incorporating a promise-keeping norm increases the descriptive, prescriptive, and pedagogical usefulness of the traditional

---

[15] In formal modeling terms, we utilize the popular joint assumptions that have become known as LEN: Linear incentive contracts, Exponential utility functions, and Normal distributions of noise terms (Lambert 2001). As is commonly done in these LEN models, we also assume that the agent is risk-averse whereas the principal is risk-neutral.

theory of the firm. Incorporating a promise-keeping norm allows the principal-agent model to *describe* the existence of salary contracts in practice and predict when such salaries will include a premium to induce additional effort from the agent. Incorporating a promise-keeping norm also allows the model to *prescribe* ways of increasing the efficiency of the principal-agent relationship. By demonstrating the benefits of norm sensitivity to the principal, the agent, and the economy in general, for example, our model justifies the emphasis placed upon professional norms by practitioners, regulators, and educators. Finally, incorporating a promise-keeping norm allows the model to be used to teach the importance of social and moral norms to one's career, the firm, and the economy. Thus, our model demonstrates that incorporating social norms increases the *pedagogical* usefulness of agency theory in business education.

Our principal-agent model demonstrates that a norm for promise-keeping causes other social and moral norms to arise endogenously in the model. For example, the promise-keeping norm raises the possibility of a "work ethic" in the agent that promotes an expectation for a fair amount of effort for a fair wage. The promise-keeping norm also raises the possibility of an "employment ethic" in the principal that requires her to compensate the agent for higher levels of productive effort. Thus, the promise-keeping norm generates the possibility of reciprocity and fairness norms arising in the model. This supports Jon Elster's (1989, 101) assertion that "(t)he workplace is a hotbed for norm-guided action." Finally, our model supports the importance of Adam Smith's moral theory to his economic theory in *The Wealth of Nations*. Because the productivity of the agent's effort is affected by his skill, moral sensitivity allows the agent to directly profit from improvements in his skill through the salary premium. Absent moral sensitivity, however, the agent can only expect an incentive contract that inflicts significant financial risk and only pays the minimum amount required by the labor market. Thus, our model suggests that moral sensitivity represents a type of human capital that fuels the specialization and division of labor that Adam Smith theorized as the basis for economic growth and the wealth of nations.

2.5 CONCLUSION

This chapter dispels many of the myths regarding Adam Smith propagated by classical and neoclassical economists. In contrast to his popular caricature today, Smith was a moral philosopher of the highest caliber who incorporated important moral perspectives throughout his writings.

Smith presented his moral theory based on social norms and culture in *The Theory of Moral Sentiments* and maintained it as the moral foundation for his economic theory in *The Wealth of Nations*. Smith's moral theory is based on the principle of sympathy and the behavioral norms that arise due to past social experiences that reveal standards of right and wrong behavior. Similar to the other philosophers of the Scottish Enlightenment, he attributes moral judgment and the moral conscience to the *impartial spectator*, but he also reserves important roles for religion and moral codes such as the Stoic virtues. When nineteenth-century classical economists adopted narrow self-interest as the first principle of their discipline, therefore, they adopted a principle that Smith and the other Scottish Enlightenment philosophers had adamantly rejected.

Smith's moral foundation for capitalism is best summarized by the sixth and final edition of *The Theory of Moral Sentiments*, which he published in the final year of his life (1790) and reflects his lifelong reflections on commerce and society. The following points of that final edition are worth emphasizing: (1) As with every edition of his classic work in moral philosophy, he begins by refuting narrow self-interest as the main motivation for human behavior. He does this by condemning Mandeville's view of virtue and by distinguishing between good self-interest (prudence) and bad self-interest (selfishness). (2) Smith grants mankind the ability to empathize with others, which he calls *sympathy*, and makes it the major force behind moral judgment and behavior. (3) Smith uses the concept of the *impartial spectator* to explain moral judgment and the moral conscience. Individuals observe what constitutes praiseworthy behavior over time and internalize these behavioral norms. (4) Smith adds a new section on moral virtue to emphasize that individuals are motivated by both the desire for *praise* and the desire to be *praiseworthy*.

It is a sad irony that shortly after Adam Smith's death, his writings on moral philosophy nearly disappeared from the cannon and his writings on political economy were reinterpreted to support the discipline's new defining principle of self-interest. A recent survey of 150 papers referencing Smith in two leading business ethics journals in the United States and Europe finds that an overwhelming majority endorsed the view that "Adam Smith established and defended the proposition that the worlds of ethics and economics are unrelated and that, in effect, society fares best when allowing individual self-seeking to roam freely" (Hühn and Dierksmeier 2016, 119). Only 2 percent of the papers reflected a correct view of Smith's two major works and their interconnectedness. In addition to dispelling many of the popular myths surrounding Adam Smith, this chapter presents a formal principal-agent model supporting his moral foundation for capitalism. This model demonstrates the importance of Smith's moral theory to his economic theory and reveals that any failure to incorporate his moral theory into the traditional theory of the firm reflects the economist's straightjacket of self-interest rather than difficulties in formal modeling.

The following chapter begins to explain how Adam Smith's moral foundation for capitalism was lost. By the time Max Weber and R. H. Tawney provided their detailed moral critiques of capitalism in the early twentieth century, Smith's writings had already been reduced to ideological statements pulled out of context in support of laissez-faire, free-market capitalism. In particular, classical economists after Smith narrowed their focus to individual utility maximization and largely ignored important social and moral aspects of capitalist society. Particularly devastating to Smith's moral foundation, neoclassical economists continued this narrowing by developing an increasingly mathematical economic theory that was void of human sympathy. Thus, Weber and Tawney had to face the growing economic and social challenges of industrial capitalism without the benefit of Smith's moral theory. The source of the hijacking of Smith's legacy is a mystery that involves the German Historical School, the modernist view of economics as a natural science, and the powerful influence of the Chicago School. That mystery is a major theme of this book.

3

Religion as a Moral Foundation
Max Weber and R. H. Tawney

Modern man, on the whole, is rarely able, with the best will in the world, to imagine just how significant has been the influence of religious consciousness on conduct of life, "culture," and "national character." However, it cannot, of course, be our purpose to replace a one-sided "materialist" causal interpretation of culture and history with an equally one-sided spiritual one. *Both are equally possible*, but neither will serve historical truth if they claim to be the *conclusion* of the investigation rather than merely the *preliminary work* for it.

Max Weber
The Protestant Ethic and the "Spirit" of Capitalism

Following his death in 1790, Adam Smith's legacy began to be reshaped by those who came after him. Based on differing readings of *The Wealth of Nations*, Smith became associated with conflicting political causes with Whig, Tory, republican, conservative, and liberal leanings. The reshaping of Smith's legacy began right away with his first biographer, Dugald Stewart (1753–1828), whose account of Smith's life in 1793 emphasized his writings in support of conservative politics and laissez-faire economics. The editors of subsequent editions of *The Wealth of Nations* in 1814 and 1828 further embellished his legacy in that direction. Another major reshaping of Smith's legacy was performed by John Stuart Mill (1806–73), who formed Smith into his own image in his *Principles of Political Economy* in 1845 (Milgate and Stimson 2009). Classical economists followed J. S. Mill's lead in narrowing the motivations of economic man to self-interest with preferences only for wealth and leisure. A group of historical economists in Germany, however, rose up to resist this narrowing of their discipline. A German economist from that group and a British economist from the London School of Economics wrote seminal works that highlighted the role of religion in the rise of capitalism. In this chapter, I address religion as a moral foundation for capitalism by discussing the lives and writings of Max Weber and R. H. Tawney.[1]

3.1 THE NARROWING OF ARGUMENTS FOR CAPITALISM IN THE NINETEENTH CENTURY

As capitalism triumphed in the West, it left in its wake new social, political, and economic challenges. In the face of these challenges, arguments in favor of capitalist systems turned into detailed critiques (Hirschman 1982). To be sure, Adam Smith provided a list of potential weaknesses as well as strengths in his critique of commercial society, which accounts for his usefulness to both the political Left and Right. In a recent study of passages in *The Wealth of Nations*, Graafland and Wells (2021, 38–39) find that of 208 references related to the impact of free markets on society, Smith associates free markets positively with virtues in about 60 percent of those references and negatively with vices in the other 40 percent. Graafland and Wells conclude that "Smith was no ideologue but a thoughtful and rigorous academic who paid very careful attention to the critiques of commercial society brought by his contemporaries like Rousseau even though his final conclusion was firmly in its favor."

Hirschman (1982) identifies three views of capitalism that became part of its detailed critique in the nineteenth century. Consistent with early arguments in the eighteenth century, capitalism continued to be viewed by some as a powerful moralizing agent. Hirschman calls this positive view the *Doux-commerce Thesis*.[2] An opposing view that rose to prominence during this period, however, was that capitalism dissolves social traditions and ideologies, such as religion, and thereby chips away at its own moral foundation. Hirschman calls this negative view, which was held by both Marxist and religious thinkers, the *Self-Destruction Thesis*. Finally, a third view rose to explain why capitalism didn't live up to its potential in various regions of the world. Hirschman calls this view the *Feudal-Shackles Thesis*, which describes the inability of a society to

---

[1] As the epigraph to this chapter reveals (Weber 1905/2002, 122), Weber maintained a broad view of economic life that included culture and religion. He became particularly interested in religion as a social institution that conveyed social and moral norms in capitalist society.

[2] *Doux* is the French word for gentle or soft, which characterizes Montesquieu's civilizing view of commerce leading to peace and tranquility in society.

entirely throw off the former feudal culture when transitioning to the merchant culture of capitalism.[3]

Hirschman (1982, 1483) concludes that capitalism imposes both *doux-commerce* and *self-destructive* effects upon society. Thus, the prosperity or "flourishing" of society under capitalism is determined by which mechanism dominates the other:

Once this view is adopted, the moral basis of capitalist society will be seen as being constantly depleted and replenished at the same time. An excess of depletion over replenishment and a consequent crisis of the system is then of course possible, but the special circumstances making for it would have to be noted, just as it might be possible to specify conditions under which the system would gain in cohesion and legitimacy.

Similarly, Adam Smith warned of the natural tendency for commercial society to corrupt the virtues and moral sentiments, leading to the vices of dishonesty, vanity, greed, and a willingness to exploit others (*TMS* I.iii.3). These vices became evident during the industrial revolutions generated by early capitalism in Britain in 1760–1840 and America in 1870–1920. Griswold (1999, 295) highlights three key points regarding Smith's view of the importance of civic virtue to capitalism:

First, competition and liberty, protected by a spectating "night-watchman state," are in themselves insufficient to sustain a peaceful and just society, for they cannot be counted upon always to generate the requisite civic virtue.... Without a modicum of habituated virtue (moral and intellectual) in the citizens, the invisible hand behaves like an iron fist. Second, there is no single solution to the problem of civic virtue; a mix of interdependent institutions and arrangements will always be required. Third, what mix is appropriate will depend on the historical circumstances; there is no a priori Smithean dogma about that. His policy prescriptions are, just as in the case of the impartial spectator's responses to the particular, sensitive to the context, within a general conception of virtue (including, of course, justice), human psychology, and relevant considerations of utility.

These three points help explain Smith's balanced critique of commercial society, including his insistent moral reservation regarding the unfettered operation of the market. In *The Wealth of Nations*, Smith grants commerce, religion, education, the family, and government important roles in preserving civic virtue and high moral character. Rather than promoting narrow self-interest in his classic work of political economy, therefore, Smith promotes the proper structuring of social institutions to

---

[3] This third view of capitalism has also been used to explain the persistence of feudalism in France until the 1790s and in parts of Central and Eastern Europe as late as the 1850s. See Chapter 4 for an extended discussion of the persistence of feudalism in Europe.

establish and maintain proper virtues and social norms (Stevens 2019). These three points also help explain why Smith spent his final years adding important extensions to *The Theory of Moral Sentiments* dealing with the virtues, and why Smith demonstrated an increasing concern for what Hirsch (1977) has labeled the "depleting moral legacy" of commercial society.[4]

By the end of the nineteenth century, the *doux-commerce* view of capitalism was largely eclipsed due to the harsh reality of industrial capitalism. In the midst of this harsh reality, however, economists began to model the economic world as one of isolated, individual decision making under conditions of perfect competition. Further, they applied mathematical formalism which required increasingly narrow behavioral assumptions. Thus, at the precise moment when classical economists needed to address the social challenges of capitalism, they tied their own hands by removing political and social issues from their discipline. Hirschman (1982, 1473) highlights the inability of economists to mount a legitimate defense of capitalism at this critical time:

Should not the praisers (of capitalism), at least, have had an interest in keeping alive the thought that the multiple acts of buying and selling characteristic of advanced market societies forge all sorts of social ties of trust, friendliness, sociability, and thus help hold society together? In actual fact, this sort of reasoning is conspicuously absent from the professional economics literature. The reasons are several. First, economists, in their attempt to emulate, in rigor and quantitative precision, the natural sciences, had little use for the necessarily imprecise ("fuzzy") speculations about the effects of economic transactions on social cohesion. Second, those trained in the tradition of classical economics had only scorn for the concern of sociologists over the more disruptive and destructive aspects of capitalism.

Milgate and Stimson (2009) have documented the narrowing of political economy after Adam Smith in their book, *After Adam Smith: A Century of Transformation in Politics and Political Economy*. They identify four historical periods that shaped the view of commerce and capitalist society in the West: *ancient, mercantilist, classical,* and *neoclassical.* Ancient philosophers, characterized by Aristotle and the Greco-Roman tradition, tended to merge economic life into political, social, and ethical perspectives. For example, "the household and city economies of ancient Greece comprised a nexus of relations between persons, determined by

---

[4] Griswold (1999, 295, Footnote 64) concludes that the conjunction of these three points "makes it impossible to see Smith as either 'conservative' or 'liberal,' 'right' or 'left' in the contemporary American sense of these terms."

moral and political norms" (Milgate and Stimson 2009, 62). Under mercantilism, however, economic life was considered subservient to political ends. In particular, trade was viewed as a "zero-sum game" that was to be conducted on a warlike footing and understood as politics by another means. Thus, mercantilism is best viewed as "an artifact of seventeenth-century statecraft overriding competing religious as well as economic norms" (Milgate and Stimson 2009, 66).

Smith devoted a large part of book four of *The Wealth of Nations* to attacking the antiquated mercantilist system of the French physiocrats. As he had surmised from his trip to Paris in 1766, the physiocrats had managed to combine an *economic* philosophy of liberty of trade with a *political* philosophy of despotism. He viewed the major error of this system as "its representing the class of artificers, manufacturers and merchants, as altogether barren and unproductive" (*WN* IV.ix.29). The French physiocrats thought they could raise up this important but "unproductive" class apart from free trade and individual liberty. It is in this context that Smith lends his most ardent support to the economic system of "perfect liberty" (*WN* IV.ix.16–17). In contrast to the mercantilist view that economic and religious liberties were subservient to political aims, Smith viewed the aims of government as subservient to the individual liberties of its citizens. "It is beyond debate that Smith believed that three liberties – the liberty of private property, the liberty of trade, and an expanding personal liberty – would go together" (Milgate and Stimson 2009, 69).

The publication of *The Wealth of Nations* is commonly viewed as the beginning of the classical period. Two views emerged regarding the relationship between economics and politics during this period. First, classical economists reduced the significance of politics by establishing economic life as the foundation of political life. David Ricardo (1772–1823) and Thomas Malthus (1766–1834) applied this *reductionist view* in their debates regarding constitutional reform in Britain. Next, classical economists severed economic life completely from political life. This *separability view* is reflected in J. S. Mill's classic work of political economy, *On Liberty*. These two views represented a significant narrowing of Adam Smith's original view of political economy, which incorporated moral aspects of capitalist society that he had outlined more fully in his first major work on the moral sentiments.

Throughout the nineteenth century, classical economists continued to narrow the discipline of political economy until it was no longer recognizable. Ricardo reduced political economy to an exercise in mathematical modeling, with his well-known tendency to utilize abstract economic models labeled the "Ricardian Vice" (Milgate and Stimson 2009, 161). For his part, Malthus developed a steady state model of the market economy where wages are at subsistence levels and grinding poverty prevails. This fatalistic vision gave economics its reputation as "the dismal science."[5] J. S. Mill (1836/1967, 323) narrowed the definition of political economy to "the science which traces the laws of such of the phenomena of society as arise from the combined operations of mankind for the production of wealth, in so far as those phenomena are not modified by the pursuit of any other object." To fit his narrow definition of political economy, Mill also limited the motivations of economic man to a desire for wealth and a dislike of work (Stevens 2019).[6]

The publication in 1890 of Alfred Marshall's (1842–1924) first edition of his famous treatise, *Principles of Economics*, represented a watershed event in the new "neoclassical" period. Neoclassical theory was largely an invention of mathematicians and engineers from France, Germany, and Austria such as Antoine Cournot (1801–77), Jules Dupuit (1804–66), Johann Thünen (1783–1850), Hermann Gossen (1810–58), and Carl Menger (1840–1921). Marshall systemized the mathematical, marginalist approach to economic theory that dominates the discipline today. To reflect this new approach, Marshall (1890, 36) expunged the "political" label from political economy: "(Economic study) shuns many political issues, which the practical man cannot ignore: and it is therefore a science, pure and applied, rather than a science and an art. And it is better described by the broad term Economics than by the narrower term Political Economy."[7]

As Milgate and Stimson (2009, 56) point out, "the classical economists' vision managed to preserve the array of institutions and associations that comprised the social and moral order... The same cannot be said of the principles of neoclassical economics that were introduced in

[5] According to classical economists, this fatalistic vision was to be avoided on two fronts. To Malthus, the answer was to curb population growth by a moral constraint on reproduction. To Ricardo, the answer was to encourage economic growth through globalization and technological innovation (Milgate and Stimson 2009).
[6] Morgan (2006, 7) describes J. S. Mill's narrow view of economic man as "a fiction in the service of science." Although Mill never used the term himself, his narrow view of economic man has been labeled *homo economicus*.
[7] In hindsight, it is remarkable that Marshall viewed economics as the broader label given that he had created it by removing political and social issues that were at the heart of political economy. See Chapter 4 for an extended discussion of Marshall's motivation for narrowing political economy at Cambridge.

the marginalist revolution of the 1870s." In the process of continuing the formalization of their discipline, neoclassical economists moved from a vision of "a civil society composed of social classes, professional groups, corporate entities, trade unions, and cooperative societies, to a civil society of isolated individual utility maximizers." In narrowing their focus to Jeremy Bentham's (1748–1832) world of individual utility maximization, they ignored the social, cultural, and moral context undergirding that world. Of particular significance to Adam Smith's moral foundation for capitalism, "neoclassical theory lacked any concept of human sympathy ... that might serve as the effective cement of a society" (Milgate and Stimson 2009, 59).

In the middle of the nineteenth century, a group of German economists rose up to challenge the narrowing of their discipline by classical economists. Led by Wilhelm Roscher (1817–94), Karl Knies (1821–98), and Bruno Hildebrand (1812–78), they sought to supplement the economic theory of classical economists by incorporating important social and historical insights. Roscher's *Principles of Political Economy* (1854/1877), for example, demonstrated a skilled attempt to supplement and complete Ricardo's classical economics (Ekelund and Hébert 2014). Later, however, a new German historical school led by Gustav von Schmoller (1838–1917) rejected classical economic theory completely due to its mathematical formalism and general lack of social and moral content. Schmoller's stance drew a strong response from Carl Menger, the founder of the "Austrian School of Economics." The ongoing conflict between the German Historical School and the Austrian School became known as the *Methodenstreit* or "battle of the methods." At the dawn of the twentieth century, however, a historical economist out of Germany published a broad critique of capitalism that would become famous for its focus on religion.

3.2 MAX WEBER'S CRITIQUE OF CAPITALISM

In the fall of 1909, the *Verein für Sozialpolitik* (Association for Social Policy) held its annual convention in Vienna. Founded in 1873 by German economists Georg Friedrich Knapp (1842–1926), Gustav von Schmoller, and Adolf Wagner (1835–1917), the association sought to address the rising challenges of modern industrialism and develop public policy suggestions for the new German Empire. The end of the Franco-Prussian War of 1870 led to the unification of thirty-nine German states into a new monarchy that lasted until the end of World War I, when

Wilhelm II was forced to abdicate the throne and the German Empire became a republic. The German unification of 1871 produced a period of accelerated economic growth and the development of heavy industry, but the explosion of wealth further separated the lifestyles of the wealthy aristocrats from the laborers who worked the fields or entered the growing cities to find work.

The founders of the association were concerned not only by the rising disparity of wealth but by a host of social and economic challenges that modern industrialism had unleashed upon German society. In contrast to the growing indifference of classical economists, "they demanded that economics orient itself to ethical ideals again" (Weber 1975, 127). The association "rejected socialistic experiments, and recognized the existing forms of production and property, but it fought for an improvement in the situation of the working classes." Three generations of scholars had gathered at the convention in Vienna in 1909. The older founders of the association were present as were their former students – including Max Weber (1864–1920) and his brother Alfred Weber (1868–1958), Heinrich Herkner (1863–1932), and Werner Sombart (1863–1941). A younger generation of scholars had appeared on the scene, however, and was beginning to assert itself against the political-metaphysical historicism of Schmoller.

Between speeches, one would frequently see a group of scholars huddled around an animated and fiery figure. Max Weber was one of the leading coordinators and speakers at the convention, and he took a particular interest in the ideas of the participants. His wife Marianne was also in attendance, and she observed her husband's intensity with both pride and concern. She knew the physical and mental toll it would take on him. The continuing conflict between Weber's deeply religious mother and his unreligious, politically liberal father had come to a head in 1897, causing the eldest son to explode in a fit of rage at his father's intolerant and domineering personality. When his father suddenly died four weeks later, Weber went into a deep depression that left him largely incapacitated for the rest of his life. As a result of his illness, Weber's longest full-time academic position was remarkably limited to only five semesters at the University of Freiburg from 1894 to 1896. Weber was barely able to work from 1898 to 1903 (Scaff 1989).

As a college student, Weber had pursued a broad education including jurisprudence and history along with philosophy, theology, political science, and political economy. He had attended Karl Knies's (1821–98) lectures on political economy at Heidelberg, which included material on Adam Smith and his political economy.[8] Weber joined the *Verein für Sozialpolitik* in 1888. Seeing his special promise, the founders gave him a special assignment upon the completion of his doctorate at the University of Berlin in 1889.[9] This assignment involved a study of the plight of agricultural workers east of the Elbe River, which gave Weber a further taste of political economy. Similar to Knapp and Schmoller, Weber's interest in political economy came with a "radical and postliberal concern for the social question" that led him to pursue contact with economists "committed to an activist social policy" (Scaff 1989, 28). Further, his political economy had a strong nationalist flavor. More precisely, Weber placed political economy in the service of "the permanent economic and political power interest of the nation," which explains his insistence that "the science of political economy is a *political* science" (Scaff 1989, 31).

The theoretical and empirical rigor with which Weber attacked his assignment cemented his reputation as a German scholar of political economy. At the session of the *Verein für Sozialpolitik* where Weber presented his work in 1893, Knapp declared that "this work above all has led to the perception that our expertise has been surpassed, that we must start to learn all over again" (Scaff 1989, 40).[10] After a brief stint replacing the ailing Levin Goldschmidt as a lecturer of commercial law at the University of Berlin, Weber accepted the offer of a chair in political economy at the University of Freiburg in the fall of 1894. His decision to focus on political economy was driven by three trends that had evolved after the German unification of 1871. First was the demise of middle-class "liberal" politics and culture which his father was a leading part of as a prominent member of the National Liberal Party in Berlin. Second was the steady growth of Marxist socialism as an ideology and cultural movement in response to the struggles of the working class and the indifference of the ruling elite. Third was the appearance of an uneasy concern over the prospects of a "cultural decline" driven by the shallow "rationalization" of modern life.

---

[8] Given that Weber covers much of the same moral terrain but fails to mention Smith's moral theory, it is highly unlikely that Knies incorporated content from *A Theory of Moral Sentiments* in his lectures.

[9] Weber completed two doctoral dissertations at the University of Berlin, one on the history of trading companies in the Middle Ages and one on the agrarian history of imperial Rome.

[10] Scaff (1989, 23) calls Weber's 1893 speech to the *Verein für Sozialpolitik* "the single episode responsible more than any other for establishing his reputation."

Weber viewed these trends with growing concern. Overall, he held a gloomy assessment of the political and economic conditions that had emerged under the new German empire. After the collapse of negotiations between Bennigsen and Chancellor Bismarck in 1878, prospects for increasing parliamentary power came to an abrupt end.[11] "The record of middle-class liberalism and its twelve years of legislative achievements, beginning with the North German Confederation in 1866, was simply obliterated in the prevailing political climate" (Scaff 1989, 15). Weber suspected that the conditions had been set for political paralysis, bureaucratic domination of the authoritarian state, and "feudalization" of the social order. He was proven correct. The new political-economic reality in Germany included widespread protectionism and an "unholy" alliance between industrial capitalism and the large Junker estates in the East.[12]

The German historical economists believed that the question "*What is capitalism?*" could best be grasped by the broader question, "*When and where did capitalism begin?*" Knapp had provided evidence that the origins of capitalism could be traced back to the sixteenth-century agriculture of the English leasehold system and the large-scale farms in the East Elbia region of Prussia. In both instances, "one could observe the formation of large enterprises, accumulation of profits by an entrepreneurial class, and commercial production for a market – for Knapp the sufficient conditions for capitalist development" (Scaff 1989, 37). Knapp concluded that capitalist enterprises could be consistent with either "free" or various forms of "unfree" labor. While in England free agrarian labor was already present by the sixteenth century, in Prussia free labor did not appear until the legal emancipation of the peasantry in 1807.

In his early work on the East Elbian territories, Weber largely accepted Knapp's views regarding the sixteenth-century transformation of traditional farming into capitalist production. To provide a more complete picture of the development of capitalism and the question of the status of labor, however, Weber looked more closely at the systematic relationships connecting economic production, social stratification, and political

---

[11] Rudolf von Bennigsen (1824–1902) was president of the National Liberal Party for thirty years and Otto von Bismarck (1815–98) was the conservative German statesman who helped Wilhelm I unify the thirty-nine German states into a new monarchy in 1871 and served as its chancellor until he was removed by Wilhelm II in 1890.

[12] The Junker estates were named after the "Juncherre" or landed nobility in Prussia who owned large estates that were maintained and worked by peasants with few legal rights. Chancellor Bismarck himself was a famous member of the Junker class.

power. He identified four main types of economies in Western civilization: (1) the *"slave state,"* which assured a continuous labor supply through military conquest and strict control of laborers' social institutions; (2) the *"colonial"* system, which relied on nomadic labor, piece-wages, and surplus land; (3) the *"patriarchal"* system, which bound labor to the land by enforcing complex forms of economic, social, and legal dependency; and (4) the emerging *"capitalist"* system, which was characterized by "free labor," wage payments, intensive cultivation, technological innovation, and capital accumulation (Scaff 1989).

Weber's comparative studies of the four types of economies, using questionnaire data as well as historical and contemporary observations (he used the colonial economy of contemporary Argentina), convinced him that the *slave, colonial,* and *patriarchal* types were incapable of providing sustained technological innovation and economic growth. All three types relied on the persistence of specific historical conditions – continual military conquest, access to surplus land, isolation from market forces, etc. – that were difficult to sustain in the modern world. Only the fourth type of economy, *capitalist,* was conducive to the development of a rational system of production and exchange that led to sustained technological innovation and economic growth. Yet Weber's analysis of each type of economy exposed the potential for socioeconomic and political conflicts and objective possibilities for transformation over time. In what would become known as the "Weberian approach," he insisted on objectivity and the use of "ideal types" for the construction of theory, hypotheses, and suggested relationships for further investigation.

Similar to Karl Marx (1818–83), Weber based his critique of capitalism on capitalist systems as they had evolved in industrialized cities and lingering patriarchal systems in agrarian areas of Germany. In contrast to Marx's pessimistic view based on alienation and class conflict, however, Weber concluded that capitalism "represents an irreversible 'developmental tendency,' and therefore the question to ask is not whether it can be stopped or reversed, but rather, what its social, political, and cultural consequences are" (Scaff 1989, 59). Weber observed that both reliable peasants and self-assured Junkers (large landowners) were dying breeds and that the *patriarchal* system would eventually break down as large landowners sold plots of land or passed their land on to their descendants. Further, Weber foresaw that alienation and exploitation would become less of a concern with these smaller landholders because they would own the means of production and thereby view their labor as a freely chosen activity based on material interest.

While Weber and Marx shared a similar historical context and concern for the working class, their critiques of capitalism were fundamentally different. Scaff (1989, 65) emphasizes that while Weber's views did not clearly align with any given scientific school or political party, "it is nevertheless also correct to emphasize that Weber did not doubt the long-term strength of either capitalist development or pressures for increasing social and cultural democratization." His trip to America in 1904 confirmed his faith in capitalism and its potential to yield widespread opportunity and freedom. The same cannot be said of Marx, whose political economy was a product of the political left. Marx's theory of historical materialism predicted that capitalism would collapse due to the growing alienation and exploitation felt by the working class (proletariat). While Weber took Marx seriously and learned from him, he did not seek to build upon what he called "Marx's theoretically shattered system" (Scaff 1989, 49).

Karl Löwith (1993) has provided the most detailed comparison of Weber and Marx and their critiques of capitalism. Marx based his critique of capitalism on the narrow utilitarianism of the classical economists (e.g., Ricardo, Malthus, and J. S. Mill), whereas Weber maintained a broad perspective that incorporated social, cultural, and moral influences. As Löwith (1993, 63) explains:

> Weber did not regard capitalism as a power made up of "relations" of the forces and means of production which had become autonomous, so that everything else could be understood therefrom in terms of ideology. According to Weber, capitalism could only become the "most fateful" power in human life because it had itself already developed within the framework of a "rational way of life".... Weber conceived of this rationality as an original totality – as the totality of an "attitude to life" and "way of life" – which is subject to a variety of causal conditions but is nevertheless unique: as the occidental "ethos." This determinant ethos manifests itself in the "spirit" of (bourgeois) capitalism as well as in that of (bourgeois) Protestantism. Both religion and the economy are formed in their living religious and economic reality within the current of this determinant totality, and they, in turn, concretise this totality by leaving their imprint upon it.

Weber viewed Marx's critique of capitalism as narrow, materialistic, and utopian. Specifically, Weber questioned Marx's view that the abolition of private property and free enterprise would end the domination of man by man. Whereas Marx envisioned the demise of both religion and capitalism and the rise of a utopian communist state run by the "dictatorship of the proletariat," Weber envisioned an increasingly enlightened capitalism that would be supported by religion and the effective public policy of a democratic government. Such a public policy would be committed to not only promote justice and the needs of the disadvantaged, but to "protect and sustain that which appears *valuable* in people: self-responsibility, the deep impulse toward achievement, toward the spiritual [*geistig*] and moral excellence of humanity" (Scaff 1989, 71). In this regard, the Weberian approach closely resembled the broad social and moral approach of Adam Smith. However, the German Historical School had invented a conceptual conflict between Adam Smith's two major works that obscured his moral foundation for capitalism from Weber and other institutional and historical economists.

By the time of the Vienna Convention in 1909, Weber's views on political economy had matured in a number of important ways. First, he had separated himself from the political-metaphysical historicism of Schmoller. Weber proposed a middle-ground between the German Historical School and the Austrian School which he called "social economics" (Baehr and Wells 2002).[13] Second, he had developed a more hopeful view of capitalism after journeying to America for three months in the summer of 1904. Weber's fascination with American society was "born in part from the sense that the United States offered a unique opportunity to observe the practice and culture of modern 'rational' capitalism in an especially concentrated form" (Scaff 2011, 61). Weber's institutional and historical view of economics would be imported back to the United States through the efforts of Frank Knight at the University of Chicago. In a strange twist of fate, however, Knight's students at Chicago would be instrumental in crushing that view.

3.3 R. H. TAWNEY AND THE CHRISTIAN LEFT

The moral conviction of the British economist Richard Henry (Harry) Tawney (1880–1962) can best be conveyed by his actions during World War I. The rising power of the German Empire at the turn of the century had become a concern for Britain and France as well as the rest of Europe. Wilhelm II dismissed Chancellor Bismarck in 1890 and gave the military increasing control over the Empire, which he had expanded further after the German unification of 1871. When a young Serbian nationalist assassinated Archduke Franz Ferdinand, the heir to the Dual Monarchy of Austria-Hungary, Wilhelm II encouraged his Austrian counterpart, Franz Joseph I, to adopt an aggressive stance against Serbia

---

[13] The term "social economics" emerged originally in France in the early 1800s and is typically associated with Jean-Baptiste Say (Baehr and Wells 2002, xxxv).

by promising military support. After Austria-Hungary declared war on Serbia on July 28, 1914, Britain, France, Russia, and Belgium lined up against Austria-Hungary and Germany. The Great War had begun.

Although he was nearly thirty-four years old, and had no obligation to do so, R. H. Tawney volunteered with his fellow countrymen on November 26 as a private in the Manchester Regiment of the British Army. Tawney's strong association with the working class of Britain began soon after his graduation from Balliol College at Oxford University in 1903. He came from a deeply religious family that had fought for Parliament and Cromwell in the English Civil War and become successful capitalists involved in banking, brewing, and building. Tawney's father, Charles Henry Tawney (1837–1922), was a Cambridge "Apostle" who had taught English, literature, and history at the University of Calcutta in India and had become a notable scholar and translator of Hindu epics.[14] He had served as the Principal of Presidency College at the University of Calcutta for much of the period from 1875 to 1892. In his research, teaching, and service, the elder Tawney brought Western culture to India as he made Indian culture accessible to the West.

R. H. Tawney's family background and education made him a member of the late-Victorian intellectual aristocracy. He had won the top classical entrance scholarship to Balliol, one of the most influential of Oxford's colleges, known for its ethic of public service and social responsibility. While at Oxford (1899–1903), Tawney had joined the Christian Social Union, which was founded in 1889 on the principle that economic and social life must be organized and conducted in accordance with Christian principles. As a forerunner of things to come, he had also joined the Independent Labour Party which was founded by industrial workers in the North of England in 1893. But things did not end well for Tawney at Oxford. In addition to his growing social and political activities, he became burdened with the care of his younger brother Stephen, who had suffered a nervous breakdown. While he took a first-class score in Classical Moderations at the end of his first two years, he took a second in Literae Humaniores ("Greats") in the summer of 1903. This dismayed his prominent father, who purportedly wrote to his son, "How do you propose to wipe out this disgrace?" (Goldman 2014, 22).

---

[14] The "Apostles" is the common name for the Cambridge Conversazione Society, an elite secret society founded in the 1820s that became well known for the stature of its members and its impact on those who came under its influence. Famous members of the Apostles included such celebrities as John Maynard Keynes, G. E. Moore, Bertrand Russell, Henry Sidgwick, and Leonard Woolf.

Tawney's inferior performance at the end of his fourth year meant that he was not a candidate for a college fellowship and future study at Oxford. Instead, Tawney had to content himself with an exhibition and residence at Toynbee Hall, a settlement house established in East London in the 1880s to provide humanitarian relief for the poor. Tawney was able to acquire a temporary position lecturing in economics at the University of Glasgow from 1905 to 1907.[15] His social and political activism, however, never stopped. In 1907, Tawney joined a campaign to open the University of Oxford to students from working-class and lower-middle-class backgrounds. The campaign resulted in the creation of a tutorial post under the joint auspices of Oxford and the Workers' Educational Association (WEA), an association founded in 1903 to pro- mote higher education to working adults in Britain. Tawney joined the WEA in 1905 and was quickly placed on its executive committee. He began teaching two experimental classes for the WEA in January 1908 in the northern industrial towns of Longton and Rochdale, but was not formally appointed as its first tutor until November of that year.

The temporary nature of the tutorial position generated considerable uncertainty and caused another crisis in Tawney's life as he had recently proposed to the sister of his best friend, William Beveridge. Tawney was still living in Glasgow when his experimental classes began, and he would leave the city on a Friday morning and not return home until Sunday after teaching his Friday evening class at Longton and his Saturday afternoon class at Rochdale. After his marriage and his three-month honeymoon in Germany, Tawney moved to Manchester to be closer to the industrial dis- tricts where he was teaching, which now included Chesterfield, Longton, Rochdale, and Wrexham. He taught tutorial classes for Oxford and the WEA for the next five years, including classes in economic and industrial history, seventeenth-century political history, economic theory, and local government (Goldman 2014).

Tawney's experience teaching in the cities of the industrial north changed his perspective in critical ways. While he remained genuinely interested in the concerns of "Outcast London" – including unemploy- ment, casual labor, homelessness, and overcrowding – he became con- vinced that "the social question" in Britain was changing to the concerns

[15] The position at Glasgow came open when William Smart, Adam Smith Professor of Political Economy, was asked to write the majority report of the Royal Commission on the Poor Laws. Tawney also assisted Smart with a massive project that came out of his work for the Royal Commission – an economic history of the nineteenth century.

of the working class. In an entry in 1912 in his *Commonplace Book*, a journal he kept before the war, Tawney summarized the new perspective drawn from his tutoring experiences:

> One whole wing of social reformers has gone, it seems to me, altogether astray. They are preoccupied with relieving distress, patching up failures, reclaiming the broken down. All this is good and necessary. But it is not the social problem and it is not the policy which would ever commend itself to the working classes. What they want is security and opportunity, not assistance in the exceptional misfortunes of life, but a fair chance of leading an independent, fairly prosperous life.... It is no use devising relief schemes for a community where the normal relationships are felt to be unjust.

This background helps explain why, in 1914, Tawney signed up for the war as a private in the Manchester Regiment and refused a position as a commissioned officer. At the Somme offensive on July 1, 1916, Tawney, who by this time was a sergeant, led his platoon out of their trenches at 7:30 a.m. in the first wave of attacks on the German front. Most of his men were immediately killed or wounded, and the rest were pinned down, unable to move under heavy machine gun fire. Volunteering to go on a reconnaissance mission to find the promised second wave of support, Tawney was hit with bullets that went through his abdomen and took away part of one of his kidneys. He lay in no-man's land for thirty hours, and the few medics who passed by did not think he would survive. Tawney had received communion prior to the final order to move out and, as he told his wife in a fateful letter on June 29, he believed that he was "in the hands of the Lord." It was one of the bloodiest battles in the war, with almost 60,000 British casualties that day. Miraculously, Tawney would be among the 54 out of 350 members of the 22nd Manchester who survived the battle. However, he would carry the pain of his wounds for the rest of his life.[16]

Tawney's biographer, Lawrence Goldman, describes the perception among Tawney's students, colleagues, and the general public that he was a Christian, a democrat, and a socialist in that descending order. His political views, however, reflected an indigenous British socialism that was based on a Christian worldview and opposed Marxist materialism.[17]

---

[16] In August 1916, Tawney wrote a detailed essay describing his battle experience for the *Westminster Gazette* called "The Attack." It became a vital source for a BBC docudrama entitled *Battle of the Somme* nearly ninety years later.

[17] Tawney reminded his readers that while Marx was born and raised in Germany, he had spent much time in London and was well aware of the indigenous English socialism based on Christian ethics.

Although Tawney was a member of the Fabian Society after 1906 and was good friends with its founders Beatrice and Sidney Webb, he rejected their state-centric view of socialism. In particular, he rejected their arguments for state control of key industries based on utilitarianism and efficiency. In his *Commonplace Book* in 1912, for example, Tawney wrote, "All experience seems to me to prove that people, or at any rate English people, will not accept efficiency as a substitute for liberty." Tawney particularly rejected the Marxist rationalization of all statements into expressions of class interest: "If truth is merely what a group finds it convenient to declare to be truth then that statement is itself an example of that fact, and the attack on bourgeois morality possesses no more validity than that morality" (Goldman 2014, 177).

Goldman, however, detects a noticeable shift in Tawney's socialist views toward the more state-centric variety after the war. This shift was caused, Goldman argues, by Tawney's involvement with the problems of the coal industry from the Royal Commission of Inquiry of 1919 until the General Strike of 1926. Despite Tawney's recommendation of state control in the coal industry and his involvement in the Labour Party, he "remained deeply attached to a Christian world view and … his earliest religious ideas in the *Commonplace Book* retained their importance to him" (Goldman 2014, 180). Tawney took up a teaching post at the London School of Economics in 1920 where he spent the rest of his professional life until 1949. After the disastrous outcome of the nationalization of the coal industry and the increased narrowing of the Labour Party along Marxist lines, a new centrist party named the Social Democratic Party (SDP) established itself in 1981–82 around Tawney's moderating ideals. The Christian socialist movement which arose in Britain in the late nineteenth century and was well represented by Tawney, however, died with him.

3.4 THE ROLE OF RELIGION IN THE DEVELOPMENT OF CAPITALISM

Both Max Weber and R. H. Tawney possessed a deep knowledge of economic history and shared an appreciation for the social challenges of early capitalism. Further, both had religious upbringings and theological training, although Weber considered himself "unmusical" when it came to religious faith. While they both were concerned with the growing disparity of wealth in capitalist society, their critique of capitalism went much deeper to include critical social and moral issues arising during the industrial revolution. Thus, Weber and Tawney rejected the narrow self-interest and utilitarianism that had captured classical and neoclassical economics. Despite their dramatically different backgrounds and temperaments – Weber was known for his vindictive temper, whereas Tawney was widely revered for his gentility and humility – they both wrote seminal works addressing the role of religion in the development of capitalism.

Weber wrote his seminal essay, *The Protestant Ethic and the "Spirit" of Capitalism*, in stages between the summer of 1903 and the winter of 1905. It contained many of the themes covered in the lectures he attended as a young student under Karl Knies at the University of Heidelberg. It also contained many new insights from the trip that he and his wife Marianne took to America during the summer of 1904. Coming as it did after his prolonged nervous illness from 1898 to 1903, it also represented what Marianne called "the first work to make Weber's star shine again" (Weber 1975, 333). Perhaps that is why he spent the rest of his life passionately defending it, including publishing a revision aimed at addressing critics just before his death in 1920.[18]

Weber published *The Protestant Ethic* in a prestigious German journal of social science in two parts in 1904 and 1905.[19] It was not translated into English until Talcott Parsons completed his translation of the 1920 version in 1930. Parsons had spent a year at the London School of Economics in 1924–25 and attended lectures by Tawney, but Tawney had not mentioned Weber's seminal work of economic history. It wasn't until Parsons went to Heidelberg in 1925 to begin a Ph.D. in sociology and economics that he was exposed to Weber's work. Parsons was enamored with Weber's narrative of the founding of America and its unique moral order, and was anxious to make it accessible to an English-speaking audience. Because of his strong reputation and command of the German language, Tawney was chosen by the publisher to provide editorial advice on Parson's translation and write an introduction. It is generally agreed that Parson's translation, although defective in important aspects, made Weber's seminal work famous in America.[20]

---

[18] According to Baehr and Wells (2002), Weber's revision served only to generate new problems and ambiguities.

[19] Weber published his seminal work in the *Archiv für Sozialwissenschaft und Sozialpolitik* (Archives for Social Science and Social Welfare), an academic journal where he had accepted a position as co-editor in 1903 and which occupied his energies for the rest of his life (Scaff 2011).

[20] To address the criticism that Parson's translation was defective in important aspects, and to show changes between the two versions, Baehr and Wells provided a new English translation in 2002 based on Weber's original version of his classic work in 1904–5.

Weber could see the gathering clouds when it came to his native country. He became increasingly convinced that Germany lacked the combination of discipline and freedom that the Puritan tradition had bestowed upon America. Thus, *The Protestant Ethic* reflected Weber's concern for contemporary public policy and the future of Germany. According to Baehr and Wells (2002, x), Weber included a number of important themes that were relevant to this debate:

Not least of them is a plea for Imperial Germany to grow up: to cast off a politically authoritarian, outmoded system, dominated by the Junker landed class and embrace the modern industrial order. Weber located the origins of modern freedom not in the Enlightenment, but in the Puritan Anglo-American tradition; the struggle to establish liberty of conscience and worship, he argued, was the cornerstone of all other human rights. The vanguard of that struggle was the Protestant sects – Baptists, Quakers, and others – whose influence in Germany had been eclipsed by the Lutheran Church and its "aura of office." Weber acknowledged that Lutheranism began life as a radical movement, but he viewed its trajectory as moving in an increasingly illiberal direction, endorsing state power against individual freedom and, allegedly like Catholicism, encouraging passive adaptation to existing conditions rather than soliciting innovation and risk.

According to Weber, the Protestant sects, inspired by a powerful sense of the divine, created a social and economic order that their forebearers would have condemned as godless, materialist, and devoid of any ultimate purpose. In particular, the rational, individualistic world of modern capitalism was the unintended consequence of a deep religious devotion to God. *The Protestant Ethic*, however, has been narrowly interpreted as a "work ethic." Scaff (2011, 146) argues that this notion is at best a poor caricature of Weber's seminal work:

(T)he ethos Weber was attempting to describe (was) an ethos characterized by constant, methodical, ascetic mastery of the self and the world as an end in itself that required no independent justification. This kind of asceticism was transformative in its unintended consequences; it sought to discipline the natural self and change the everyday world by bringing both self and world under "rational" – that is to say, "conscientious" and "mindful" – control. The ethic was thoroughgoing and continuous, not episodic; it defined a totality, a specific kind of life conduct, a complete way of life.

Weber emphasized how religions hold out to believers differing kinds of "psychological rewards" or "premiums" – including what Weber called "premiums of salvation." He also emphasized, however, the uniqueness of the psychological premium of Calvinism in that it provided little support for the belief that human beings could affect their eternal destiny by works of righteousness.

(O)n the contrary, the weight of the doctrine pulled overwhelmingly against such a heretical notion, championing a God so transcendent as to have little interest in his creatures and so all-powerful as to confound any notion of significant human agency…. Weber's conclusion was that Calvinism promoted, despite itself, an emotional inducement in the faithful to look for "proof" of "election"; and that methodical, systematic work in a calling was the social product of this religious quest.

Lutheranism and Catholicism, in contrast, offered psychological premiums by "rewarding … an adaptation to the world and providing pressure valves (e.g., through the confessional) to release the pent-up, agitated anxiety typical in Calvinism or among the Puritan sects" (Baehr and Wells 2002, xxxix).

Weber became fully convinced by Georg Jellinek's (1895) argument that the idea of legally established, inalienable rights for the individual was not the work of the French Revolution but a fruit of the Protestant Reformation. The Bills of Rights issued from Virginia and across the American Colonies "bore the impress of the uncompromising struggles for freedom of conscience that characterized the northern European Puritan movement whose seeds had fallen on American shores" (Baehr and Wells 2002, xl–xli). Weber stated this link explicitly in *Economy and Society*:

Such freedom of conscience may be the oldest Right of Man – as Jellinek has argued convincingly; at any rate, it is the most basic Right of Man because it comprises all ethically conditioned action and guarantees freedom from compulsion, especially from the power of the state. In this sense the concept was as unknown to Antiquity and the Middle Ages as it was to Rousseau's social contract, with its power of religious compulsion. The other Rights of Man or civil rights were joined to this basic right, especially the right to pursue one's own economic interests, which includes the inviolability of individual property, the freedom of contract, and vocational choice.

R. H. Tawney published his seminal work, *Religion and the Rise of Capitalism*, in 1926 (Tawney 1926/2017). This work began as a set of lectures in honor of Henry Scott Holland, the British theologian and social reformer who had died in 1918. The Holland Memorial Lectures were to be delivered every three years having for their subject "the religion of the incarnation in its bearing on the social and economic life of man." Tawney delivered his lectures in March and April of 1922 at King's College, London, but it took him over three years to prepare them for publication. He dedicated the book to the Anglo-Catholic theologian Charles Gore, whose social teaching had made Balliol College a hotbed of social activism and who was later Bishop of Oxford and mentor to

Tawney. There is no evidence that Tawney read Weber's essay prior to writing his own seminal work. According to Goldman (2014, 229), the authors had two different motivations:

Weber had wanted to understand the effect of reformed religion on the inner life, motives and economic behavior of individuals specifically, and to explain the role of religious ideas in the formation of a capitalistic personality. Tawney, on the other hand, focused on a broad transformation in social ethics, the slow retreat over centuries of a Christian social tradition.

Religion and the Rise of Capitalism was largely based on the English pamphlet literature of the sixteenth and seventeenth centuries, and represented a rigorous historical study in its own right. Always the moralist, however, Tawney began by reflecting on contemporary efforts to revive a Christian social ethics and involve the modern church in the challenges of industrial capitalism. As such, his work shared Weber's concern for contemporary public policy. While Weber set a strictly objective, "scientific" tone in his essay, however, Tawney often used colorful, normative language in his book. His detailed historical synthesis included the waning of the middle ages, the corruption of the Roman Catholic Church, the Reformation response in Luther and Calvin, the rise of Puritanism, the Civil Wars in Britain, the triumph of the landed aristocracy after the Restoration, the growth of the middle class, and the origins of industrialization. According to Goldman (2014, 231), however, Tawney's book revealed an ambivalence regarding the effects of Puritanism in England:

Puritanism in England had vanquished not only the surviving elements of "feudalism" but also the monarchical state "with its ideal of an ordered and graded society." In this way, battling on these two fronts, it had prepared the way "for the commercial civilization which finally triumphed at the Revolution." It had also turned religion from the rule of all conduct in society into a purely personal and private affair: by the eighteenth century "it is in the heart of the individual that religion has its throne, and to externalize it in rules and institutions is to tarnish its purity and to degrade its appeal."

In contrast to Weber, Tawney emphasized the role of Catholicism in the early development of capitalism (Tawney 1926/2017, 84):

If capitalism means the direction of industry by the owners of capital for their own pecuniary gain, and the social relationships which establish themselves between them and the wage-earning proletariat whom they control, then capitalism had existed on a grand scale both in medieval Italy and in medieval Flanders. If by the capitalist spirit is meant the temper which is prepared to sacrifice all moral scruples to the pursuit of profit, it had been only too familiar to the saints and sages of the Middle Ages.

Further, up until the Spanish Armada against Britain in 1588, "it was predominantly Catholic cities which were the commercial capitals of Europe and Catholic bankers who were its leading financiers." According to Tawney's historical account, it was the extravagance of the capitalist spirit in the Roman Catholic Church that led to the Protestant Reformation.

Tawney (1926/2017, 110) identified three separate responses to the corruption, luxury, and ostentation of the Roman Church. The German reformers represented by Martin Luther "preached a return to primitive simplicity," whereas the Humanists attempted "the gradual regeneration of mankind by the victory of reason over superstition and brutality and avarice." The Swiss Reformers represented by John Calvin, however, took a third approach. Also based on reason, these reformers sought a moral regeneration of mankind based on purification, industry, and thrift.

Was it not possible that, purified and disciplined, the very qualities which economic success demanded – thrift, diligence, sobriety, frugality – were themselves ... Christian virtues? Was it not conceivable that the gulf which yawned between a luxurious world and the life of the spirit could be bridged, not by eschewing material interests as the kingdom of darkness, but by dedicating them to the service of God?

Tawney (1926/2017, 112) argued that Calvin did for the *bourgeoisie* of the sixteenth century what Marx did for the *proletariat* of the nineteenth.

(T)he doctrine of predestination satisfied the same hunger for an assurance that the forces of the universe are on the side of the elect as was to be assuaged in a different age by the theory of historical materialism. (Calvin) set their virtues at their best in sharp antitheses with the vices of the established order at its worst, taught them to feel that they were a chosen people, made them conscious of their great destiny in the Providential plan and resolute to realize it.

In contrast to Calvin, Marx's historical materialism was based on the feudal system that had evolved in medieval Europe and lingered in parts of Germany until well into the twentieth century. His moral denunciation of capitalism, therefore, resembled Luther and the doctrines of the medieval Schoolmen. As such, Tawney (1926/2017, 36) famously labeled Marx "The last of the Schoolmen."

Calvin and the Puritan moralists who derived their Christian doctrine most directly from him, including John Knox and the Presbyterians in Scotland, changed the plane on which the discussion of economic systems was conducted. In sharp contrast to the feudal world of Luther and Marx, Calvin assumed an advanced economic system based on commerce, banking, and trade. Thus, Calvinism was an urban faith targeted for life in large merchant cities such as Geneva, Antwerp, Amsterdam, and London. For example, Calvin relaxed the medieval condemnation of money lending and the charging of interest. According to Tawney (1926/2017, 113), "Both an intense individualism and a rigorous Christian Socialism could be deduced from Calvin's doctrine. Which of them predominated depended on differences of political environment and of social class."

Tawney (1926/2017, 131) emphasized that the religious zeal of Calvinism in France, Switzerland, England, Scotland, and the New England colonies initially bred a social system more tyrannical than the medieval Church: "Its meshes were finer, its zeal and its efficiency greater. And its enemies were not merely actions and writing, but thoughts." But mature Calvinism, especially when joined with Locke's political system of individual rights and liberties, brought forth a culture of liberalism and religious freedom that proved to be the most fertile ground for capitalism. In Italy, the Netherlands, Britain, and America, this fertile ground brought forth unparalleled advances not only in science and technology but also in literature, music, and art. These advances have been labeled the "Italian Renaissance," the "Dutch Golden Age," and the two "Industrial Revolutions," respectively.

Recent studies of economic history affirm the role of religion in the development of capitalism. Soll (2014, xii), for example, uses historical evidence to demonstrate how the discovery of double-entry accounting precipitated the birth of capitalism first in medieval Italy then in the Netherlands, Britain, and America. Similar to Weber and Tawney, he concludes that the development of capitalism was aided by religious devotion and moral norms that arose in support of a merchant culture, which included the norms of transparency and accountability: "Those societies that have succeeded are not only those rich in accounting and commercial culture but also the ones that have worked to build a sound moral and cultural framework to manage the fact that humans have a regular habit of ignoring, falsifying, and failing in accounting." In my book, *Social Norms and the Theory of the Firm* (Stevens 2019, Chapter 2), I provide a history of capitalism and the firm that incorporates social norms. Consistent with Soll, I conclude that the survival of capitalism is constantly threatened by a lack of transparency and accountability.

66   *Religion as a Moral Foundation: Weber and Tawney*

Recent evidence in psychology supports Weber's thesis that religion satisfies important emotional needs and supports capitalist institutions. Based on detailed questionnaires and clinical experience, Steven Reiss and his colleagues have identified sixteen psychological needs or "basic desires" that motivate individuals and explain the continuing appeal of religion in modern capitalist society. Reiss (2015, 140) summarizes his findings as follows: "People embrace religion because it provides them with opportunities to satisfy their basic desires again and again." One basic desire, for instance, is honor. Reiss has found that people with a strong need for honor are loyal, responsible, trustworthy, righteous, and self-disciplined. In contrast, those with a weak need for honor are expedient and opportunistic. His findings suggest that religion appeals to a significantly larger percentage of honorable than opportunistic people. This evidence supports Weber and Tawney's assertion that religion provided the values and virtues necessary for capitalism to arise and flourish in the West.

3.5 CONCLUSION

Although Adam Smith provided a moral foundation for capitalism based on social norms and culture, and maintained that foundation in all of his writings, classical economists after him largely removed issues of social and moral significance from their discipline. There were two responses to the narrowing of political economy by classical economists. Neoclassical economists continued to narrow political economy until it was no longer recognizable and was relabeled "economics." Marx and his followers, in contrast, "generated a repository of ideas and arguments concerning the alienating and exploitative character of capitalism, and the limited efficacy of social and political reform, that inspired revolutionaries and radical critics alike" (Milgate and Stimson 2009, 259). Weber and Tawney articulated a third critique of capitalism based on social and moral factors which included the influence of religion. That moral critique has largely been lost in the modern-day struggle between supporters of capitalism on the political Right and Marxist sympathizers on the Left.

Weber's seminal essay made reasoning related to the role of religion in capitalism popular and resurrected concerns that the faltering of religious faith posed a serious threat to its survival (Hirschman 1982). As for Tawney's seminal work, it was a best-seller during his lifetime and has been cited by Nobel prize-winning economists such as Kenneth Arrow and Amartya Sen. Tawney was particularly motivated by the growing number of indigent laboring poor in England under industrial capitalism and saw education as a major tool to lift the masses out of poverty. In his attempt to address the needs of the poor under capitalism, he promoted a Christian socialism that was popular with the political Left of his day. Recent research in economic history and psychology support the importance of religion in the development and survival of capitalism. Researchers and practitioners who use religion as a moral foundation for capitalism, therefore, appear to build on solid historical and scientific ground. As the following chapter reflects, however, this moral foundation fell out of favor among many intellectuals in the West by the end of the nineteenth century.

4

Humanism as a Moral Foundation

Karl Polanyi and John Maynard Keynes

> In actual fact, man was never as selfish as the theory demanded. Though the market mechanism brought his dependence upon material goods to the fore "economic" motives never formed with him the sole incentive to work. In vain was he exhorted, by economists and utilitarian moralists alike, to discount, in business, all other motives but material ones. On close investigation he was still found to be acting on remarkably "mixed" motives, not excluding those of duty towards himself and others – and maybe secretly even enjoying his work for its own sake.
>
> Karl Polanyi
> *Economics and the Freedom to Shape Our Social Destiny*

Adam Smith and the other eighteenth-century Scottish Enlightenment philosophers were heavily influenced by the teachings of John Calvin and the Presbyterian Kirk, but they were also influenced by recent developments in natural philosophy by Francis Bacon and Isaac Newton. This led them to pursue a moral system that was scientifically based and generalizable across multiple ages, cultures, and religious traditions. Over time, this enlightened humanism became highly influential and replaced religion as the source of moral truth for many in the West. Events in the first half of the twentieth century, however, tested the *Doux-commerce* view that capitalism could tame the violent passions and bring widespread peace and prosperity. Weber's concerns regarding Germain society proved prescient as uncontrolled global ambitions from first Wilhelm II and then Adolf Hitler embroiled Europe in two world wars. These wars brought suffering and death along with social unrest throughout Europe. In this unstable environment, Marxist socialism rose to threaten democracies from the political left and fascism rose to threaten from the political right. To meet the socialist and fascist threats and solve the economic and social challenges of the period, two economists built a moral defense of capitalism based on its ability to promote liberty and freedom and meet the broader needs of society. In this chapter, I address humanism as a moral foundation for capitalism by discussing the lives and writings of Karl Polanyi and John Maynard Keynes.[1]

4.1 THE RISING INFLUENCE OF HUMANISM IN THE TWENTIETH CENTURY

Tawney (1926/2017, 166) argued that the psychology of a nation that lives predominantly by the land differs significantly from a nation that lives predominantly by commerce: "In the latter, when all goes well, continuous expansion is taken for granted as the rule of life, new horizons are constantly opening, and the catchword of politics is the encouragement of enterprise. In the former, the number of niches into which each successive generation must be fitted is strictly limited; movement means disturbance, for, as one man rises, another is thrust down; and the object of statesmen is not to foster individual initiative, but to prevent social dislocation." This fundamental difference between agrarian and commercial societies was at the heart of Adam Smith's attack on the mercantilist system of the French physiocrats. This difference also helps explain the social and political upheaval of the twentieth century and the rising influence of humanism during this era.

Tawney (1926/2017, 57) criticized the role of the medieval Church in keeping peasants enslaved in the agrarian system of feudalism. The very essence of this economic system was human exploitation, including "compulsory labor, additional *corvées*[2] at the very moments when the peasant's labor was most urgently needed on his own holding, innumerable dues and payments, the obligation to grind at the lord's mill and bake at the lord's oven, (and) the private justice of the lord's court." Yet medieval canon law enforced this economic system and prominent ecclesiastics, including Aquinas, failed to speak out against it. Martin Luther's

---

[1] As the epigraph to this chapter reveals (Polanyi 1947/2014, 35), Polanyi rejected the narrow utilitarianism of classical economists. However, he came to view Marx's moral critique of capitalism as too wedded to that same utilitarianism. In the end, Polanyi offered a way through the impasse by returning to Adam Smith's original moral foundation for capitalism (Rogan 2017).

[2] The term *corvées* captures unpaid labor demanded by the lord or landowner to cover taxes or other obligations of the peasants such as military service. The injustice of the *corvée* system in France helped bring about the French Revolution.

(1483–1546) protestant reformation in sixteenth-century Germany assumed the continuation of the Feudal system, which he pointed out required heavy civil rule "lest the world become wild, peace vanish, and commerce and common interest be destroyed.... No one need think that the world can be ruled without blood. The civil sword shall and must be red and bloody" (quoted in Tawney 1926/2017, 101–102).

In contrast to Luther's reformation in Germany, John Calvin's (1509–64) reformation in Switzerland was specifically tailored for the commercial societies that had emerged in the West. Calvinism ushered in a moral system designed for the rising middle class based upon individual responsibility and unparalleled civil liberties. This moral system rewarded hard work and discipline and required relatively light civil rule. Tawney (1926/2017, 111–112) emphasized the role of the middle class in maintaining law and order in Calvin's reformation: "Once the world had been settled to their liking, the middle classes persuaded themselves that they were the convinced enemies of violence and the devotees of the principle of order." Similarly, Weber (1905/2002, 117) emphasized the Puritan aversion to the feudal lifestyle and the power of Calvin's Puritan worldview to bring about a "middle-class, economically *rational* conduct of life, of which it was the most significant and only consistent support." This worldview spread and became the fertile soil upon which capitalism took root in the Netherlands, Britain, and America.

Weber's trip to America in the summer of 1904 confirmed his optimistic view of the future of capitalism. Although he witnessed the same struggles of industrial capitalism that plagued England and Germany, including widespread labor unrest in the industrial cities of the north, Weber saw in America the capitalist spirit's "highest development" and "emancipation" (Scaff 2011, 6–7). The young nation had never experienced the stratified system of feudalism and lacked the tradition of a privileged upper class. Further, it had avoided forming a European-style state church which "*inevitably* drove all of the individual's striving for emancipation ... and 'liberalism' in the broadest sense of the word, in the direction of *hostility* toward the religious communities" (Weber 1905/2002, 215). Weber observed that America was the world's oldest self-governing democracy at the time of his visit, and her perception of capitalism was sharply different from that of Europe. Scaff (2011, 64) highlights Weber's surprising conclusion from his trip to America:

These social and historical differences led Weber to a surprising conclusion – namely, that "European capitalism, at least on the Continent, has a peculiar authoritative stamp." In continental Europe capitalism developed as an unwelcome imposition and threat to lost independence among the privileged, and as an alien and exploitative power among the underprivileged. Expressed in other terms, we can say that the culture of capitalism was experienced differently among social groups in North America. The meaning of a capitalist system of production and exchange was altered for historical and social reasons ... creating in America an association between the culture of capitalism and equal rights, equal opportunities and a sense of freedom from authoritarian traditions; and by contrast in Europe an association with an imposed, alienating, exploitative rationalization of life.

Weber's interest in agrarian societies attracted him to the post-Civil War South. He sought out leaders of the African American community to discuss the problems of race relations in the former Confederacy only forty years after the end of the Civil War.[3] Weber viewed the great conflict as a struggle between the Puritanism of the Industrial North and the aristocratic traditionalism of the Agrarian South. According to Scaff (2011, 63), Weber saw that struggle as necessary to allow America to avoid Europe's anti-capitalist movements. "(In Weber's view) it was the resolution of this struggle in the Civil War that made possible the subsequent path of American 'bourgeois capitalist' development. The defeat of traditionalism meant the death of reactionary anti-capitalism, except as nostalgia for a disappearing way of life" (Scaff 2011, 63).[4]

Upon his return to Germany, Weber grew increasingly anxious regarding the stability of his native country, given its long history of state religion and a privileged Junker class. Regarding the former, he believed that Lutheranism and its "aura of office" had become too much like Catholicism, endorsing state power against individual freedom and encouraging passive submission to traditional autocratic structures.[5] Regarding the latter, the Junker class consisted of only a few thousand families, yet they owned over eight million acres and held privileged positions in government, industry, and the military. It was not until the Russian

[3] For example, Weber met with both Booker T. Washington and W. E. B. Du Bois during his trip to America and continued to correspond with them after his return to Germany. He also commissioned a paper from Du Bois on "The Negro Question in the United States," which he published in 1906 in his academic journal *Archiv für Sozialwissenschaft und Sozialpolitik* (Baehr and Wells 2002, xv).

[4] America's unique experience with capitalism – including avoiding the stratified system of feudalism, the tradition of a privileged upper class, and the state religions of Europe – is why Marxist revolutionaries have not been successful in establishing a foothold in the former British colony.

[5] In response to Bismarck's history of discrimination against Catholics in civil service positions, German Catholics were pressing for occupational quotas. Weber saw this as the continuation of the unhealthy relation between church and state in Germany (Baehr and Wells 2002, xi).

Army invaded the East-Elbian territories in 1945 that the scourge of this patriarchal system was finally lifted from the laboring poor in Germany. Hirsch (1946, 151) highlighted the role of the Junker class in the unending turmoil that rocked Germany and the rest of the world in the first half of the twentieth century:

> The few thousand Junker families keeping tight control of Prussia's Army and administration bear the chief responsibility for the fact that Germany was never able to catch up with the spirit of the western democracies, in spite of all the technical progress she made. If it had not been for the selfishness and narrow-mindedness of this retarding social element, modern ideals might have prevailed in Germany at the turn of the century and the world might have been spared unending turmoil.

In response to the growing desperation of peasants and impoverished urban workers, Europe was rocked with an outbreak of revolutions in 1848. Leftist organizations with socialist, communist, and anarchist sympathies rose up and asserted their influence. Karl Marx (1818–83) was instrumental in forming a worldwide association to unite these leftist organizations. Marx attended the first meeting of the International Workingmen's Association (IWA) in 1864 at St. Martin's Hall, London, and wrote the founding documents of the new organization.[6] Due to deep divisions within the organization, however, it soon splintered into a statist, communist group led by Marx and a global, anarchist group led by Mikhail Bakunin (1814–76). Bakunin argued that Marx's views were dangerous and would lead to concentrated power as oppressive as anything they had seen from the ruling classes. Marx's historical materialism proved irresistible, however, as it provided the Left with a theory to support its view of capitalism as alienating and exploitive as well as the motivation to topple Western democracies and their capitalist systems.[7]

The civil unrest that suddenly erupted across Europe in the twentieth century was rooted in its deep feudal history. Although feudalism was abolished in England by 1660, it was not eradicated in France until the 1790s in the wake of the French Revolution. Germany, however, held on to forms of agrarian feudalism much later. While Frederick II formally abolished feudalism on all Crown lands in Prussia in 1763, feudalistic systems persisted in southern parts of Germany until the 1850s, and

---

[6] Because of its international participants and global ambitions, the IWA of 1864–76 has been labeled the "First International."

[7] As discussed in Chapter 3, Marx's theory of historical materialism predicted that capitalism would collapse due to the growing alienation and exploitation felt by the working class (proletariat).

the Junker system existed east of the Elbe River until the 1940s. Russia outlawed feudalism in 1861, but the freed peasants were condemned to a life of poverty as they typically were prohibited from owning land. Opportunities for work in the cities also collapsed in 1899–1900 when the contraction of Western money markets plunged Russian industry into a deep and prolonged crisis. The resulting 1905 peasant revolts in Russia foreshadowed the Russian Revolutions of 1917. The lingering agrarian economy in Russia, along with its oppressive monarchy and ruling class, had clearly betrayed the Russian people and lit the flames of Marxist revolution that would soon spread to all of Europe.

Weber's writings on religion and capitalism were a direct afront to Marx's historical materialism. Yet Weber knew that many cultured people in the modern West ignored religion. Thus, he turned increasingly to humanism rather than religion for his own moral foundation for capitalism. For example, he began to emphasize moral responsibility and use Benjamin Franklin as an example of the highly responsible life that undergirded capitalism. Weber's emphasis on moral responsibility expanded to science and politics as well as individual behavior. As Scaff (2011, 193) concludes, Weber came to believe that "(t)he problems of meaning are resolved not transcendentally but with a matter-of-fact appeal to 'self-clarification' and the sense of 'responsibility' – in science, responsibility for knowledge and its uses, and in politics, responsibility for the exercise of power and its consequences for history."

Weber's shift in emphasis away from religion reflected the rising influence of humanism in twentieth-century Western thought. In contrast to classical economists, however, Weber maintained a strong emphasis on social and moral concerns. "(H)is leading political slogan was 'dynamic capitalism instead of bureaucratic socialism,' and his main scientific purpose was to forge the weapons of 'bourgeois sociology' in order to slay the dragon of 'historical materialism'" (Scaff 1989, 175). Weber also condemned the rising nationalism on the right as exhibiting unrivaled irresponsibility and the potential for destruction. "Setting aside these possible competitors *within* the political value-sphere, Weber turned to a conception of responsibility or accountability as a vocational *ethos*" (Scaff 1989, 183). Due to his untimely death in 1920, however, Weber did not live to battle the rising influence of communism and fascism across Europe. That task was taken up by other leading political economists of his era, including an Austro-Hungarian economist bearing the scars of war and a British economist trained by Alfred Marshall at the University of Cambridge.

4.2 KARL POLANYI'S CRITIQUE
OF CAPITALISM BASED ON HUMANISM

Karl Polanyi (1886–1964) was broken in body and spirit as he lay in a military hospital in Budapest. The year was 1917, and he had just passed his 30th birthday. It would take two more years for him to heal sufficiently from his physical wounds to leave his hospital bed. The wounds to his psyche, however, would never completely heal. Polanyi had been called up to the Russian front as a cavalry officer in the Austro-Hungarian army in 1915 and had witnessed the horrors of war up close. In addition to replaying the senseless violence and loss of life, including the eerie sight of rotting horses comingled with human corpses, Polanyi spent his days pondering the sudden collapse of Western Civilization. The individualism of laissez-faire capitalism had proven too unstable, yet the collectivism of Marxism robbed people of their freedom. He wondered if it was possible to get beyond that binary choice ... was there a middle way?

At the beginning of World War I in 1914, Russia possessed the largest standing army at 1.4 million soldiers and quickly mobilized another three million. Knowing that it was severely outnumbered, the Austro-Hungarian Army attacked the Russian Army on the plains and rolling hills of Galicia in southern Poland in the late summer. The two armies engaged in outdated but lethal warfare, "featuring great columns of infantry, eager battalions stacked deep, meeting each other with bayonets fixed as mounted cavalry dueled and artillery decided the day with fire" (Schindler 2015, 9). In just three weeks, over four hundred thousand Austro-Hungarians were dead, wounded, or captured. Russian casualties were nearly as great, but they had ample reserves. By the time Polanyi was called up to the Russian front in 1915, the Austria-Hungary Empire had already lost over a third of its military strength. The war to end all wars, however, would drag on for three more years, culminating in the collapse of the empire and the Habsburg monarchy.

Polanyi's two years on the Russian front left an indelible mark on his soul. The peasant army he and his compatriots confronted in Galicia exhibited the same depleted morale that plagued the Russian people. After crushing the Austro-Hungarian Army in the first battle of Galicia a year earlier, Russia was doing poorly against the German Army in the north and the Ottoman Army in the south. The Tsar Nicholas II had made the situation worse by taking personal control of the Imperial Russian Army in 1915, which was a challenge far beyond his skills and only made him personally responsible for Russia's continuing defeats. To finance the war, the Russian government had printed millions of ruble notes, which led to rampant inflation and disruptions in both farm and industrial production due to hoarding and strikes. Thus, the cities and towns were constantly short of food, and the environment was ripe for revolution.

After the Tsar was ousted in the 1917 February Revolution, German authorities allowed Vladimir Lenin (1870–1924) to cross Germany in a sealed railway carriage from Zurich to Petrograd (now St. Petersburg). He would play a leading role in overthrowing the Provisional Government in the October Revolution that same year. Lenin and the Bolsheviks campaigned on ending Russia's participation in the war, granting land to the peasants, and providing bread to urban workers. Once in power, however, the Bolsheviks established a security service to weed out "enemies of the people" in campaigns consciously modeled on those of the French Revolution. The war's aftermath brought even greater horrors and loss of life in Russia, including six years of civil war (1917–23), the Red Terror, and the heavy hand of Stalin. The pullout of Russia from the war in 1917 freed the Germans from having to fight on two fronts but caused America to commit troops on the side of the Allies, which brought a rapid end to the war in the fall of 1918.

Polanyi was born in Vienna in 1886. His father, Mihaly Pollacek, was unquestionably the most important influence in his life (Polanyi-Levitt and Mendell 1987). Having studied engineering in Zurich and Edinburgh, Mihaly became a successful railway contractor and moved his family from Vienna to Budapest in the late 1880s. He maintained the Pollacek surname but changed the names of his five children to Polanyi, including his third child Karl and his fifth child Michael.[8] He also changed their religion from Jewish to Protestant-Calvinist. In 1900, the financial fortunes of the family plummeted after three months of rain washed away a railway line Mihaly was building for the Hungarian government in the Danube Valley. The government insisted that the risk was his and refused to pay for the work that he had completed. Mihaly paid his workers what they were owed, returned his shareholders' capital, and declared bankruptcy. Physically and emotionally drained, he died of pneumonia in January 1906 (Rogan 2017).

---

[8] Michael Polanyi is commonly known among economists for questioning positivism as the only source of knowledge and for promoting the concept of spontaneous order in his opposition to central economic planning.

The untimely death of his father pushed Polanyi into a progressive melancholia. In a letter to a close friend in 1925, he described his state of mind during this time as "a tormenting senseless inner excitement, a poisoned feel of life, a narrowed down consciousness, suicide as a fate already consummated, preordained." In his hospital bed from 1917 to 1919, however, the darkness began to lift as Polanyi contemplated his future. He pondered the collective guilt of his generation for its mindless participation in a war that had sacrificed men, women, and children for a cause nobody understood. He also pondered the parties responsible for the war and the ensuing social unrest, including nobles and aristocrats, the business class, revolutionaries, and organized labor. At the end of his convalescence, Polanyi rose from his hospital bed, determined to confront the burden of responsibility he felt for himself and his generation. He concluded his letter by stating, "I do not know what was choking me then, as a rope chokes a man going to be hanged. Something else has taken its place; the ethical world, to live and comprehend the ethical reality…" (quoted in Polanyi-Levitt and Mendell 1987, 20).

Under the supervision of Gyula Pikler, his law professor at the University of Budapest, Polanyi had helped found the Galileo Circle in 1908 and served as its first president. The student-led group sought "a philosophic and scientific renaissance, a challenge to the backward and reactionary character of the University and the general pervasive morass of clericalism, corruption, opportunism, privilege and bureaucracy" (Polanyi-Levitt and Mendell 1987, 17–18). Upon completing his doctorate in law in 1912, Polanyi entered and then quickly abandoned the law profession, choosing instead to become editor of the Galileo Circle's journal, *Szabadgondolat* (Free Thought).[9] The monthly journal originally followed the preoccupation of Hungarian intellectuals with the problem of social alienation under industrial capitalism. The goal had originally been to develop techniques to perfect a market-based social order using innovations in social science. By the time the war had broken out, however, this aspiration had been abandoned as naïve and Polanyi had made moral renewal his focus (Rogan 2017).

After the high hopes of Enlightenment had been dashed due to the war, some members of the Galileo Circle tended toward the Marxism of Lenin, whereas others tended toward the institutional and moral reform

---

[9] His future wife, Ilona, would say of his decision to leave the profession, "He was not merely the man who would not tell a lie, but also the man who found his true vocation in telling disagreeable truths at all times and in all circumstances" (Polanyi-Levitt and Mendell 1987, 20).

of Oscar Jaszi (1875–1957). Polanyi gravitated to the latter camp. In October 1918, the social democrats who had rallied around Jaszi joined two left-wing parties to constitute a Hungarian National Council with Mihaly Károlyi as the president. After the assassination of the former Prime Minister István Tisza, Karl I appointed Károlyi the new prime minister. Ties to the Habsburg monarchy, however, were soon dissolved, and the People's Republic of Hungary was proclaimed in November 1918. The Károlyi government was immediately destabilized by the Hungarian Communist Party, which had been emboldened by the Bolshevik revolution in Russia. Seeing the gathering threat, Polanyi devoted the December 1918 issue of his journal to Bolshevism. In March 1919, socialist elements within Károlyi's government joined forces with the communists to proclaim a Soviet Republic. By August 1919, however, that Republic had been overthrown by counterrevolutionary forces led by former members of the military.

Despairing of Hungarian politics and fearing for his safety, Polanyi left Budapest for Vienna by the end of 1919. He had recovered enough from his wounds by the time of the Soviet Republic to accept a post in the People's Commissariat for Social Production, but he resigned in frustration three months later. "That direct experience as part of the bureaucracy in charge of a command economy helps to explain why he became interested in socialist alternatives to the centralization of production once he moved to Vienna" (Rogan 2017, 60). Within three years of arriving in Vienna, Polanyi had discovered the Christian socialism of Tawney in Britain. He was heavily influenced not only by the writings of Tawney and G. D. H. Cole, but also by contacts made with British relief workers after the war. In 1920, Polanyi went to the University of Vienna to enlist help in resettling his future wife, Ilona Duczynska, who had spent some time in jail in Budapest for her revolutionary socialist activities.[10] The British relief worker who received Polanyi was a Scot named Donald Grant, a devoted Presbyterian and committed follower of the Christian socialism of Tawney and Cole.

Vienna had a rich history as the cultural, political, and economic center of Continental Europe. Located in northeastern Austria on the banks

---

[10] The socialist activities of Duczynska during this period kept her from receiving a visa to live in the United States toward the end of Polanyi's career. As a result, the couple moved to Canada and Polanyi commuted to New York City during his time at Columbia. Under the influence of her husband, however, Duczynska eventually came to view the Hungarian Communist Party as "militaristic, immoral, and corrupt" (Rogan 2017, 63).

of the Danube River, Vienna became the resident city of the Habsburg dynasty in 1440 and eventually grew to be the *de facto* capital of the Holy Roman Empire. Due to its importance as the seat of the Habsburg monarchy and its location on a major shipping route through the heart of Europe, Vienna developed great riches which funded unparalleled cultural achievements in architecture, art, education, and music. By 1910, Vienna had more than two million inhabitants and was the third-largest city in Europe after London and Paris. In 1913, Leon Trotsky, Josip Broz Tito, and Joseph Stalin lived within a few miles of each other in central Vienna, which contributed to its reputation as "Red Vienna" in the early twentieth century.

Under the new federal constitution enacted in Austria two years earlier, Vienna was proclaimed an autonomous state in 1922. Although out of power federally, Jaszi and the social democrats were now able to embark upon a radical experiment in democratic socialism evolving around moral responsibility. Tax reform enabled the city to tap its immense wealth to fund new education and welfare programs. Vienna built new hospitals, nurseries, schools, and public housing. At the same time, however, ultra-nationalist parties in the federal government were developing plans to drive socialists out of Vienna. While Polanyi had originally focused on the threat of Bolshevik communism on Western democracy, his new preoccupation became the threat posed by Nazi fascism (Rogan 2017).

As the social democrats in Vienna awaited their confrontation with the Austrian ultra-nationalists, a confrontation they were destined to lose, Polanyi planned his escape to democratic England. Jaszi had shut down the magazine where Polanyi worked and emigrated to America in 1924, taking a teaching position at Oberlin College. As a result, Polanyi was having an increasingly difficult time supporting himself, his wife, and their young daughter. As with Jaszi, he was also beginning to despair of the prospects for democracy in Continental Europe. Polanyi sought to follow in Tawney's footsteps and find a lecturer position in political economy at a worker's college, but he found his prospects limited. Therefore, he began his academic career outside of Europe by embarking on a grueling series of lecture tours through the American Midwest in 1934 and 1935.

Polanyi's reputation in England was enhanced by his role as editor of a book of essays entitled *Christianity and the Social Revolution*. Tawney reviewed the book for the *New Statesman* in November 1935. Tawney was particularly impressed with Polanyi's essay called "The Essence of

Fascism." Polanyi argued that in their attempt to eradicate the influence of the communists, Nazi fascists had found it necessary to eradicate Christianity. Tawney recognized that Polanyi's essay "described the social philosophy of Hitler's Germany in terms commensurate with the critique of capitalism which he had developed in the 1920s. Polanyi's essay on fascism, moreover, was readily identifiable with the attempt to move beyond the binary choice between individualism and collectivism" (Rogan 2017, 66). Polanyi had begun to develop his "middle way."

Following in Tawney's footsteps, Polanyi eventually acquired a lecturer position at the WEA in 1936. However, he did not find a permanent faculty position until he left London for America in 1940. Polanyi joined the staff of Bennington College in Vermont in 1940 as a visiting scholar before finally receiving a teaching position at Columbia University in 1947. Rogan (2017, 53) attributes Polanyi's lack of success in England to his attempt to build a new foundation for capitalism based on humanism. "Polanyi was not content simply to reiterate Tawney's critique. He believed that it needed reformulation if it was to remain relevant. That need arose in part from the emergence of fascism.... The critique of capitalism to which Tawney had assigned Christian meanings (Polanyi believed) should be broadened to give that reverence for human personality a secular grounding."

The need for a moral foundation for capitalism based on secular alternatives was not yet obvious or urgent in Britain. Thus, Polanyi was ahead of his time. He had initially attempted to replace Tawney's moral critique with the early writings of Karl Marx, who had argued that the rising capitalist system corroded all traditional values and institutions (Hirschman 1982). As he looked closer, however, Polanyi realized that Marx's arguments exhibited the same narrow utilitarianism that plagued classical economics. By the time Polanyi had written his own moral critique of capitalism, *The Great Transformation*, he no longer believed that Marx had successfully provided a secular alternative to Tawney's moral critique. Published in 1944, Polanyi's moral critique of capitalism based on humanism ended up encompassing a direct attack on Marxism.

4.3 JOHN MAYNARD KEYNES'S RADICAL HUMANISM

In contrast to the large standing armies of Continental Europe, the relatively small British army relied on volunteers at the beginning of World War I. Tawney's Manchester Regiment was part of the large number of volunteers who answered the call to enlist from 1914 to 1916.[11] During this early period, John Maynard Keynes (1883–1946) chose not to volunteer for the war. In fact, when rising casualties forced Britain to introduce conscription in 1916, Keynes declared himself a conscientious objector. That declaration, however, was likely a signal of solidarity with his elite friends at Cambridge and Bloomsbury as the Treasury Department had already exempted him from active service. Over the course of the war, Keynes worked exhaustingly at the Treasury to finance the war. According to his biographer Robert Skidelsky (1994, xvii), this inner conflict drove Keynes to the breaking point: "(H)e did finally break down at the Paris Peace Conference in 1919, returning, shattered, to England, to denounce Lloyd George's peace policy with a vehemence made more savage by pent-up hostility to his war policy."

Keynes had displayed a unique ability to address the complex financial problems of the war. This earned him the position of chief Treasury representative at the Paris Peace Conference. As Keynes observed the peace negotiations, however, he grew increasingly agitated with the terms being suggested by the "Big Four" – Britain, France, Italy, and America. Rather than cool reason and rational economic policy, the negotiations were dominated by politics and settling old scores. In March 1919, Keynes circulated a paper at the conference warning that overly burdensome reparations imposed upon Germany would poison and perhaps destroy the global capitalist system. After realizing that his warnings had gone unheeded, and that the new German government would never be able to meet the onerous terms of the treaty, Keynes resigned from the Treasury in June 1919 out of protest. He withdrew from the world stage to his country retreat at the Charleston Farmhouse in Sussex.

In a letter to his mother from Charleston, Keynes stated that he had begun to write a new book "on the economic conditions of Europe as it now is, including a violent attack on the Peace Treaty and my proposals for the future." He was worried, however, whether his "temper" would remain high enough to "carry it through." (Skidelsky 1986, 376). He needn't have worried. The book was published in December of that same year. According to Skidelsky (1986, 384), *The Economic Consequences of the Peace* has a legitimate claim to be Keynes's best book:

---

[11] The initial call across Britain was for 100,000 volunteers, but almost 500,000 men enlisted in the first two months, including many underage boys who enlisted by lying about their age or giving false names.

In none of his others did he succeed so well in bringing all his gifts to bear on the subject in hand. Although the heart of the book was a lucid accounting of the reparation problem, the book was no mere technical treatise.... (T)he failings of Clemenceau, Wilson and Lloyd George are displayed with cruel precision. The writing is angry, scornful and, rarely for Keynes, passionate: never again were his denunciations of bungling and lying, or his moral indignation, to ring so loud and clear.

The book exposed how the war had damaged the delicate economic mechanism supporting the people of Europe before 1914, and how the Treaty of Versailles, far from repairing this damage, would complete its destruction. Keynes predicted that the treaty would perpetuate the social unrest that had lit the fire of leftist revolution across Europe. In particular, the terms of the peace would generate the very conditions that threatened capitalism most, including ruinous inflation and the absolute falling off of the standard of living. Keynes's moral outrage was heightened by the fact that he was present at the negotiations and had personally witnessed the injustice of the process. The shapers of the Treaty of Versailles had based their deliberations primarily on political and territorial concerns and had largely ignored important financial and economic concerns that would inevitably determine the success of the peace. Amazingly, the Allies who gathered for the Paris Peace Conference chose not to invite any of the defeated Central Powers. Therefore, the process itself was destined to generate continued resentment and hatred between the belligerents.

Many within Britain, especially in the Lloyd George government, saw Keynes's book as a betrayal of the homeland. As the British economy sputtered in the 1920s and unemployment soared, however, Lloyd George turned again to Keynes to provide an economic program that would help the Liberal Party win back power. Keynes persuaded Lloyd George that going off the gold standard and increasing government spending would help Britain cure its economic ills. In contrast to Britain, America was experiencing robust economic growth in what became the "Roaring Twenties." The US presidents during this period, Warren Harding and Calvin Coolidge, were therefore able to refuse the kind of government involvement in the economy that Keynes was asking for. The stock market crash of 1929, however, precipitated an economic depression in America that would infect the rest of the world and last for a decade. During this time, Keynes's economic insights would be highly sought after, and he would focus his moral indignation on those who turned a blind eye toward the suffering of the unemployed.

Keynes's strong sense of duty and moral responsibility came from his upbringing as the son of a Cambridge don at the end of the nineteenth century. After struggling with the field of mathematics, his father John "Neville" Keynes (1852–1949) switched to the study of moral sciences at Cambridge in 1873. Similar to the Scottish universities in the eighteenth century, the ancient universities in England were awakening to a new sense of their "responsibility to provide leadership in an age of industrialism, declining religious faith, rising democracy, and intellectual ferment." By the 1870s, the moral sciences – which at the time included moral and political philosophy as well as political economy – were seen as a replacement for religion as a source of social and moral wisdom. Thus, John Maynard Keynes "was a product of the Cambridge moral science tradition, in which Cambridge economics developed side by side with Cambridge moral philosophy" (Skidelsky 1986, 10).[12]

Neville studied under Henry Sidgwick (1838–1900) and Alfred Marshall (1842–1924). Sidgwick, who had transferred over to the moral sciences from the classics and had tried to construct a coherent system of secular ethics to replace religion, taught Neville his moral and political philosophy. Marshall, who had transferred over from mathematics and remained "socially minded" despite losing his faith, taught Neville his political economy. Although Sidgwick tried to keep moral philosophy a major part of the curriculum in moral sciences, Marshall continued to strip away requirements in ethics and politics. By the time John Maynard Keynes took economics from Marshall after completing his mathematics degree in 1905, the field was a mere shadow of its former self: "It was another fragment of a vanishing whole, soon to disappear into the black hole of mathematics" (Skidelsky 1994, xxv).[13]

Keynes's Treasury experience during the war, and the uses to which he put it in *The Economic Consequences of the Peace*, made him a highly sought-after world figure. Yet the major economic achievements

---

[12] John Neville Keynes had plenty of opportunities to distinguish himself in the course of his career. For example, he was declared "Senior Moralist" after placing first in the first class of the moral science tripos in 1875. He also received an offer of a professorship of political economy at the University of Chicago in 1894, which he promptly rejected in a letter stating he was "far too firmly rooted at Cambridge to be able to think of moving" (Skidelsky 1986, 65).

[13] Upon reviewing Keynes's papers in mathematics, Marshall continually urged him to take an economics degree. However, the young prodigy was adamant. "He never did take an economics degree. In fact, his total professional training came to little more than eight weeks. All the rest was learnt on the job" (Skidelsky 1986, 166). Given the continued narrowing of the discipline of economics, this may have been to Keynes's advantage.

that he would be famous for lay ahead of him. "In 1920, Keynes was thirty-seven, and had given no hint of greatness in the sphere in which he would excel – economics. But for the war, it is not clear that he would have stuck to economics, or the life of a Cambridge don" (Skidelsky 1994, xvi). Although Keynes was responsible for the economics teaching at King's College in Cambridge after the war, he made no important theoretical contribution to his discipline until the appearance of his *Treatise on Money* in 1930. His greatest work, *The General Theory of Employment, Interest, and Money*, did not appear until 1936.

Over his lifetime, Keynes defended capitalism against "the attacks and criticism of Socialist and Communist innovators" (Skidelski 1994, 149). He was part of the modernist movement of his times, which was dedicated to undermining any "delusion" that put limits on human freedom and the play of reason. Keynes was particularly attracted to solving problems that socialists drew attention to without resorting to socialism. This included finding solutions to business cycles, unstable currencies, and high unemployment. After the stock market crash of 1929 and the prolonged depression of the 1930s, Keynes became particularly obsessed with solving the problem of prolonged unemployment. The Great War and the depression that followed convinced him that the economic health of a nation was too important to be left to *laissez-faire*.

Before the war, the fading influence of religion in society had not concerned Keynes. He had taken full advantage of the fruits of his elite education at Eton and Cambridge to enter the secret world of the Apostles at Cambridge and, eventually, the Bloomsbury group.[14] This contrasted with Tawney, who abandoned his unique privilege as the son of a Cambridge Fellow and Apostle to embrace the humble life of the working class. Keynes was an active Apostle from 1903 to 1910 and interacted with the Bloomsbury group throughout the rest of his life. As an Apostle, Keynes participated in weekly meetings to present papers and discuss scholarly topics in literature, politics, religion, and philosophy. Keynes was the financial muscle behind the Bloomsbury group, spending lavishly or organizing financial backing for their enterprises in literature, theater, and art. The radical humanism of the Bloomsbury group, however, became increasingly irrelevant due to the puritan revival after World War I (Skidelsky 1986).

---

[14] Andrews (2010, 5) argues that membership in the Apostles "was by far the most important experience that shaped the intellect of the young Keynes and it impacted him for the rest of his life."

At age fifty-five, Keynes wrote a memoir describing and critiquing his moral outlook prior to the war. In the memoir, entitled *My Early Beliefs*, Keynes labeled his early beliefs and those of his close friends at Cambridge and Bloomsbury as "utopian." Reflecting the new age of modernism, they held a strong belief in the possibility of continuing moral progress apart from tradition and religion (quoted in Keynes 2015, 21–22):

> We entirely repudiated a personal liability on us to obey general rules. We claimed the right to judge every individual case on its merits, and the wisdom, experience and self-control to do so successfully.... We repudiated entirely customary morals, conventions and traditional wisdom. We were, that is to say, in the strict sense of the term, immoralists. The consequences of being found out had, of course, to be considered for what they were worth. But we recognized no moral obligation on us, no inner sanction, to conform or to obey.

After World War I, however, the utopian view of Keynes and his elite friends became unsustainable. Keynes came to see that tradition, custom, and convention were critical to maintaining social order. As he neared the end of his life (he died at the age of 62), Keynes saw that he and his friends had overlooked a key element of human nature (quoted in Keynes 2015, 22–23):

> In short, we repudiated all version of the doctrine of original sin, of there being insane and irrational springs of wickedness in most men. We were not aware that civilization was a thin and precarious crust erected by the personality and the will of a very few, and only maintained by rules and conventions skillfully put across and guilefully preserved. We had no respect for traditional wisdom or the restraints of custom.... It did not occur to us to respect the extraordinary achievements of our predecessors in the ordering of life (as it now seems to me to have been) or the elaborate framework which they had devised to protect this order.

Whereas Keynes had fully participated in the erotic lifestyle of the Bloomsbury group prior to the war, he fell in love with a Russian ballerina named Lydia Lopokova shortly after the war and they were married in 1925. By all accounts, Keynes had a fulfilling and happy marriage and continued to support the arts through his wife's projects and the projects of friends associated with Bloomsbury. He also chose an active life of increasing duty and social responsibility. For example, he became the bursar at King's College and had exclusive control over its budget and funds. He was also appointed chairman of the National Mutual Life Assurance Society and acquired several directorships and consultancies. Of particular importance, he took on the challenge of chronic unemployment under capitalist economies, which he always approached from his experience as a monetary economist. Toward the end of his life, therefore, Keynes adopted a more traditional humanism and fully embraced his role as the "savior of capitalism" (Skidelsky 1994, xxii).

4.4 HUMANISM AS A MORAL FOUNDATION FOR CAPITALISM

Polanyi's moral foundation for capitalism is contained in his major treatise published in 1944, *The Great Transformation: The Political and Economic Origins of Our Time*. Although he wrote his treatise at the height of World War II while he was at Bennington College in Vermont, the purpose of his major work was to explain the outbreak of World War I. Polanyi opens the book by placing it within this historical context (Polanyi 1944/2001, 3): "Nineteenth-century civilization has collapsed. This book is concerned with the political and economic origins of this event, as well as with the great transformation which it ushered in." This opening passage conveys the great tension of the period and sets up the main puzzle Polanyi means to address in his seminal work: "Why did a prolonged period of relative peace and prosperity in Europe, lasting from 1815 to 1914, suddenly give way to a world war followed by an economic collapse?" (Block 2001, xxii).

Polanyi laid the blame for the sudden collapse of nineteenth-century civilization at the feet of classical economists and their idea of a self-regulating market (Polanyi 1944/2001, 3–4): "Our thesis is that the idea of a self-adjusting market implied a stark utopia. Such an institution could not exist for any length of time without annihilating the human and natural substance of society; it would have physically destroyed man and transformed his surrounding into a wilderness. Inevitably, society took measures to protect itself...."

The global economy that had evolved by the dawn of the twentieth century was the creation of four institutions: the balance-of-power system, the international gold standard, the self-regulating market, and the liberal state. The self-regulating market, however, was the unique innovation behind the entire system. "The gold standard was merely an attempt to extend the domestic market system to the international field; the balance-of-power system was a superstructure erected upon and, partly, worked through the gold standard; (and) the liberal state was itself a creation of the self-regulating market" (Polanyi 1944/2001, 3). Because the idea of a self-regulating market was a stark utopia, the system was destined to fail. The four institutions governing the global economy, according to

Polanyi, were destined to generate increasing social and political tensions within and among the great nations of the West.

Similar to Keynes, Polanyi saw the terms of the Treaty of Versailles as a threat to both capitalism and democracy. First, the unilateral disarmament of the defeated nations forestalled any reconstruction of the balance-of-power system. The League of Nations proved incapable of restoring this balance of power. Second, the exorbitant reparations imposed upon Germany assured the complete collapse of the gold standard. These reparations, combined with the soaring war debt, led to excessive printing of currencies in Germany and across Continental Europe, leading to rampant inflation. Thus, returning to the gold standard became impossible even for Britain and America. Britain's adherence to the gold standard generated a prolonged recession through the 1920s, while America's overdue slump arrived in 1929. Britain finally went off the gold standard in 1931, and America followed suit in 1933. By that time, however, the liberal state had been replaced by fascist totalitarian regimes in many countries including Germany, Italy, and Austria.[15]

While global capitalism was born in England, as Polanyi pointed out, its collapse yielded the most tragic repercussions on the European continent (Polanyi 1944/2001, 32):

The Industrial Revolution was an English event. Market economy, free trade, and the gold standard were English inventions. These institutions broke down (in the nineteen-twenties) everywhere – in Germany, Italy, or Austria the event was merely more political and more dramatic. But whatever the scenery and the temperature of the final episodes, the long-run factors which wrecked that civilization should be studied in the birthplace of the Industrial Revolution, England.

To find the political and economic origins of the sudden collapse of Western Civilization, therefore, Polanyi focused on the development of global capitalism in England. He discussed the disruption caused by sixteenth-century enclosures and the change from arable land to pasture that benefited England's wool industries (Polanyi 1944/2001, 39):

Yet, but for the consistently maintained policy of the Tudor and early Stuart statesmen, the rate of that progress might have been ruinous, and have turned the process itself into a degenerative instead of a constructive event. For upon this rate, mainly, depended whether the dispossessed could adjust themselves to changed conditions without fatally damaging their substance, human and economic, physical and moral ... and whether the effects of increased imports induced by increased exports would enable those who lost their employment through the change to find new sources of sustenance.

---

[15] Polanyi believed that the supersession of liberal capitalism by some form of fascism could already be foreseen before 1914 (Polanyi-Levitt and Mendell 1987).

Polanyi provided historical evidence that the Tudors and early Stuarts used the power of the Crown to slow down the process of economic improvement until it became socially bearable.

Similar to the enclosures in sixteenth-century England, Polanyi argued, the Industrial Revolution in England (1760–1840) brought with it social alienation and dislocation in addition to great economic growth. By this time, however, the idea of self-regulating markets had grabbed the imagination of classical economists and policymakers. "The effects on the lives of the people were awful beyond description. Indeed, human society would have been annihilated but for protective counter-moves, which blunted the action of this self-destructive mechanism" (Polanyi 1944/2001, 79–80). Polanyi labeled the tendency of society to protect itself from the perils of a self-regulating market system the *double movement*:

While the organization of world commodity markets, world capital markets, and world currency markets under the aegis of the gold standard gave an unparalleled momentum to the mechanism of markets, a deep-seated movement sprang into being to resist the pernicious effects of a market-controlled economy. Society protected itself against the perils inherent in a self-regulating market system...

Polanyi found early evidence for his double movement in England's Poor Laws, which were implemented in the late sixteenth century and remained in effect until after World War II. These Poor Laws were administered through parish overseers who provided relief for the aged and infant poor as well as work for the able-bodied in workhouses. Polanyi (1944/2001, 82) emphasized that England's Poor Laws were further supported by the so-called "Speenhamland Law" from 1795 to 1834, which provided allowances to the working poor who received wages from their employers below what was considered a subsistence level:

The justices of Berkshire, meeting at the Pelican Inn, in Speenhamland, near Newbury, on May 6, 1795, in a time of great distress, decided that subsidies in aid of wages should be granted in accordance with a scale dependent upon the price of bread, so that a minimum income should be assured to the poor irrespective of their earnings...

The resulting increase in expenditures on public relief was so great, and the decline in productivity and work ethic so abhorrent, that the Speenhamland Law was repealed in 1834 and replaced with a new Poor Law that provided no relief for the able-bodied poor except employment in the workhouse.[16] While humanitarian feelings for the poor led many

[16] Polanyi used the Speenhamland Law not only as an example of the double movement but also to explain the brutal view of capitalism created by classical economists in the nineteenth century. This is discussed further in Chapter 5.

parishes to mitigate the harshness of the new law in practice, social legislation in the 1930s and 1940s eventually replaced the Poor Laws with a comprehensive system of public welfare services.

Polanyi stressed the large gap between the narrow utilitarian views of nineteenth-century classical economists and Adam Smith, who always emphasized the social and moral aspects of political economy (Polanyi 1944/2001, 117):

Smith wished to regard the wealth of the nations as a function of their national life, physical and moral.... A broad optimism pervades Smith's thinking since the laws governing the economic part of the universe are consonant with man's destiny as are those that govern the rest. No hidden hand tries to impose upon us the rites of cannibalism in the name of self-interest. The dignity of man is that of a moral being, who is, as such, a member of the civic order of family, state, and "the great Society of mankind." Reason and humanity set a limit to piecework; emulation and gain must give way to them.

Tawney rejected the narrow utilitarianism of classical economists based on his Christian belief in the Incarnation of Christ, which inscribed human personality with infinite value. Polanyi viewed Tawney's attempt to contradict utilitarian reasoning from within Christian social ethics as innovative and exemplary, but he insisted that the necessary innovation had to come from outside the Christian tradition. Tim Rogan (2017, 87) describes Polanyi's journey to replace Tawney's moral critique of capitalism with a humanist foundation:

In the late 1930s he had pointed to the early writings of Marx as sources of the requisite "elucidation." But if the early Marx harbored a conception of the human comparable to Tawney's Christian emphasis on the infinite importance of human personality, Marx's eventual critique of political economy effaced that early humanism almost entirely. Polanyi came to believe that this was because Marx had assimilated the premises of his polemical opponents to the point where he could not think outside of them. Marx's aim had been to challenge the estrangement of ethics and economics. But Marx's "too close adherence to Ricardo and the traditions of liberal economics" confounded the attempt.

It is from the perspective of this journey that Polanyi's major treatise must be understood. In addition to explaining the disruption of Western Civilization at the beginning of the twentieth century, *The Great Transformation* represents Polanyi's search for a humanist moral foundation for capitalism. "Polanyi followed the intellectual history back beyond Marx in search of a displaced humanism. That path led him back to Adam Smith."

It was somewhere between the publication of *The Wealth of Nations* in 1776 and the public policy debates of Thomas Malthus and David Ricardo in the early 1800s that the moral foundation provided by Adam Smith had been lost. These debates had focused on the biological nature of man instead of his distinctively human qualities, manifest as an overemphasis on population growth and limits to the wealth of nations imposed by the natural world. As Rogan (2017, 88) points out, "Polanyi identified the source through which this new naturalism had been assimilated into political economy with impressive precision. The key document was Joseph Townsend's *Dissertation on the Poor Laws* (Townsend 1786)":

Townsend's tract – an attack on the English poor laws, which Townsend saw as perpetuating the problems of "poverty and wretchedness" they were supposed to solve – revolves around an apocryphal story. On the South Sea island of Juan Fernandez, a pair of goats is landed to provide a supply of food for seafarers. The goats multiply, their food supply runs short, the weaker starve, and in time an equilibrium is established in which the population size is regulated by the availability of food. Before long, Spanish authorities become concerned that the goats are provisioning the privateers who are plundering their ships. They land a pair of greyhounds to kill off the goats. The dogs feast and multiply, goat numbers decline, until at length the stronger goats retreat to rocky peaks where the dogs cannot follow, leaving only the weak and reckless to be eaten. A new equilibrium is established...

This apocryphal story, whose validity Polanyi could not verify, "would be cited again and again in early nineteenth-century social and political thought, notably by Malthus and then Darwin. The lesson drawn was that social problems were best solved by leaving things be. Poverty was a problem created and sustained by the poor laws: by allowing hunger and scarcity to do their grim work, the abolition of the poor laws would limit the population to a level the country could support, lifting the living standards of the laboring poor. This – for Polanyi – was the inauguration of the social philosophy of laissez faire" (Rogan 2017, 89).

As the Great Depression dragged on, John Maynard Keynes saw that the tendency for markets to "self-adjust" and approach full employment was much weaker than classical economists believed. Thus, he added a moral obligation for government. In addition to advancing civil society with wise and prudent policy, government had a duty to do all it could to maintain full employment. Yet "Keynes emphatically rejected socialism as an *economic* remedy for the ills of *laissez-faire*. Its doctrines were ideological, obsolete, irrelevant, inimical to wealth-creation, and likely to involve gross interferences with individual liberty" (Skidelsky 1994,

233). Like Polanyi, he promoted a middle way between the individualism of laissez-faire capitalism and the collectivism of Marxist socialism.[17]

Keynes's moral foundation for capitalism based on humanism has largely been overlooked by philosophers, economists, and policymakers. This may be attributable to the fact that the details of his moral foundation are spread out over several of his published works including *The Economic Consequences of the Peace* (Keynes 1919), *The End of Laissez-faire* (Keynes 1926), *Economic Possibilities for Our Grandchildren* (Keynes 1930a), and *My Early Beliefs* (Keynes 1938). These four works all appeared after World War I and, thus, reflect his renewed appreciation for duty, responsibility, and moral norms. As Skidelsky (1986, 402) points out, after the war, Keynes and his generation returned to a more traditional humanism based on the Victorian values of the previous generation:

> Yet it must be remembered that a sense of precariousness was always implicit in the world view of Keynes's generation. Their parents had, after all, relied on God to maintain social cohesion. When belief in God waned they could not help feeling that the moral capital which sustained the accumulation of economic capital had been severely depleted. Keynes and his friends had not worried about this before the war. The death of God meant to them liberation from false beliefs and irksome duties. By 1919 it appeared in a different light. The vanished nineteenth-century certainties seemed curiously comforting in retrospect.... In the last resort Keynes's post-war fear for the future of capitalism was profoundly influenced by the Victorian fear of a godless society.

David Andrews (2010) has written a detailed account of Keynes and the rich humanist tradition of nineteenth- and early twentieth-century Britain. This tradition was largely a response to David Hume's (1711–76) skepticism regarding religion and morals. "Hume concluded that ordinary knowledge and experience of the physical world is grounded on no firmer a foundation than custom and habit, which are ultimately unreliable. The result for Hume was a thoroughgoing skepticism with regard to both the physical and moral worlds" (Andrews 2010, 12). The British Humanist Tradition that shaped Keynes's views rejected Hume's moral skepticism but looked beyond religion as a source of social and moral wisdom.[18] That moral tradition also followed the philosophy of Plato

---

[17] Skidelsky (1994, 229) concludes that the argument is not over. "Capitalism may have vanquished socialism, but the debate between *laissez-faire* and Keynes's philosophy of the Middle Way is still fiercely joined."

[18] As discussed above, Cambridge had established a Moral Sciences department by the 1870s, which at the time included moral and political philosophy as well as political

and the teachings of Christ, which both "claimed that some activities or experiences are higher than others, in some important spiritual sense, and thereby asserted a claim that is both *positive* in that it purports to be factually true and *normative* in that it asserts that one manner of being is morally superior to others" (Andrews 2010, 32, italics added).

The British humanist moral tradition that Keynes learned as a student at Cambridge was shaped by the British philosopher Samuel Taylor Coleridge (1772–1834) and the Cambridge moral philosophers Henry Sidgwick (1838–1900) and G. E. Moore (1873–1958). These moral philosophers reflected the modernist movement away from religion and toward scientific rationalism as the main source of moral truth. Although he was a devout Christian, for example, Coleridge's moral philosophy was distinguished by its opposition to the exclusivity of truths. "He took the accumulated wisdom, the insights, and the judgments of humans throughout the course of their history as data to be explained. A great many doctrines had been proclaimed and some of them had consistently resonated with large numbers of people while others had not. The fact that certain beliefs had been held by thoughtful educated people and that they resonated with many people did not lead Coleridge to conclude that they were therefore necessarily correct; it led him to ask what it was about such beliefs that made them persuasive" (Andrews 2010, 13).

Sidgwick applied this same anthropological approach in his treatise, *The Methods of Ethics* (Sidgwick 1874/1907). "There he gave a sympathetic account of the major approaches to ethics that were current in the late nineteenth century, namely, intuitionism, utilitarianism, and egoism. He argued that each of them expresses a truth, and he attempted to show that they could be reconciled. He succeeded, at least to his own satisfaction, in reconciling intuitionism and utilitarianism, but he deeply regretted his failure to reconcile these with egoism" (Andrews 2010, 15). Sidgwick found intuitionism (following general principles in moral decision-making) to be in harmony with utilitarianism (promoting everyone's well-being). When attempting to reconcile egoism (promoting one's own well-being) with utilitarianism, however, he found an irreconcilable duality of practical reason.

Sidgwick's treatise reflected the classical utilitarian tradition of his times. By the end of the nineteenth century, however, classical economists had significantly narrowed that tradition. In particular, Jeremy Bentham

economy. It was not until 1903 that Economics was dropped from the Moral Sciences under the influence of Alfred Marshall and made a separate subject of study.

(1748–1832) and James Mill (1773–1836) had come to view political economy as based exclusively on egoism, and John Stuart Mill (1806–73) had gone even further to join utilitarianism with egoism. "Sidgwick argued that Bentham adopted egoism in addition to utilitarianism, evidently under the assumption, which Sidgwick rejected, that it was always in an individual's true interest to act so as to promote the general happiness…. Sidgwick also claimed that John Stuart Mill's writings 'veiled' the 'profound discrepancy' between egoism and utilitarianism by allowing the appearance that they should typically coincide" (Andrews 2010, 53). According to Sidgwick, therefore, classical economists had addressed his irreconcilable duality between egoism and utilitarianism by simply exalting the ethical principle of egoism.

G. E. Moore went further than Sidgwick in his critique of the growing tendency within political economy to equate egoism with utilitarianism. He concluded that egoism was self-evidently absurd as an ethical principle. In *Principia Ethica* (Moore 1903, 99), he asserted that if something is an ultimate end, then it must be so for everyone: "What Egoism holds … is that each man's happiness is the sole good – that a number of different things are each of them the only good thing there is – an absolute contradiction! No more complete and thorough refutation of any theory could be desired." Because of this glaring contradiction, Moore dismissed egoism out of hand and saw no need to reconcile it with utilitarianism, as Sidgwick had attempted and failed.

This background on the British Humanist Tradition of nineteenth- and early twentieth-century Britain helps explain why Keynes, like Polanyi, rejected the increasingly narrow utilitarianism that had evolved in classical economics. In contrast to Malthus and Ricardo, he viewed the central problem of society as "the greedy, selfish and materialistic attitude expressed in the philosophy of Jeremy Bentham…. From this perspective, Keynes came to view religion and tradition in a positive light, because they stood in opposition to the selfish and materialistic tendency" (Andrews 2017, 959). In an essay written in 1930, *The Economic Possibilities for Our Grandchildren*, Keynes predicted that the great wealth created by capitalism would eventually allow humanity to escape from Benthamism. "I see us free, therefore, to return to some of the most sure and certain principles of religion and traditional virtue" (quoted in Keynes 2015, 84–85).

The narrow utilitarianism of the classical economists, which has been passed down to neoclassical economists, has been widely criticized for its inability to describe behavior. Stanford economist Tibor Scitovsky tested the descriptive validity of utilitarianism using the methods of behavioral psychologists. In his book, *The Joyless Economy: The Psychology of Human Satisfaction* (Scitovsky 1976/1992), he presented survey evidence that countries with the highest standard of living do not necessarily exhibit the highest levels of satisfaction and happiness. His evidence showed that while income and wealth are high in America, for example, the happiness of Americans is not higher than that of many nations with lower income and wealth. His evidence also revealed that increasing income only improves happiness if the income of others is not increasing as much. Therefore, "keeping up with the Joneses" was reflected in the surveys. The evidence also showed that happiness is higher when one's income relative to others is rising than if it is already high. Finally, Scitovsky found evidence that behavior consistent with altruism and charity is associated with higher satisfaction and happiness. His evidence suggests that human motivation is not adequately described by the narrow utilitarianism of classical and neoclassical economics.[19]

4.5 CONCLUSION

Seeing that most intellectuals in the West had rejected religion, Polanyi moved away from Tawney's critique of capitalism based on Christianity toward a secular critique based on the infinite value of humanity. This put him in conflict not only with the religious views of Tawney, but with the increasingly naturalistic view of humanity inspired by Darwinism. In contrast, Keynes moved away from his early radical form of humanism based on the rejection of Victorian values toward a more traditional humanism based on those same values. Polanyi and Keynes, however, were united in their rejection of both the narrow utilitarianism of classical economists and the radical socialist theory that had been constructed on that same utilitarianism by Marx. They became convinced that the problems highlighted by socialists could best be addressed by an enlightened capitalism that incorporated moral norms and values. In this regard, their moral foundation for capitalism converged toward Adam Smith's moral foundation. Only Polanyi, however, fully recognized the significance of Smith's contribution to his moral foundation.

[19] A major weakness of Scitovsky's (1976/1992) survey evidence is that it was not gathered in economic settings with real financial pay and incentives. In the final chapter, I discuss evidence of economic behavior consistent with preferences for social and moral norms gathered from experimental and capital market settings.

While Keynes learned his economics from Alfred Marshall at Cambridge, he was heavily influenced by the moral philosophy of Henry Sidgwick and G. E. Moore. Marshall came to view ethics as useless and relied increasingly on his training in mathematics to hone his narrowing field of "economics." Keynes, in contrast, maintained the broad "political economy" perspective of Sidgwick and Moore, who viewed the question of what ends and goals to pursue in life as a moral question that must be answered before political or economic issues are addressed. Political and economic issues were still important, in their view, because they represent the means to achieving those moral ends and goals. Only Robinson Crusoe, stranded alone on his island, could practically address economic issues with no concern for political, social, and moral issues. After Marshall, however, this would become the primary setting of interest to neoclassical economists.

5

Self-Interest as a Moral Foundation

The Chicago School and Ayn Rand

The Wealth of Nations is a stupendous palace erected upon the granite of self-interest. It was not a narrow foundation: "though the principles of common prudence do not always govern the conduct of every individual, they always influence that of the majority of every class or order." The immensely powerful force of self-interest guides resources to their most efficient uses, stimulates laborers to diligence and inventors to splendid new divisions of labor – in short, it orders and enriches the nation which gives it free rein.

George J. Stigler
Smith's Travels on the Ship of State

As the political and economic upheaval of the early twentieth century subsided, and immediate threats to capitalism and Western democracies abated, neoclassical economists continued the narrowing of their discipline begun by classical economists. Karl Polanyi (1944/2001) argued that capitalist societies are continually influenced by two opposing movements: the movement to unleash the power of markets and the counter-movement to shield society from the resulting vulnerabilities and excesses of those markets. He demonstrated the overarching influence of this *double movement* in his history of capitalism and used it to explain the political and economic turmoil of the early twentieth century. Polanyi attributed the rise of the totalitarianism movements of Marxist social-ism and fascism to a market society that refused to work. In the post-war period, however, the excesses of the protective countermovement became the dominant concern as the threat of Marxist socialism contin-ued to plague the West. In the midst of this threat, an Austrian economist helped establish a beachhead of laissez-faire capitalism at the University of Chicago. Neoclassical economists at the University of Chicago ignored the vulnerabilities and excesses of unregulated markets and made self-interest the first principle of their economic theory. In this chapter, I address self-interest as a moral foundation for capitalism by discussing the rise of the Chicago School and the life and writings of Ayn Rand.[1]

5.1 THE CONTINUED NARROWING OF NEOCLASSICAL ECONOMICS

As discussed in the previous chapter, economics was originally a branch of ethics. Over the twentieth century, however, neoclassical economists "took their discipline on a path of ever increasing formalization and sought an approach free of normative or ethical considerations" (Force 2003, 170). In the *Treatise of Human Nature*, David Hume (1739/1975, III.2.5) started with the assumption that men are naturally selfish or endowed only with a confined generosity. Yet he followed Adam Smith in rejecting narrow self-interest as the main motivation in political economy. In particular, both Scottish Enlightenment philosophers rejected what Hume called "the selfish hypothesis" or "the idea (associated with Mandeville and the Epicurean/Augustinian tradition) that self-interest was a general explanatory principle for human behavior" (Force 2003, 256). In continuing Marshall's mathematical formalism, however, neo-classical economists eventually removed all normative considerations and made self-interest the first principle of their discipline.

In his book, *Self-Interest before Adam Smith*, Pierre Force (2003) presents a "genealogy" of economic science that explains how the narrow self-interest promoted by neoclassical economists became associated with Adam Smith. Force begins by critiquing George Stigler's (1971a) metaphor characterizing *The Wealth of Nations* as a stupendous palace erected upon the granite of self-interest. First, he points out that Stigler's metaphor manifests the special reverence economists have for the founder of their discipline. Second, he argues that since Adam Smith's seminal work is itself the foundation of modern economic science, Stigler's metaphor identifies self-interest as the first principle of economics. Finally, Force confronts Stigler's interpretation of Smith's seminal work on political economy by stating the obvious: *Because self-interest is a concept of*

---

[1] As the epigraph to this chapter suggests (Stigler 1971a, 265), neoclassical economists associated with the Chicago School continued the reshaping of Adam Smith's legacy begun by classical economists in the nineteenth century.

such fundamental importance, one would expect Adam Smith to mention it quite often.

As Force points out, however, the term "self-interest" appears only once in *The Wealth of Nations*. Even then, the term is used in the context of Smith's speculation that the tradition of paying Catholic priests based on voluntary gifts keeps their industry and zeal alive by "the powerful motive of self-interest" (*WN* V.i.g.2). As discussed previously in Chapter 2, the commonly quoted passage linking Adam Smith's seminal work to self-interest doesn't even contain the term. In analyzing the motives we should address when negotiating with "the butcher, the brewer, or the baker" for our supper (*WN* I.ii.2), Smith does not refer to *self-interest* but *self-love*: "We address ourselves, not to their humanity but to their self-love, and never talk to them of our own necessities but of their advantages." Consistent with leading economic historians and philosophers such as Albert Hirschman and Charles Griswold Jr., Force concludes that the adoption of self-interest as the first principle of economics has less to do with Adam Smith and more to do with the development of economic science in the two centuries after Smith.

According to Polanyi (1944/2001), Townsend's (1786) *Dissertation on the Poor Laws* marks the beginning of the end for Adam Smith's social and moral perspective on political economy. Although Townsend's apocryphal story of the goats and dogs on the island of Juan Fernandez could not be authenticated, it had a significant influence on both Thomas Malthus in his economic theory and Charles Darwin in his evolutionary theory. By conflating humanity with the animal kingdom, Townsend bypassed important questions regarding the foundations of government and law. Polanyi (1944/2001, 119) described the influence of making the biological nature of man the foundation of economic and public policy:

> But on the island of Juan Fernandez there was neither government nor law; and yet there was balance between goats and dogs. That balance was maintained by the difficulty the dogs found in devouring the goats which fled into the rocky part of the island, and the inconveniences the goats had to face when moving to safety from the dogs. No government was needed to maintain this balance; it was restored by the pangs of hunger on the one hand, the scarcity of food on the other. Hobbes had argued the need for a despot because men were like beasts; Townsend insisted that they were actually beasts and that, precisely for that reason, only a minimum of government was required.

To Adam Smith and the Scottish Enlightenment philosophers (including David Hume), political economy was a human science that dealt with what was natural to mankind, not to Nature. As a result of developments

in natural philosophy and the biological sciences, however, classical economists increasingly relinquished Adam Smith's humanistic foundation
for political economy and incorporated Townsend's naturalistic foundation. For example, the public policy debates of Malthus and Ricardo
in the early 1800s focused on the biological nature of man instead of
his distinctively human qualities. These debates reflected an emphasis on
population growth and limits to the wealth of nations imposed by the
natural world.

Polanyi (1944/2001, 129) argued that England's early Poor Laws,
including the so-called "Speenhamland Law" from 1795 to 1834, created an environment that confirmed the new "dismal science" view of
economics promoted by Malthus and Ricardo:

Smith's own view was that universal plenty could not help percolating down to
the people; it was impossible that society should get wealthier and wealthier and
the people poorer and poorer. Unfortunately, the facts did not seem to bear him
out for a long time to come; and as theorists had to account for the facts, Ricardo
proceeded to argue that the more society advanced the greater would be the difficulty of procuring food and the richer would landlords grow, exploiting both
capitalists and workers; that the capitalists' and the workers' interests were in
fatal opposition to one another, but that this opposition was ultimately ineffective as the workers' wages could never rise above the subsistence level and profits
were bound to shrivel up in any case.

According to Polanyi, the Speenhamland Law helped create "the facts"
that Malthus and Ricardo had to explain in their classical economic theory. During a time of great distress, the justices of Berkshire decided that
subsidies in aid of wages should be granted in accordance with a scale
dependent upon the price of bread, so that a minimum income should
be assured to the poor irrespective of their earnings. Meant as a supplement to the Poor Laws in effect since the late sixteenth century, however,
the new law worsened the suffering of the laboring poor. As Polanyi
(1944/2001, 101–102) described it, "(Speenhamland) was started as aid-
in-wages, ostensibly benefitting the employees, but actually using public
means to subsidize the employers…. In the long run, a system as uneco-
nomical as that was bound to affect the productivity of labor and to
depress standard wages."

The ultimate effect of the Speenhamland law was to prevent the creation of a labor market during the most active period of the first Industrial
Revolution. By the time of its repeal in 1834, the same law that had been
ushered in to protect rural England against the full force of the market
economy had become a moral scourge that "was eating into the marrow
of society" (Polanyi 1944/2001, 106–107):

By the time of its repeal huge masses of the laboring population resembled more the specters that might haunt a nightmare than human beings. But if the workers were physically dehumanized, the owning classes were morally degraded. The traditional unity of a Christian society was giving place to a denial of responsibility on the part of the well-to-do for the condition of their fellows. The Two Nations were taking shape. To the bewilderment of thinking minds, unheard-of wealth turned out to be inseparable from unheard-of poverty.

Polanyi's history of capitalism in England reveals two economic truths about government involvement in the economy. First, market societies *need* the state to play an active role in reducing the vulnerabilities and excesses of free markets. Second, any efforts by the state to reduce such vulnerabilities and excesses must be carefully conducted in view of unintended consequences. While Polanyi's interpretation of the Speenhamland Law has been debated by historical economists, his two economic truths and his historical theory of the double movement have been consistently supported over time.

According to Fred Block in the new introduction to the 2001 reprint of Polanyi's seminal work, Polanyi's double movement suggests that the binary choice between laissez-faire, free-market capitalism and Marxist socialism is a false choice (Block 2001, xxix):

Polanyi's thesis of the double movement contrasts strongly with both market liberalism and orthodox Marxism in the range of possibilities that are imagined at any particular moment. Both market liberalism and Marxism argue that societies have only two real choices: there can be market capitalism or socialism. Although they have opposing preferences, the two positions agree in excluding any other alternatives. Polanyi, in contrast, insists that free market capitalism is not a real choice; it is only a utopian vision.

Polanyi also attacked socialism as a utopian vision. Given his brief experience with economic planning in the Soviet Republic of Hungary after World War I, he fully grasped that markets were more efficient at managing supply and demand than government planning. He also understood, however, that free-market economies always required planning. The challenge for public policy, according to Polanyi, was determining which mix of markets and planning was most efficient in expanding output and fostering innovation while protecting civil liberties. His experiences living in Hungary, Austria, England, and the United States during the tumultuous early twentieth century, combined with his deep sense of moral responsibility and love of individual liberty, shaped Polanyi's broad view of capitalist society.

Despite the political and economic upheaval of his world, Polanyi remained optimistic about the future of capitalism. In particular, Polanyi viewed Roosevelt's market reforms initiated during the 1930s as a model of future possibilities. "Roosevelt's reforms meant that the US economy continued to be organized around markets and market activity, but a new set of regulatory mechanisms now made it possible to buffer both human beings and nature from the pressure of market forces" (Block 2001, xxxv). Reforms initiated in the United States during the 1930s included the establishment of Social Security to provide the elderly with a source of income and the creation of depositor's insurance to protect communities against bank closures. Again, Polanyi viewed these reforms positively as society deciding through democratic means to protect itself from the vulnerabilities and excesses of free-market capitalism.[2]

As the political and economic upheaval of the early twentieth century subsided and immediate threats to capitalism and Western democracies abated, however, neoclassical economists continued the narrowing of their discipline begun by classical economists in the nineteenth century. Just as the humanist tradition of nineteenth- and early twentieth-century Britain incorporated David Hume's skepticism regarding religion and morals, the narrowing of neoclassical economics incorporated Hume's utilitarianism. As discussed in the previous chapter, the classical utilitarian tradition which Hume initiated and Sidgwick explored in *The Methods of Ethics* (1874/1907) drew a clear distinction between intuitionism (following general principles in moral decision-making), utilitarianism (promoting everyone's well-being), and egoism (promoting one's own well-being). In his attempt to reconcile the three philosophical perspectives, Sidgwick found an irreconcilable duality of practical reason when attempting to reconcile utilitarianism with egoism. According to Sidgwick, classical economists had addressed this irreconcilable duality by simply exalting the ethical principle of egoism. Neoclassical economists continued that tradition by making each individual in capitalist society a utility maximizer with preferences only for wealth and leisure.

As for Adam Smith, we have seen that he strongly rejected both the utilitarianism of Hume and the egoism (narrow self-interest) of Hobbes and Mandeville. In the opening lines of *The Theory of Moral Sentiments*, for example, Smith directly refutes Mandeville's selfish hypothesis (*TMS* I.i.1.1). In the rest of his seminal work of moral philosophy, Smith explains the moral sentiments or "passions" that arise due to sympathy and the

---

[2] It is generally agreed, however, that the New Deal policies of the 1930s were ineffective at lifting America and the world economy out of the Great Depression (Bernstein 2001).

formation of the moral conscience based on the impartial spectator. In a later passage refuting the selfish hypothesis he writes (*TMS* VII.ii.I.20):

The wise and virtuous man is at all times willing that his own private interest should be sacrificed to the public interest of his own particular order or society. He is at all times willing, too, that the interest of this order or society should be sacrificed to the greater interest of the state or sovereignty, of which it is only a subordinate part. He should, therefore, be equally willing that all those inferior interests should be sacrificed to the greater interest of the universe, to the interest of that great society of all sensible and intelligent beings, of which God himself is the immediate administrator and director.

Despite Smith's rejection of both utilitarianism and narrow self-interest, neoclassical economists associated with the Chicago School used a few isolated passages from his other seminal work to make him the poster child of their modern economic theory. Force (2003, 201) concludes that, rather than being a stupendous palace erected upon the granite of self-interest, *The Wealth of Nations* represents a frontal attack on the narrow self-interest of neoclassical economics:

As we have seen ... in "The Wealth of Nations," self-love is a motive of human behavior only to the extent that it is used as an argument to persuade others to engage in commercial exchange. The drive behind commerce and the division of labor is the propensity to barter and trade, and this propensity is itself based on the faculties of reason and speech and the urge to persuade others. The "desire to better our condition," which Smith invokes as a quasi-universal motive of action in commercial society, is ultimately grounded in neo-Stoic assumptions regarding sympathy and the desire for sympathy, not in Epicurean principles of pleasure or happiness. In that sense, the conventional reading of "The Wealth of Nations" as a paradigm of the interest doctrine is an Epicurean interpretation of a work that is fundamentally anti-Epicurean.

Given the above errors in interpretation, and the fact that Smith never refuted his moral theory in his lifetime, it is clear that Stigler's metaphor represents a mischaracterization of Adam Smith's seminal work of political economy. This is particularly puzzling given that Stigler completed his Ph.D. under the supervision of Frank Knight at the University of Chicago in 1938, and his dissertation dealt with the history of economic thought. Knight was a scholar of Max Weber and shared his broad institutional and historical view of economics.[3] In particular, he

---

[3] Knight had translated Max Weber's lectures from German into English just before arriving at Chicago, and while there, he taught a seminar on Weber and the German Historical School (Mitch 2010).

arrived at the University of Chicago from the University of Iowa in 1927 with the expectation of teaching institutional economics and, like Weber, was particularly interested in the question of the development of capitalism and its effects on society (Rutherford 2010). By 1945, however, the growing influence of the Keynesian revolution within the economics profession led to a counter-revolution at Chicago spearheaded by Friedrich Hayek, Milton Friedman, and George Stigler. Through the influence of these prominent neoclassical economists, the Chicago School went from the birthplace of institutional economics in America to the bastion of laissez-faire, free-market capitalism. How this dramatic transformation occurred is the topic of the following section.

5.2 HOW SELF-INTEREST CONQUERED THE CHICAGO SCHOOL OF ECONOMICS

At the end of World War II, Keynes and other world leaders were determined to avoid the missteps that characterized the peace negotiations of World War I. The driving force behind Keynes's vision for postwar planning was his conviction that modern society could no longer stand "nature's cures" of inflation and unemployment for the malfunctioning of the global financial system. He took the decisive lead with his proposal for an International Clearing Union and was also highly influential in the negotiation of the Bretton Woods Agreement of July 1944. Keynes spent his final days in early 1946 negotiating a major loan with America to see Britain through the early postwar years and planning the new International Monetary Fund and World Bank. However, on the morning of Easter Sunday, April 21, his weak heart finally gave out. Prominent British economist Lionel Robbins said that Keynes had given his life for his country "as surely as if he had fallen on the field of battle" (Skidelsky 2001, 472).

In the same year that Polanyi's seminal work was published (Polanyi 1944/2001), Friedrich A. Hayek (1899–1992) published his highly influential book, *The Road to Serfdom* (Hayek 1944/2007). Similar to Polanyi, Hayek was born in Vienna and fought in the Austro-Hungarian Army during World War I in an artillery regiment on the Italian front. Like Polanyi, he also was drawn to democratic socialism in his youth but eventually rejected socialism as an ineffective economic system that threatened liberty and freedom. He earned doctorates in law and political economy at the University of Vienna in 1921 and 1923, respectively. During that time, Hayek's economic thinking shifted away from socialism toward classical liberalism. Upon his reading of Ludwig von Mises's book *Socialism: An Economics and Sociological Analysis* (first published in German in 1922), Hayek began attending von Mises's bi-weekly private seminars and became a leading proponent of the Austrian School of Economics.

While Keynes was busy financing World War II for the Allies and planning for postwar Europe, Hayek spent his time teaching and writing from his chaired position at the London School of Economics (LSE). After acquiring a lecturer position with the help of Robbins in 1931, Hayek engaged in a public debate with Keynes over his recent book, *A Treatise on Money* (Keynes 1930b). The deep economic recession of the 1920s, followed by the worldwide depression of the 1930s, had increased the popularity of socialist ideology and economic planning in Britain. In the inaugural lecture for his faculty chair in March 1933, Hayek attacked such economic planning as inconsistent with rational economic thinking. Toward the end of his lecture, he criticized the German Historical School for having paved the way for such misguided thinking.

Hayek's inaugural lecture was not well received by many students and faculty at LSE (Caldwell 2007).[4] Britain had not yielded to the radical socialism gripping much of Continental Europe, but Hayek could see the warning signs. What troubled Hayek most was "the nearly universal sentiment among the intelligentsia in the 1930s that a planned system represented 'the middle way' between a failed capitalism and totalitarianisms of the left and right" (Caldwell 2007, 11). In *The Road to Serfdom*, written from 1940 to 1942, Hayek sought to reverse the trends that he saw in Britain. But he sought to do more than make the case against socialist planning. He also sought to remind the British of their liberal democratic heritage and contrast it with the collectivism of both Marxism and Naziism. Because of his conviction that flawed socialist thinking had permeated all of British society, Hayek dedicated his book "To the Socialists of All Parties."

Hayek sent a copy of his book to his old nemesis and found him a kindred spirit when it came to pushing back on the lingering threat of Marxist socialism in Britain. Keynes wanted Hayek to directly address, however, the legitimate role of government in capitalist economies (Caldwell 2007, 23–24):

---

[4] It is important to recall that English social reformers Sidney (1859–1947) and Beatrice Webb (1858–1943), early members of the Fabian Society, were cofounders of the London School of Economics.

John Maynard Keynes read the book on the way to the Bretton Woods conference, and delighted Hayek when he wrote him that it was "a great book" and that "morally and philosophically I find myself in agreement with virtually the whole of it; and not only in agreement with it, but in a deeply moved agreement." Keynes went on to say, though, that "You admit here and there that it is a question of knowing where to draw the line. You agree that the line has to be drawn somewhere, and that the logical extreme is not possible. But you give us no guidance whatever as to where to draw it."

After its publication in England by Routledge, three American publishing houses rejected the manuscript before it was finally published by the University of Chicago Press. Until its final acceptance, its success in America was very much in doubt. At the time, the Economics Department at Chicago had a reputation for being highly diverse. That reputation was no better exemplified than by the Chicago economist Frank H. Knight (1885–1972). During the interwar period, Knight was involved in translating the works of Max Weber into English. In addition to his deep knowledge of the German language, Knight began studying Weber because of his common interests in economic history, institutional economics, and ethics. In contrast to the neoclassical economists who would later dominate the Economics Department at Chicago, "Knight's interest in ethics and social science broadened as he came to focus more attention on the problems of liberalism" (Emmett 2010, 282).

When the University of Chicago Press asked Knight to evaluate Hayek's manuscript for potential publication, he provided a lukewarm endorsement that could easily have doomed the project. Knight found fault with both Hayek's theoretical and historical arguments. Regarding the former, he pointed out, "There is little or no economic theory in the book." Regarding the latter, he took issue with Hayek's interpretation of German history and the events that precipitated the Nazi dictatorship of Hitler. "It seems to me that there are many factors in German history which would call for consideration in a balanced treatment." Knight cited as examples "the late survival of feudalism, retarding of national unification and industrialization, and the special circumstances surrounding these changes and the establishment of responsible government after the First World War." He concluded, "In sum, the book is an able piece of work, but limited in scope and somewhat one-sided in treatment. I doubt whether it would have a very wide market in this country, or would change the position of many readers" (Caldwell 2007, 249–250).[5]

---

[5] Knight's review of Hayek's manuscript reflects his expertise as a German scholar and translator of Max Weber's writings from German into English.

Hayek's book ended up being accepted by the University of Chicago Press largely through the lobbying efforts of a former instructor in the Economics Department at Chicago, Aaron Director. Interestingly, his book was reviewed and given a strong vote of support by a new member of the Economics Department at Chicago, Jacob Marschak (1898–1977). Marshak had come to Chicago in 1943 to serve as Director of the Cowles Commission for Research in Economics, which had moved there from Colorado Springs in 1939.[6] Like most of the highly mathematical modelers and statisticians at Cowles, Marschak was a devoted Keynesian with socialist leanings. He also found problems with Hayek's book, including that "the book is almost exclusively critical not constructive. Its technique is black-and-white. It is impatient of compromises...." Yet Marschak concluded "Hayek's style is readable and occasionally inspiring. This book cannot be by-passed."

Not only did the University of Chicago not bypass Hayek's book, its publication played a central role in Chicago's conversion from the birthplace of institutional economics in America to a bastion of laissez-faire, free-market economics. In sharp contrast to the initial review provided by Knight, Milton Friedman's introduction to the fifty-year anniversary edition of *The Road to Serfdom* expressed unqualified admiration (Caldwell 2007, 259–260):

On rereading the book before writing this introduction, I was again impressed with what a magnificent book it is – subtle and closely reasoned yet lucid and clear, philosophical and abstract yet also concrete and realistic, analytical and rational yet animated by high ideals and a vivid sense of mission. Little wonder that it had so great an influence. I was impressed also that its message is no less needed today than it was when it first appeared.... The same collectivist fallacies are abroad and on the rise today, but the immediate issues are different and so is much of the jargon. Today we hear little of "central planning".... Instead the talk is of the urban crisis ... the environmental crisis ... social responsibility ... here the jargon is still "poverty in the midst of plenty," though what is now described as poverty would have been regarded as plenty when that slogan was first widely use.

A note from the publisher in the fifty-year anniversary edition admits that, right up until the original publication date, they couldn't get a bookstore even in New York excited about the book. An initial review in

[6] The presence of the Cowles Commission was another sign of the diversity of the Economics Department at Chicago prior to the arrival of Hayek in 1950. In 1955, however, the Cowles Commission moved to the Yale Department of Economics and became the Cowles Foundation.

the *New York Times* called it "this sad and angry little book." However, future reviews were more positive, and the prospects of the book were bolstered by the publication of a condensed version in the *Reader's Digest* and the Book of the Month Club in 1945. In the fifty years after its original publication, the University of Chicago Press sold over a quarter of a million copies of Hayek's book including 81,000 in hardback and 175,000 in paperback.

The differing critiques of Hayek's book between 1943 and 1994 reflect the radical transformation at Chicago from the institutional economics of Knight to the neoclassical economics of Friedman and Stigler. Friedman and Stigler, however, took Hayek's critique of socialism much further than he originally intended. *The Road to Serfdom* reflects Hayek's experience with socialism in Austria and what he saw as the growing threat of economic planning in postwar Britain. A little more than a year after its initial publication, Britain had a socialist government that remained in power for six years. The new Labour government even put through an order (Control of Engagement Order of 1947) allowing the conscription of labor in peacetime and had a plan to require British workers to acquire work through an employment exchange of the Ministry of Labour (Caldwell 2007, 47). Thus, Hayek's deep concerns regarding the growing influence of socialism in Britain appear to have been warranted.[7]

Despite the historical perspective of Hayek's book as a response to the looming threat of socialism in postwar Britain, it was used by Friedman and Stigler to support their increasingly narrow view of economics based on self-interest. By the time Hayek penned his forward to the 1956 American paperback edition, he had to concede that the "hot socialism" of Marx that had motivated his book – "that organized movement toward a deliberate organization of economic life by the state as the chief owner of the means of production" – was nearly dead in the West. He stated, "The century of socialism in this sense probably came to an end around 1948" (Caldwell 2007, 44). Unlike Friedman and Stigler, Hayek never equated the modern welfare state of the West with socialism. Further, Hayek never equated free-market capitalism with laissez-faire economics or narrow self-interest. "He explicitly disavowed the ideal of laissez-faire and distanced himself from the sort of free market utopianism common among more extreme libertarians" (Feser 2006, 6). Under the influence of Friedman and Stigler, however, the Chicago School

---

[7] His lecturer position at largely progressive LSE likely heightened Hayek's concerns regarding the influence of socialism in Britain.

would eventually surpass Hayek's free-market views by equating most all government involvement in the economy with socialism and embracing libertarianism.

Edward Nik-Khah (2011) identifies the major players in the formation of the postwar Chicago School. Using unexploited archival materials and letters between the protagonists, he argues that Milton Friedman (1912–2006), George Stigler (1911–91), and Aaron Director (1901–2004) were central figures in the formation of the Chicago School and that their association with Fredrich Hayek and the Mont Pélerin Society played a decisive role. Nik-Khah identifies three main pillars of the Chicago School within the university: one located in the Business School and led by Stigler, one located in the Economics Department and led by Friedman, and one located in the Law School and led by Director. Stigler became known as "Mr. Micro," and Friedman became known as "Mr. Macro," reflecting the former's emphasis on industrial and labor economics and the latter's emphasis on monetary policy. While Director did very little writing and publishing and never distinguished himself as a scholar, Hayek won a Nobel Prize in Economic Sciences in 1974, Friedman won his Nobel Prize in 1976, and Stigler won his Nobel Prize in 1982.

As Stigler himself has noted in his memoirs (Stigler 1988, 148), there was no Chicago School of Economics prior to the first meeting of the Mont Pélerin Society (MPS) in 1947. While on a book tour promoting *The Road to Serfdom* in the spring of 1945, Hayek met with businessman Harold Luhnow in Chicago. Luhnow was then president of the William Volker Fund, and he was in the process of converting the purpose of the Fund, which existed from 1932 to 1965, into a foundation to promote a rethinking of liberal government policies in America (Van Horn and Mirowski 2015). Before returning to London, Hayek began corresponding with Luhnow on a plan to commission the writing of *The American Road to Serfdom*.[8] Hayek handed the responsibility for the new book project over to Director and it never was written, but his correspondence with Luhnow resulted in a more ambitious project.

After establishing a connection with Luhnow at the Volker Fund, Hayek began to correspond with his "great friend" Henry Simons at the Chicago Law School about gathering like-minded scholars for a

---

[8] Luhnow found Hayek's original book less useful for his purposes because it "had been composed with a British audience in mind and perhaps had been pitched at too elevated a level of discourse for American audiences" (Van Horn and Mirowski 2015, 141).

long-term project promoting classical liberalism and free-market capitalism.[9] Simons viewed Frank Knight's wider interests in social science, moral philosophy, and economic history as evidence that he was not deeply interested in concrete problems of economic policy. As a result of his growing correspondence with Hayek, Simons drew up an ambitious plan to reshape the Chicago landscape with the help of Aaron Director and economists with similar political leanings such as Milton Friedman, George Stigler, and Allen Wallis. His plan involved the creation of an institute to facilitate academic discussion, bring in libertarian visiting professors, and promote the publication of scholarly and semi-popular literature in support of free-market capitalism (Van Horn and Mirowski 2015).

The Economics Department at Chicago had refused to renew Director's teaching contract in 1934 (Van Horn 2010). Consequently, he went to work for the US Treasury Department in Washington. In 1937, however, Director attempted to restart his academic career by moving to London to conduct research for a dissertation under Jacob Viner on the quantitative history of the Bank of England. Director eventually stopped working on his dissertation due to difficulty getting data. Soon after arriving in London, however, he met Hayek at the LSE, "and they came to regard each other as intellectual comrades in arms. Director later became one of Hayek's staunchest political allies in the United States, persuading the University of Chicago Press to publish *The Road to Serfdom* after numerous commercial publishers had turned it down.... Director's deep respect for Hayek would later prove pivotal in Director's decision to return to Chicago" (Van Horn and Mirowski 2015, 147–148). Director's younger sister, Rose, married Milton Friedman in 1938.[10]

As negotiations between Luhnow, Hayek, Simons, and Director dragged on, Simons began to despair of the eventual success of the institution he and Hayek had envisioned. A major snag remained – the ongoing negotiations with the central administration at the University of Chicago. The original proposal had included the stipulation that the Law School

---

[9] Hayek and Simons's friendship dated back as early as 1934 when Hayek sent Simons a personal note of appreciation for his tract *Positive Program for Laissez Faire*, which advocated for a free price system uninhibited by political or monopolistic intervention (Van Horn and Mirowski 2015).

[10] In her part of the joint memoirs with her husband (Friedman and Friedman 1998, 14), Rose admitted that her older brother Aaron was a committed socialist as an undergraduate at Yale – an example of the old adage, "If one is not a socialist before age thirty, one has no heart; if one remains a socialist after thirty, one has no head."

"extend to Mr. Director an appointment as Research Associate with the rank of Professor and with permanent tenure, on condition that his salary be underwritten for a period of five years with funds from outside the University" (Van Horn and Mirowski 2015, 153). Although the Chicago Law Faculty formally approved the proposal, the central administration objected to giving Director automatic tenure as a Full Professor after a Volker-funded five-year stint as an administrator of "a Free Market Study."

Luhnow, who was aggravated by the latest setback, fired off a note to Hayek on June 18, 1946 stating that the outcome was now in his hands. Hayek later responded to Luhnow's note with tragic news. Simons had committed suicide on June 19. Director was also thinking about backing out of the proposal. After reassurance from Hayek, however, Director agreed to the new terms of the administration and the foundation for "The Chicago School" was laid by the fall of 1946. Friedman had already been hired away from the University of Minnesota in the spring of 1946 to replace Viner as the Economic Department's price theorist, and Wallis was hired away from Stanford that same year by the Business School. While Stigler's arrival was delayed, he was eventually hired by the School of Business in 1958 with a joint appointment in economics. As for Hayek, he was unable to secure a faculty position in the Economics Department and only came to Chicago due to a Volker-funded position in the Committee of Social Thought in 1950.[11]

As Van Horn and Mirowski (2015, 158–159) reveal, Hayek planned to establish a beacon of neoliberalism and free-market capitalism at Chicago. However, that was only part of his plan.

Once we acknowledge Friedrich Hayek's pivotal role in getting the Chicago School up and running by the fall of 1946, and then turn our attention to the first meeting of the Mont Pélerin Society in Vevey, Switzerland, in April 1947, we can begin to appreciate the extent to which the dual start-ups of the two landmarks of the history of postwar neoliberal thought were intimately connected. The MPS is generally regarded as the central locus of the development of neoliberal doctrine in the postwar world. Yet we observe that Hayek provided both the intellection impetus and the organizational spade-work for both the Chicago School and the MPS.... That MPS and the Chicago School were joined at the hip from birth is verified by the fact that most of the major protagonists were present at the creation of both organizations: Director, Friedman, Wallis, and Knight.

---

[11] The Committee of Social Thought was a multi-disciplinary graduate department founded in 1941 by Frank Knight, historian John Nef, and anthropologist Robert Hutchins. Nef had worked with R. H. Tawney in England to complete a major work on the history of the British coal-mining industry in 1932 (Rutherford 2010).

The neoliberalism that evolved at the Chicago School under Friedman and Stigler, however, transcended the classical liberalism of Hayek by collapsing all political and economic issues within the market paradigm of neoclassical price theory.[12] "Notoriously, it was the Chicago School that innovated the idea that much of politics could be understood as if it were a market process, and therefore amenable to formalization through neoclassical theory" (Van Horn and Mirowski 2015, 162). By embracing narrow self-interest as their first principle and rejecting all social and moral responsibility for the market, Friedman and Stigler eventually drove both Hayek and their mentor Frank Knight out of the Economics Department at Chicago.

5.3 AYN RAND AND THE GLORIFICATION OF NARROW SELF-INTEREST

The development of Friedman and Stigler's radical form of neoliberalism can be seen in their interaction with another major advocate for narrow self-interest in America – Ayn Rand (1905–1982). Historian Jennifer Burns (2009) has written the most recent and detailed biography of Rand: *Goddess of the Market: Ayn Rand and the American Right.* Burns's biography shows how an escapee from the turmoil and violence of the Bolshevik Russian Revolution could bring her experiences with her to America and, like Milton Friedman, become a major political figure in American conservative circles. Despite the complexity of her interactions with Friedman and other neoclassical economists associated with the Chicago School, Rand's unique moral philosophy was a natural extension of their neoclassical economic theory based on narrow self-interest.

In addition to providing funding for the establishment of the Chicago School and the Mont Pélerin Society, Harold Luhnow and the Volker Fund also provided funding for the oldest free-market think tank in the United States in 1946, the Foundation for Economic Education (FEE).[13] Rand was an important advisor or "ghost" to the founder and long-time president of FEE, Leonard Read (1898–1983). Given her rising reputation as a strong proponent of free-market capitalism, Read tapped Rand

---

[12] The term neoliberalism ("new" liberalism) was apparently coined at the Walter Lippmann Colloquium in Paris in 1938 to herald the appearance of the new orientation toward the previous liberal tradition, and the term was used by Friedman in 1951 to indicate the ambitions of Chicago and MPS (Van Horn and Mirowski 2015).

[13] FEE also received generous funding from other corporate supporters such as Chrysler, General Motors, Monsanto, Montgomery Ward, and U.S. Steel (Burns 2009).

to review material he intended to publish to make sure the foundation was ideologically coherent. From the beginning, Rand pushed Read to make decisions and adopt positions that supported her radical new philosophy based on narrow self-interest (Burns 2009).

Troubles began right away with FEE's inaugural pamphlet, *Roofs or Ceilings?*, co-authored by Friedman and Stigler who were together at the University of Minnesota at the time. In the pamphlet, the two young economists argued that rent controls popular in New York and other large cities had unintended economic consequences. By interfering with the free working of the market, they argued, such controls removed incentives to create more housing units, improve existing units, or share housing. Friedman and Stigler concluded that rent controls only increased the shortage of affordable housing they were designed to alleviate. They did not question the underlying motivation of such government regulation or invoke any moral principles, but simply emphasized that such regulation was inefficient and did not achieve its stated objectives. This would become the general position of the Chicago School toward all government involvement in the economy.

According to Burns (2009, 117), "the dispassionate tone of Friedman and Stigler's pamphlet infuriated Rand, who viewed it through the lens of her experience in Communist Russia."

Friedman and Stigler's use of the word "rationing" particularly disturbed her. She did not know such usage was standard in economics, instead flashing back to her days of near starvation in Petrograd. "Do you really think that calling the free pricing system a 'rationing' system is merely confusing and innocuous?" she asked in an angry letter to … a FEE trustee. She believed the authors were trying to make the word "respectable" and thus convince Americans to accept permanent and total rationing. Focusing entirely on the hidden implications of the pamphlet, Rand saw the authors' overt argument against rent control as "mere window dressing, weak, ineffectual, inconclusive and unconvincing."

Rand displayed a similar hostility toward another major player in the formation of the Chicago School. Hayek focused his criticism of socialism on central planning and state ownership of economic enterprises and generally accepted some state action as long as it was economically efficient and protected individual liberties. Hayek defined individualism as a respect for individuals and their unique capacity as rational beings – "respect for the individual man *qua* man." However, he rooted that individualism in Christianity, classical antiquity, and the Renaissance. Although his views on religion were closely held, he found religion culturally useful and was particularly sympathetic to

Catholicism. "Hayek also believed that a revival of traditional morals would save the West, and he was receptive to Christian values" (Burns 2009, 105). These views were unacceptable to Rand, whose individualism reflected an inflamed atheism and a glorification of narrow self-interest.

Read ignored Rand's suggestion to reject Friedman and Stigler's pamphlet, making it the first publication at FEE after adding a footnote. In addition to incurring Rand's wrath, he deeply alienated the two young economists with his decision to add the unauthorized footnote. While Rand soon broke her association with FEE, Friedman and Stigler reconciled with Read through their mutual connection to Hayek's newly formed Mont Pélerin Society. Over time, however, the two economists moved away from Hayek's neoliberalism and toward Rand's radical form of libertarianism. Friedman, in particular, abandoned the label "neoliberalism" altogether in describing his political positions and adopted the label "libertarianism." Thus, the moral foundation for capitalism coming out of the Chicago School increasingly resembled Rand's glorification of narrow self-interest.

Ayn Rand's views were shaped by her early life experiences as the eldest of three daughters in a wealthy and well-connected Jewish family in Czarist Russia. She was born Alisa Zinovyevna Rosenbaum in 1905 to Anna and Zinovy Rosenbaum in the thriving port city of St. Petersburg, the capital city of Russia since 1712. Her father was a highly educated chemist and pharmacist, and she experienced a privileged childhood with a cook, a governess, a nurse, and ample tutors. The family was affluent enough to spend each summer on the Crimean peninsula and travel to Austria and Switzerland for six weeks when Alisa was nine. After extensive tutoring at home, her parents enrolled her in a progressive and academically rigorous gymnasium. As a loner, she frequently resorted to fantasy in school, "imagining herself akin to Catherine the Great, an outsider in the Russian court who had maneuvered her way to prominence" (Burns 2009, 11).

As the turmoil of Russia's revolutionary years closed in around the Rosenbaums, however, the family was forced to cut back on their lavish lifestyle. After the October Revolution of 1917, the Bolsheviks moved the seat of government to Moscow from St. Petersburg, which had been renamed Petrograd after the fall of the Russian Empire in 1914. The Pale of Settlement, a far western region of Russia where approximately 94 percent of Russian Jews were required to live and work, was abolished by the provisional government along with most of the remaining anti-Jewish restrictions.[14] In 1918, a Red Guard pounded on the door of Zinovy Rosenbaum's chemistry shop and announced that it had been seized in the name of the people. The Rosenbaums fled briefly to Crimea, but the Red Army defeated the White Army for control of the region, and the family was forced to return to Petrograd in 1921. What they found horrified them (Burns 2009, 14):

> Years later Alisa described in her fiction the grim disappointment of her family's return to Petrograd: "Their new home had no front entrance. It had no electrical connections; the plumbing was out of order; they had to carry water in pails from the floor below. Yellow stains spread over the ceilings, bearing witness to past rains. All trappings of luxury and higher culture had vanished".... Under the Soviet New Economic Plan Zinovy was able to briefly reopen his shop with several partners, but it was again confiscated. After this latest insult Zinovy made one last, futile stand: he refused to work. Alisa silently admired her father's principles. To her his abdication was not self-destruction but self-preservation. His refusal to work for an exploitive system would structure the basic premise of her last novel, "Atlas Shrugged."

Alisa soon entered Petrograd State University, which, under the Bolsheviks, had no tuition fee and a liberalized admission policy that accepted formerly restricted students, including women and Jews. Alisa was a member of the first class of women admitted to the university. These additional freedoms, however, came with stifling authoritarian rule (Burns 2009, 15):

> (T)he Bolsheviks dismissed counterrevolutionary professors, harassed those who remained, and instituted Marxist courses on political economy and historical materialism. Students and professors alike protested the new conformity. In her first year Alisa was particularly outspoken. Then the purges began. Anticommunist professors and students disappeared, never to be heard from again. Alisa herself was briefly expelled when all students of bourgeois background were dismissed from the university. (The policy was later reversed and she returned.) Acutely aware of the dangers she faced, Alisa became quiet and careful with her words.

Alisa's three years of college in Bolshevik Russia were heavily influenced by Marxist ideology. Not only did she witness government propaganda throughout the curriculum, but she also witnessed plummeting academic standards and degradation of infrastructure at the school.

---

[14] In 1791, Empress Catherine II (Catherine the Great) signed an order restricting Jews of the Russian empire to live and work within the borders of the Pale of Settlement, which included all of modern-day Belarus, Lithuania and Moldova, much of Ukraine and east-central Poland, and small parts of Latvia and western Russia.

There was a severe shortage of textbooks and school supplies, and lecture halls became cold enough to freeze ink. By the end of her three years, the school had been renamed Leningrad State University, and the name of the city had been changed again to Leningrad. Her experiences in Bolshevik Russia taught Alisa to hate all forms of collectivism. After enrolling at a state-run film school, however, she learned the usefulness of propaganda to alter reality and maintain political power.

Alisa's parents soon realized that they needed to get their eldest daughter out of Russia. They acquired English lessons for her and initiated fervent activities intended to prove the family's loyalty to the Revolution. Next, they invented a ruse to help her slip by the careful eyes of the Bolsheviks. "The Rosenbaums claimed that Alisa intended to study American movies and return to help launch the Russian film industry, a lie made plausible by her enrollment at the film institute and the fact that her relatives owned a theater." The ruse was effective at getting Alisa out of Russia. On the long trip to her relatives living in Chicago, Alisa began to plan her new life. She had experimented with using a different name that would aid her in her planned transition to Hollywood and the silver screen. "The one she ultimately chose, Ayn Rand, freed her from her gender, her religion, her past. It was the perfect name for a child of destiny" (Burns 2009, 18–19).

By the time Rand arrived in Hollywood in 1926, she had watched and ranked more than three hundred movies. She used her experience at the Russian film school in Leningrad to land a job as a junior writer at the De Mille Film Studio. "Her steady intellectual companion in these years was Friedrich Nietzsche, and the first book she bought in English was *Thus Spoke Zarathustra*. Nietzsche was an individualist who celebrated self-creation, which was after all what Rand was doing in America. She seemed to have been deeply affected by his emphasis on the will to power, or self-overcoming" (Burns 2009, 22). After De Mille closed his studio in 1927, however, Rand found herself searching for whatever work she could find. She began to write short stories, drawing from her own readings of Nietzsche. She was especially drawn to Nietzsche's concept of a "Superman" who cared nothing for the thoughts, feelings, or opinions of others.

Knowing that her visa was about to expire, in 1929 Rand married a handsome sometime actor she had met during the filming of one of De Mille's films. She soon applied for US citizenship as Mrs. Frank O'Connor. To support the couple, she took a full-time job as a filing clerk in the wardrobe department at RKO Radio Pictures and continued her writing during her off-hours. After Universal purchased a film scenario of hers in 1932, she was able to quit her job at RKO and begin writing full time. She used her newfound success to exercise more creative license in her stories and screenplays, peppering them with underlying themes inspired by her interpretation of Nietzsche. In early 1934, she began a journal to note the development of her unique moral philosophy (Burns 2009, 29):

It was only "the vague beginnings of an amateur philosopher," she announced modestly, but by the end of her first entry she had decided, "I want to be known as the greatest champion of reason and the greatest enemy of religion." She recorded two objections to religion: it established unrealizable, abstract ethical ideas that made men cynical when they fell short, and its emphasis on faith denied reason.

At the end of 1934, Rand moved to New York to bring her unique moral philosophy to Broadway. Her courtroom drama *Night of January 16th* opened on Broadway in 1935, and she published the semi-autobiographical novel *We the Living* in 1936. In 1940, Rand volunteered for Republican Wendell Willkie's presidential campaign, and she became a major political figure in American conservative circles. Her first major success as a writer came in 1943 with the publication of *The Fountainhead*, a novel about an uncompromising architect named Howard Roark. In 1957, Rand published *Atlas Shrugged*, the story of a Nietzschean Superman named John Galt who encourages America's most creative industrialists, scientists, and artists to withdraw from society and begin an independent free economy in a hidden valley. The novel included a long monologue delivered by Galt describing Rand's moral philosophy, called *Objectivism*.

5.4 SELF-INTEREST AS A MORAL FOUNDATION FOR CAPITALISM

There has been a renewed interest in the moral theory of Adam Smith, even among economists formerly associated with the Chicago School (McCloskey 2006). While that moral theory shatters the narrow self-interest narrative out of Chicago, it does not advocate the total abandonment of self-interest. As Force (2003, 200) points out, "(F)or Smith, the distinction between interested and disinterested motives does *not* constitute the foundation of morality" (emphasis in the original). Smith was highly critical of moral systems that equate virtue with altruism and emphasized the praise-worthiness of many self-interested motivations (*TMS* VII.ii.3.16):

Regard to our own private happiness and interest, too, appear upon many occasions very laudable principles of action. The habits of oeconomy, industry, discretion, attention, and application of thought, are generally supposed to be cultivated from self-interested motives, and at the same time are apprehended to be very praise-worthy qualities, which deserve the esteem and approbation of every body.

Moral philosopher Tara Smith (2006, 3) sees merit in critically evaluating the altruistic prescriptions of all moral philosophies and theories. She states, "It is only by leading a morally upright life that a person can be happy and it is for the sake of having a happy life that a person should be morally upright." She also agrees, consistent with Adam Smith, that the council of morality and the counsel of prudence are frequently aligned. She argues, however, that to reach sound conclusions about the promise of all moral systems, "we must pursue all the questions that they raise, including questions about egoism" (Smith 2006, 5). Tara Smith views Ayn Rand's moral system based on rational egoism as useful to evaluate the virtues of self-interest in their strongest form and compare her unique moral system with alternative systems.

Rand's moral philosophy is difficult to interpret, however, because it is dispersed among her various works of fiction and in brief essays. For example, the most extended presentation of her philosophy is contained in her essay, "The Objectivist Ethics" (Rand 1964), which includes only twenty-five pages of text and incorporates large passages from her novel, *Atlas Shrugged* (Rand 1957). Much of her personal history and moral philosophy is also written by individuals with a political agenda or with whom she had a personal falling out, such as Nathaniel Branden. Because Leonard Peikoff worked with her for thirty years, his systematic presentation of Rand's moral philosophy is typically viewed as authoritative (Peikoff 1991). Tara Smith attempts to explain Rand's unique moral philosophy by explaining how her rational egoism is related to conventional ethical egoism (Smith 2006, 23):

Ethical egoism is the thesis that a person should act to promote his own interest. More precisely, it is the view that each person's primary moral obligation is to achieve his own well-being and he should not sacrifice his well-being for the well-being of others. This is exactly what emerges from Rand's explanation of the basis of morality. Adherence to morality is necessary to guide a person's pursuit of values. The achievement of values, in turn, is necessary in order for a person to secure his life. It is not any value attributed to life per se or an alleged duty to serve others' lives that creates the need for morality. Rather, it is a person's self-interest, his life, that mandates adherence to a rational moral code. The reason to be moral is selfish.

As the label "Objectivism" implies, the crucial feature of Rand's form of egoism is the notion that value is *objective*. As Tara Smith (2006, 25) explains, "What is good for a person – what is in his interest – is not simply a subjective projection of that person's beliefs, attitudes, tastes, or desires, for those are not adequate guides to meeting his life's requirements. Although the choice to live is the condition of anything's being good for a person, the preference for a particular object does not, by itself, render that object conducive to his survival and therefore valuable." At the same time, Rand rejects that value is found ready-made in the external world. "Nothing can be good in itself. A value is always good *to* someone and *for* some end."

As Tara Smith (2006, 7) explains, "Rand rejects hedonism and contends that an egoist must abide by rational principles, as these offer the only effective means of advancing his interest, long range. Principles' authority stems entirely from their egoistic practicality. Rand also rejects the dog-eat-dog image of an egoist as out to unjustly exploit others." Smith identifies seven major virtues that Rand justifies on the basis of her rational egoism: *rationality, honesty, independence, justice, integrity, productiveness,* and *pride.* However, Rand significantly alters the definitions of these virtues to be consistent with her unique moral philosophy. Thus, the definitions appear distorted and unrecognizable to the untrained. For example, Rand defines *integrity* as "loyalty in action to rational principles" and *pride* as "a forward-driving commitment to achieve one's moral perfection."

Ayn Rand's moral philosophy can only be understood from the perspective of her admiration of Nietzsche's "Superman" and her complete rejection of the controlling power of religion and the state. Instead of deriving virtues that are capable of controlling self-interest in the interest of society, her moral philosophy identifies virtues that are justified and defined based on self-interest. As a result, there are many traditional virtues that are not justified according to Rand's moral system. Because self-interest is opposed to self-sacrifice, for example, such traditional virtues as *charity, forgiveness, generosity, humility, kindness, mercy,* and *temperance* are not virtues according to Rand's moral system. As Tara Smith (2006, 15) demonstrates, however, many of these virtues can be redefined and justified based on Rand's rational egoism. For example, an act of generosity would be morally permitted, according to Rand, if it "is consistent with the seven moral virtues and with an individual's hierarchy of values, when it does not require self-sacrifice and is extended to an appropriate beneficiary." Despite her glorification of narrow self-interest based on Nietzsche and the twisted view of virtue that it requires, many religious conservatives have been drawn to Rand's moral philosophy due to its unambiguous rejection of big government socialism.

Irrespective of Rand's unique moral philosophy, altruism remains an important motivational factor across all individuals, societies, and economic systems. Researchers in multiple disciplines have attempted to explain how altruism evolved and why it continues to affect behavior in modern capitalist society. A central theoretical problem in sociobiology, for example, is "how can altruism, which by definition reduces personal fitness, possibly evolve by natural selection?" (Wilson 1975, 12). As I discuss further in Chapter 6, a Nobel-prize winning economist associated with the Chicago School used neoclassical economic theory to help answer that question and address other social issues such as discrimination, education, crime, the family, and politics (Becker 1976a). To prepare for that discussion, I describe in greater detail the unique neoclassical theory that developed out of Chicago.

Friedman and Stigler's neoclassical economic theory can best be interpreted as a counter-revolution aimed at restoring Marshall's competitive price theory as the foundational mode of theorizing in economics (Kaufman 2010, 133):

> Friedman and Stigler were in the top rank of neoclassical price theorists and were arguably the two most ardent and skilled defenders/developers of Marshallian microeconomic theory, particularly in its competitive market version. One must recall that when Friedman and Stigler began their careers, competitive market theory – widely perceived as the core of the neoclassical paradigm – traded at a deep intellectual discount due to the imperfect competition revolution pioneered by Edward Chamberlin and Joan Robinson and the macroeconomic revolution pioneered by John Maynard Keynes. Both revolutions suggested that competitive demand/supply analysis was largely inapplicable to modern economies populated with large price-wage-setting corporations and trade unions and prices and wages were neither very flexible nor able to clear most product and labor markets.

Stigler (Mr. Micro) took the lead in bringing back competitive price theory by writing a textbook in 1942 entitled, *The Theory of Competitive Price* (Stigler 1942). The second edition was retitled simply, *The Theory of Price* (Stigler 1946), and microeconomic theory at the Chicago School became famously known as *Price Theory*. The last chapter of the textbook was devoted to the supply and demand of labor and excluded any mention of imperfect competition in either product or labor markets (Kaufman 2010). In essence, Stigler's price theory dismissed the institutionalists' claim that labor markets are rife with imperfections and workers bargain at a disadvantage. He simply characterized the firm as a series of supply and demand curves, and all societal concerns and norms were extracted from the economic theory of the firm (Stevens 2019).

In the early development of their neoclassical theory of the firm, Friedman and Stigler were heavily influenced by their relationship with Hayek and the highly private and exclusive Mont Pélerin Society (MPS). As such, their main concerns evolved around "economic issues such as the presumed legitimacy of neoclassical price theory, the meaning of competition in economics, the (ir)relevance of history to analysis, and the best way to argue against socialism" (Mirowski 2011, 246). The legitimacy of their price theory, however, soon came under harsh scrutiny. In the late 1930s, the Oxford Economists Research Group presented evidence that businesses did not adhere to marginalist principles of optimization but instead tended to set prices by adding a profit markup to cost. The validity of marginal theory was also questioned by Princeton economist Richard Lester, who published a study in 1946 highlighting the shortcomings of marginal analysis for wage-employment problems (Lester 1946). Because Lester's study appeared in a leading economics journal, the *American Economic Review*, it warranted a strong response from Friedman.

Austrian economist and future MPS member Fritz Machlup was the first to publicly confront Lester's attack on neoclassical price theory in a later article in the same journal (Machlup 1946). Friedman's own detailed response came years later in a series of essays published by the University of Chicago Press, *Essays in Positive Economics* (Friedman 1953). In his response to the marginalist controversy of Lester and Machlup, Friedman made use of Karl Popper's scientific methodology (Popper 1934).[15] As he stated in his published memoirs, Friedman formulated his response with the aid of Stigler and Popper at the first meeting of the MPS (Friedman and Friedman 1998, 215):

The essay had a long gestation period.... Shortly after I had completed a first draft, George Stigler and I had long discussions with Karl Popper in 1947 at the founding meeting of the Mont Pélerin Society. The part of those discussions that I remember best had to do with scientific methodology.... (T)hese discussions at Mont Pélerin were my first exposure to his views. I found them highly compatible with the views that I had independently come to, though far more sophisticated and more fully developed. That conversation had a good deal of influence on the final version of the essay.

---

[15] Friedman himself argued that he cared little for philosophy and read next to none of it. Further, Popper was an Austrian teaching at the London School of Economics and most of his writings had not yet been translated into English. Thus, Friedman had at best a superficial understanding of Popper's methodological arguments (Mirowski 2011).

As the title reflects, a major aim of Friedman's essays was to move economic researchers away from normative theory related to "what ought to be" toward positive theory related to "what is." Friedman's main purpose in writing the essays, however, was "to restore and boost confidence in maximization hypotheses and marginal analyses in economics" (Vromen 2011, 212). Friedman's (1953) defense of neo-classical price theory proceeded along three lines of argument: (1) The critics had misconstrued the very purpose of an economic theory. They had proposed rejecting neoclassical price theory because the under-lying assumptions of the theory were unrealistic. He responded that assumptions, by their very nature, must be unrealistic in a descriptive sense. The only true test of the usefulness of a theory, according to Friedman, is its ability to predict. (2) Competitive price theory in fact had a good record of prediction – although this point was more asserted than demonstrated. (3) Critics of neoclassical price theory did not have an alternative theory that was as useful at predicting or describing behavior.

Mirowski (2011, 246) argues that Friedman's essays reflect "Popper's disdain for historicism and the weakness of contemporary social science at Mont Pélerin. Indeed, one thing they would share from thenceforward was the precept that there was essentially no relevant distinction between the natural and social sciences: They were all party to the same method-ological strictures." For example, Friedman used physics and biology to argue that underlying assumptions are useful even if they are widely inac-curate. Bodies that fall in the atmosphere behave *as if* they were falling in a vacuum; leaves are positioned around a tree *as if* each leaf sought to maximize the amount of sunlight it receives, and expert billiard players make shots *as if* they knew complicated physics.

Friedman (1953, 21–23) concludes, "It is only a short step from these examples to the economic hypothesis that under a wide range of cir-cumstances individual firms behave *as if* they were seeking rationally to maximize their expected returns." He also argues for the maximization-of-returns hypothesis by applying the "survival-of-the-fittest" argument from Darwinian evolution: "(U)nless the behavior of businessmen in some way or other approximated behavior consistent with the maximi-zation of returns, it seems unlikely that they would remain in business for long." Finally, he argues that the usefulness of a hypothesis can be assessed by "the continued use and acceptance of the hypothesis over a long period, and the failure of any coherent, self-consistent alternative to be developed and be widely accepted."

While many researchers view economics as a successful discipline due to its adherence to the scientific methodology outlined in Friedman's famous essay, others view his methodology as "deeply flawed, even dangerous for the cognitive aspirations and social responsibilities of economics" (Mäki 2009, 47). I argue elsewhere that Friedman's essay shaped economists' conceptions of what constituted good theory and good empirical evidence (Stevens 2019). After his influential methodological essay, representative research in the top economic journals became "more *formal* – more mathematical, more analytical, less historical, less institutional, more standardized, and more narrow regarding admissible priors" (Hands 2009, 145, emphasis in the original). As I discuss in Chapter 6, the powerful neoclassical theory that evolved from the Chicago School impacted not only the discipline of economics, but all economics-based disciplines in business – especially accounting and finance.

5.5 CONCLUSION

In the postwar period, neoclassical economists continued the narrowing of their discipline that had begun by classical economists. Whereas Polanyi and Keynes developed a moral foundation for capitalism based on responsibility and duty, neoclassical economists associated with the University of Chicago eschewed social and moral responsibility and made self-interest the first principle of their discipline. A review of the founding of the Chicago School reveals the influence of Hayek and his battle against the postwar socialist movement that had swept Europe and was penetrating Britain. After that socialist movement had lost its momentum and influence, however, Friedman and Stigler took neoliberalism further than Hayek intended by fully embracing laissez-faire capitalism and libertarianism. Ayn Rand's unique moral philosophy based on rational egoism is a natural extension of the Chicago School's neoclassical economic theory based on narrow self-interest. That explains why some economists associated with the Chicago School, including former Federal Reserve Chairman Alan Greenspan, have become dedicated followers of Rand's moral philosophy.

While Rand's novels have been criticized for their lack of literary value and their inherent propaganda in support of her moral philosophy, there are important insights to be gleaned from their continued popularity. For example, her novels emphasize that there is a limit to how much the entrepreneurs and producers of a society can be regulated and taxed before they "shrug" and withdraw their valuable contributions. Rand's overall message of rugged individualism and personal responsibility is fully supported by Adam Smith's moral foundation for capitalism. That message is also consistent with Max Weber's vision of a strong civil society as well as Polanyi and Keynes's emphasis on responsibility and duty in their moral foundation. Rand's moral philosophy, however, provides little motivation to protect society against what Polanyi and Keynes saw as the vulnerabilities and excesses of unregulated capitalism. As we will see in the remaining chapters, the deregulatory environment encouraged by the laissez-faire economics of Rand and the Chicago School would lead to a crisis of capitalism in the twenty-first century.

6

Neoclassical Economists Join the Search

Vernon Smith and Michael Jensen

Markets economize on the need for virtue, but do not eliminate it and indeed depend on it to avoid a crushing burden of monitoring and enforcement cost. If every explicit or implicit contract required external policing resources to ensure efficient performance, the efficiency gains from specialization and exchange would be in danger of being gobbled up by these support costs. In this sense, the informal property right rules or norms of moral social engagement – thou shalt not kill, steal, bear false witness, commit adultery, or covet the possessions of thy neighbor – strongly support wealth creation through the increased specialization made possible by personal social exchange and the extended order of markets.

Vernon Smith
Rationality in Economics

In *The Ethics of Competition*, Frank Knight (1935/1976, 176) revealed the broad, institutional view of capitalism he brought with him to the University of Chicago in 1927. He wrote: "Always history is being made; opinions, attitudes and institutions change, and there is evolution in the nature of capitalism." Similar to Max Weber's dynamic view of capitalism (see Chapter 4), Knight believed that capitalism was flexible and would evolve to meet the wider needs of society as they evolved. He expressed deep concerns regarding the continued narrowing of economic theory by neoclassical economists. Knight's concerns provide "a cautionary corrective to much of the later neoclassical economic revolution his own work would inspire" (Boyd 1976, x). Through the efforts of his students, the Economics Department at Chicago went from the birthplace of institutional economics in America to the promoter of a neoclassical economic theory based on narrow self-interest. After emerging evidence in experimental economics and the global market crash in 2007–08, however, some neoclassical economists have joined Knight's quest to incorporate important social and moral factors into that theory. In this chapter, I address how neoclassical economists have joined the search for a moral foundation for capitalism by discussing the lives and writings of Vernon Smith and Michael Jensen.[1]

6.1 THE VICTORY OF NEOCLASSICAL ECONOMICS OVER INSTITUTIONAL ECONOMICS

Over the course of the nineteenth century, classical economists increasingly viewed their discipline as a natural science and sought to discover the laws of "political economy" using evolutionary biology, mathematics, engineering, and physics. In the twentieth century, neoclassical economists continued this emphasis on the natural sciences and followed Alfred Marshall's lead in renaming their discipline "economics." Under the leadership of Gustav Schmoller, the younger German Historical School split off from the group of neoclassical economists associated with Carl Menger (1840–1921) in Vienna, pejoratively labeling them the "Austrian School" as part of a bitter *Methodenstreit* or "battle of the methods." Due to Schmoller's powerful influence, economists associated with the Austrian School were shut out of German universities for decades. In the open exchange between German and American universities, historical and institutional economics crossed the Atlantic first and exerted a powerful influence on the development of economic theory in America.

As the battle between the younger German Historical School and the Austrian School raged on, Weber distanced himself from the political-metaphysical historicism of Schmoller.[2] Weber proposed a broad political economy that incorporated the neoclassical economic theory of the Austrian School, the economic history of the older German Historical School, and his unique economic sociology that incorporated the influence of religion (Baehr and Wells 2002). He developed an outline for the future development of his broad political economy, which he called "social economics," but it "became a casualty of World War I and remained a mere fragment when Weber died in 1920" (Scaff 2011, 1).

---

[1] As the epigraph to this chapter suggests (Smith 2008, 21–22), experimental economists have led the way in incorporating social and moral norms into neoclassical economic theory.

[2] Although he was part of the younger German Historical School represented by Schmoller and his student Werner Sombart, Weber maintained the moderate views of the older German Historical School represented by Roscher, Knies, and Hildebrand (see Chapter 3).

Weber's emphasis on economic theory, economic history, and economic sociology was eventually preempted by the victory of neoclassical economics over institutional economics in the West. Rather than influence the future path of economics, Weber's social economics launched other social sciences such as political science, sociology, and social psychology.

It was through the efforts of Frank Knight at Chicago and Talcott Parsons (1902–79) at Harvard that Weber's institutional economics crossed the Atlantic and was planted on American soil. After receiving a B.S. and an M.A. in German at the University of Tennessee, Knight completed a Ph.D. in economics at Cornell in 1916. His dissertation, under the supervision of Allyn A. Young, provided a theory of profit and "opened the door to a host of new questions with the introduction of a theory of uncertainty" (Emmett 2010, 280). After short stints as an instructor at Cornell (1916–17) and Chicago (1917–19), Knight received a permanent position at the University of Iowa before returning to Chicago in 1928 to teach institutional economics (Jacob Viner was teaching economic theory at Chicago at the time). By then, the University of Chicago had already changed the name of its department of "political economy," founded in 1892, to "economics."

A year before assuming his faculty position at Chicago, Knight published an English translation of Weber's *General Economic History*. Knight's publication introduced Weber to the English-speaking world as a leading political economist and economic historian. As such, it paved the way for Parsons's English translation of Weber's seminal work, *The Protestant Ethic and the Spirit of Capitalism*, published in 1930 (Scaff 2011). After earning a BA degree in biology and philosophy at Amherst College in 1924, Parsons studied at the London School of Economics for a year where he was exposed to R. H. Tawney and other socially minded political economists. It wasn't until Parsons went to Heidelberg University to begin a Ph.D. in sociology and economics in 1925, however, that he was exposed to the writings of Max Weber.[3] Parson's first appointment upon his graduation from Heidelberg in 1927 was at Harvard University as a tutor of economics.

In his dissertation, Parsons asserted that his rationale for making Weber's text available "was to explore an alternative to the

---

[3] Surprisingly, Tawney's classes at the London School of Economics did not include material on Weber even though Tawney was later selected by the publisher to supervise Parson's interpretation of Weber's classic work.

'individualistic,' 'rationalistic,' and 'unilinear' evolutionary assumptions operative in Anglo-American economic thought" (Scaff 2011, 224). Similarly, "Knight perceived in Weber's work the resources for remedying the shortcomings of American neoclassical economic theory by a recourse to the historical and institutional economics of German sociological thought" (Boyd 1976, xx). Thus, both Parsons and Knight were acutely aware of the increasingly narrow neoclassical economic theory emerging in America. Shortly after translating Weber's seminal work, however, Parsons left the Economics Department at Harvard for the newly formed sociology department.[4] As for Knight, he helped found the Committee on Social Thought at Chicago and left his faculty position in the Economics Department to take a new appointment as a professor of social science in 1942.

To expand his understanding of institutional economics, Knight spent a year at the Weber circle at Heidelberg in 1930 on a Guggenheim fellowship. His application to study with Adolf Weber and Karl Jaspers reflects his quest to expand neoclassical theory (Boyd 1976, xx–xxi):

> I wish to get a much fuller acquaintance than I (or most American economists) possess with nineteenth century German philosophy, historiography and social thought, especially the historical schools of jurisprudence and economics and the background of social legislation…. It seems to me that there would be an especial value in having such a study made by one who, like myself, would approach the problem from the background of training and sympathies leaning in the opposite direction, though with an appreciation of the limitations of the traditional, individualistic economics.

As a student at Heidelberg, Weber had attended Karl Knies's lectures on political economy which included material on Adam Smith. Knies criticized what he saw as the egoistic self-interest in *The Wealth of Nations*. Further, he dismissed *A Theory of Moral Sentiments* as outdated after Smith's trip to Paris in 1766 and what he claimed was Smith's conversion to the materialist views of French physiocrats. Weber's own writings perpetuated Knies's "French connection theory" (Montes 2003). In bringing Weber's institutional economics to America, therefore, Knight and Parsons also brought Weber's distorted view of the life and writings of Adam Smith. While neoclassical economists in America eventually

---

[4] In contrast to Chicago's pioneering sociology department, which was established in 1892, Harvard's prestigious sociology department "emerged as a new department from the Committee on Sociology and Social Ethics (only in 1931), amid a debate over whether it should be considered a social science discipline at all" (Scaff 2011, 208)

rejected his institutional economics, they maintained Weber's distorted view of Adam Smith.[5]

Weber's institutional economics collided violently with the emerging neoclassical economics of twentieth-century America. For example, neoclassical economists focused on narrow self-interest as the sole motivating factor for entrepreneurs to profit from their new innovations whereas Weber (1905/2002, 22–23) emphasized the importance of ethical qualities:

Few people are sufficiently clear-sighted to be aware of the unusual strength of character that is required from this "new type" of entrepreneur.... As well as energy and clarity of vision, he will need certain outstanding "ethical" qualities to win the absolutely indispensable confidence of the clients and of the workers when introducing these innovations and to maintain the vigor necessary to overcome the innumerable obstacles he will meet. It is these qualities above all which have made possible the infinitely more intensive work rate that is now demanded of the entrepreneur. There is no longer any place for the comfortable lifestyle. These ethical qualities are quite different in kind from those that were adequate for the traditionalism of the past.

In contrast to both neoclassical economists and their Marxist detractors, Weber maintained the importance of religion in capitalist society. According to Weber, the moral values of Calvinism and Puritanism in Scotland, England, and America aided the early development of capitalism in those countries.[6] His unique contribution to political economy, according to his wife's biography (Weber 1975, 337), was to explain how capitalism arose in the West due to the view of "rational, methodical work as a moral duty." Weber (1905/2002, 17) also emphasized the importance of a fair wage and a sense of responsibility in capitalist development:

(L)ow wages fail as a principle of capitalist development whenever the manufacturing process demands "qualified" (skilled) labor or perhaps the operation of expensive and easily damaged machines, or indeed any reasonable level of

---

[5] As discussed in Chapter 2, Adam Smith included material from both of his major works in his early lectures at Edinburgh and in his courses at Glasgow University prior to his trip to Paris with the young future Duke of Buccleuch. Thus, Smith's political economy always incorporated his moral philosophy based on social norms, institutions, and culture. Not only did his thinking incorporate both major works from the very beginning, Smith revised both works continuously up to the year of his death in 1790. "In fact, the sections that he revised demonstrate a growing concern over the importance of institutions and social norms in commerce and society" (Stevens 2019, 86).

[6] This explains why Weber had serious doubts regarding the future development of capitalism in Germany, where Calvinism had never taken root.

close attention and initiative. Here low wages do not pay; in fact, they have the opposite effect. Here a well-developed sense of responsibility is absolutely indispensable, along with a general attitude which, at least during working time, does not continually seek ways of earning the usual wage with the maximum ease and the minimum effort, but performs the work as though it were an absolute end in itself – a "calling." An attitude like this is not, however, something which occurs naturally. It cannot be directly produced either by high wages or by low wages, but has to be the product of a long, slow "process of education."

Weber (1905/2002, 121) quoted Richard Baxter to highlight the Puritan view that concern for outward possessions should sit lightly on the shoulders "like a thin cloak which can be thrown off at any time." Weber also observed, however, that "fate decreed that the cloak should become a shell as hard as steel." Translators have labeled this hard shell the "iron cage." Weber concluded his essay with his famous warning regarding the future of capitalist society:

> No one yet knows who will live in that shell in the future. Perhaps new prophets will emerge, or powerful old ideas and ideals will be reborn at the end of this monstrous development. Or perhaps – if neither of these occurs – mechanized ossification, dressed up with a kind of desperate self-importance, will set in. Then, however, it might truly be said of the "last men" in this cultural development: "specialists without spirit, hedonists without a heart, these nonentities imagine they have attained a stage of humankind [Menschentum] never before reached."

During his trip to America in the summer of 1904, Weber studied the young nation's emerging colleges and universities. According to his biographer Lawrence Scaff (2011, 49), the point of his curiosity was singular: "(I)t had to do with the ethos of education – the cultivation of habits, the formation of mind and character, and the attitude toward life related to work and accomplishment." While he observed an emphasis on the development of character in America's colleges and universities – including required attendance at weekly chapel and consistent appeals for honesty, modesty, frugality, and hard work – Weber observed another trend that greatly concerned him. Business colleges were springing up across major cities and large suburban areas. He warned educators to avoid modern pressure to turn the university "into an arena for technical training, status legitimation, political dispensations, and careerism" (Scaff 1989, 142). Specifically, Weber viewed the new trend in business education as a threat to capitalist society.

In his book, *From Higher Aims to Hired Hands: The Social Transformation of American Business Schools and the Unfulfilled Promise of Management as a Profession*, Rakesh Khurana (2007) describes how Weber's warning went unheeded. Khurana describes how the rising uncertainty and alienation of the second industrial revolution led to the establishment of business schools within America's research universities. His book reveals how the university-based business school was largely a creation of institutional economists who viewed it as an opportunity to promote high professional norms and ideals. His book also reveals, however, how the victory of neoclassical economics over institutional economics eventually destroyed this professionalism project and led to the narrow careerism feared by Weber.

After America's bloody Civil War, the young country was able to fully dedicate its energy and resources to the development of its industrial power. This led to the second industrial revolution from 1870 to 1920. During this time, America's population grew rapidly as did the demand for new products and the means of shipping those products. As a result, the transcontinental railroad was completed and hundreds of new industries were established. Thereafter, America's romance with the automobile, advances in manufacturing techniques, and the industrial buildup to World War I created the conditions for further industrial growth. As a result of the second industrial revolution, America surpassed Britain as the world's strongest economic power, and New York surpassed London as the world's center of banking and international trade (Burk 2007).

Between 1880 and 1941, an enterprising group of institutional economists and business elites leveraged its social and economic resources to articulate a bold new vision for business education in America. They accomplished this, according to Khurana (2007, 49), by associating business management with three institutions that had recently come to be seen as the pillars of capitalist society: science, the professions, and the university. "These three institutions, which would become the building blocks of the modern institution of management, were taken to constitute rational, necessary, and adequate sources of legitimacy for the new occupation.... In effect, the collective legitimacy of these other institutions was appropriated to support the creation of the new institution of management. The centerpiece of the project was to be a wholly new invention: the university-based business school."

As discussed in Chapter 1, the first university-based business school was founded in 1881 at the University of Pennsylvania with the help of a $100,000 gift by Joseph Wharton. Wharton, a devout Pennsylvania Quaker and business entrepreneur with a strong sense of social and moral responsibility, perceived a need for university education in the specialized knowledge and personal character that commercial enterprise required. The nation's growing private business schools were, in his view, inadequate to meet this need. According to Khurana (2007, 108), "Wharton's framing of the purpose of his new school, along with his personal reputation for integrity, enabled him to gain the support he required for establishing the Wharton School, even in the absence of evidence of a compelling need for it to exist." The first director of the Wharton School was Edmund J. James, a German-trained institutional economist who was a personal friend of Max Weber.

It wasn't until 1898 that the University of Chicago and the University of California at Berkeley joined Wharton's professionalism project and established a business school within their research universities. Between 1900 and 1913, twenty-five universities established business schools, including Dartmouth, New York University, Northwestern, Harvard, and the public universities at Wisconsin and Illinois. Dartmouth became the first business school to offer graduate instruction in 1900, and Chicago became the first business school to offer Ph.D.s in 1920. These university-based business schools were established by institutional economists, many with training in Germany, who viewed the new institution as an opportunity to address the pressing political and social problems of early capitalism. This included the first business school dean at Harvard, Edwin F. Gay (1867–1946), who received his Ph.D. from the University of Berlin under the supervision of Schmoller.

Upon assuming the deanship at Chicago's business school in 1909, Leon C. Marshall (1879–1966) undertook to develop curricula and a program of research that served the needs of both business and society. Despite its rapid growth and acceptance by the public, however, the university-based business school faced continuing opposition from within the university. "Business school professors, for example, continued to endure taunts from academic colleagues about the lack of 'theory' or 'discipline' in their field. This made business education subject to withering criticism to the effect that universities, by creating business schools, had simply sold out to commercial interests" (Khurana 2007, 141). To address these challenges, in 1916, the deans of sixteen major business schools formed the American Association of Collegiate Schools of Business (AACSB). Led by Gay at Harvard and Marshall at Chicago, the AACSB became the main vehicle by which institutional economists promoted their professionalism project.

The relationship between university-based business schools and traditional economics departments, however, remained conflicted. This was reflected in the curricula of the new business schools (Khurana 2007, 160–161):

Introductory economics courses were initially included in many schools' curricula. Yet a number of these same schools also made deliberate decisions, at a relatively early point, to establish their independence from their universities' economics departments, which in many instances were turning away from institutional economics – focused on history and grounded in empirical observation – toward the discipline's neoclassical school, which emphasized formal modeling and theory. Many business school faculty trained in economics, however, instinctively preferred the clean, abstract models of the discipline to the messy realities of complex systems like organizations, and the relationship between business schools and economics remained uneasy and unsettled.

As they worked to found new business schools within the university, however, institutional economists lost the battle for supremacy in their own discipline. "By 1920, American economics had taken a sharp turn in the direction of a neoclassicism that successfully privileged deductive theory over the study of economic phenomena in relation to historical and social forces. The penetrating insights of institutional economics in its heyday from 1890 to 1920 would ultimately fail to shape the direction of the discipline in the twentieth century, and scholars who continued to work in this tradition would be marginalized" (Khurana 2007, 162). This sharp turn had significant implications for the future direction of economics as well as business education in America.

6.2 VERNON SMITH JOINS THE SEARCH

He did not look altogether comfortable as he stood at the large oak podium – partly due to the enormity of the occasion and partly due to the required formal attire. His lecture would be filmed and archived along with a written copy that would later be published and become part of a larger work on rationality in economics. While he had arranged his tuxedo rental in Stockholm, the president of the Swedish Academy had personally handed him a boxed pair of patent leather shoes upon his arrival from Arlington, Virginia. It was a none-too-subtle hint that his characteristic cowboy boots would be inappropriate at the official events that week. His signature string tie was also deemed too informal, but he had rented a black satin western tie to his liking. His twenty-six-year tenure at the University of Arizona was still evident to the audience, however, in his sun-scorched skin, his thick tinted glasses, his bleached mustache, and his long blond ponytail. The southwestern appearance of the tall, slender, seventy-five-year-old man standing alone at the podium belied the fact that he was a Midwesterner born and raised in Wichita, Kansas.

Vernon Smith (1927–) squinted through his tinted glasses at the printed copy of his 2002 Nobel lecture, nervously cleared his throat, and began to read. The formal awards ceremony and banquet had been held in Stockholm several days before, but his lecture was in a large auditorium at the ancient Swedish university at Uppsala. His fidgeting and mild stuttering lessened as he focused his mind and shut out the world. Similar to his Scottish namesake, his mental hyper-focus was characteristic of Asperger's Syndrome. Only his four children, his current wife, and his past two wives knew the depth of his social challenges. Remarkably, they all had come to Sweden to support him. Some of his friends, who had been predicting this moment for over twenty years, were also in attendance. As his Nobel lecture was open to the public, however, some in the audience were less supportive. Unknown to Smith, there was a heckler in the crowd who would surface during the question-and-answer period to confront what he saw as Smith's antiquated, free-market views.

Smith was caught off guard by the open hostility of the heckler. While his hosts were anxious to silence the disturbance, however, Smith welcomed the opportunity to discuss the deeper political and moral implications of his work. Life had left him inquisitive and open-minded. Smith had briefly attended a Quaker university near his home in Wichita before traveling west to the California Institute of Technology to major in Electrical Engineering in the fall of 1947. That summer, he hitchhiked to Saskatchewan with a group of liberal-minded students to work in a lumber mill and learn about the socialist government that had popped up in the middle of the Canadian frontier. Among the group was a young economics student who had brought several books by William Henry Beveridge and John Maynard Keynes. Smith thoroughly enjoyed their conversations that summer. In his recollection of the experience in his memoirs, Smith (2018b, 118) writes, "(I)t is clear that this was the beginning of my career interest in economics."[7]

After graduating from Caltech in 1949, Smith earned an MA in Economics from the University of Kansas in 1952 before traveling east to begin a Ph.D. at Harvard University. His first semester, he attended the opening class of Edward H. Chamberlin's (1899–1967) graduate course in Monopolistic Competition to see if he needed to take it after completing a similar course at Kansas. As with many Harvard students before

---

[7] In his memoirs, Smith (2018a) recollects how his early years as an anti-war protestor and socialist sympathizer delayed his FBI clearance while working as a consultant at the Rand Corporation in the summer of 1957.

him, Smith experienced Chamberlin's classroom experiment designed to demonstrate that competitive price theory was an unrealistic idealization of real-world markets. Chamberlin gave half the class buyer-reservation values (the value of an asset if purchased) and the other half of the class seller-reservation costs (the cost of an asset if sold). Chamberlin then had potential buyers and sellers circulate among themselves, form pairs, and bargain to trade the asset. If a given trading pair successfully negotiated a price, Chamberlin would post it on the blackboard. Unsuccessful pairs would seek new trading partners until the market was closed.

As Chamberlin intended to show, the prices posted on the blackboard were highly volatile and failed to converge to the predicted price from competitive price theory. According to Marshall's price theory, however, the predicted price would only be reached if the market supply and demand conditions remained stationary long enough to reach an equilibrium. Further, the bilateral negotiation market institution used by Chamberlin did not resemble market institutions used in real-world markets. Smith's experience with Chamberlin's experimental market stayed with him when, three years later, he found himself facing the challenges of teaching microeconomic theory to undergrad students as a young assistant professor at Purdue University (Smith 2018a, 197):

I could bend the curves ... and manipulate the equations as good as anyone, but how does any market actually approximate a competitive equilibrium, if it ever could or does? What was the connection between the economists' theory of supply and demand and what real people did on the ground in markets? I and nobody else, and none of the pretty books, could answer these questions. Some students, finding no answers to these questions, leave or never enter economics; those of us who stay perhaps forget that we ever wondered – theirs not to reason why, theirs only to do and lie. Not having any answers bugged me in teaching what I had been taught.

One night, unable to sleep, Smith's thoughts returned to Chamberlin's opening class experiment. He resolved that he would attempt a similar experiment the following semester. This would give students an opportunity to experience an actual market with supply and demand curves known only by the instructor. The use of a classroom experiment would also provide Smith an opportunity to examine different market institutions and parameters of supply and demand. Smith altered the market institution, however, to more closely resemble naturally occurring capital markets. After researching markets in New York and Chicago, Smith selected the "double auction" market where buyers make public "bids to buy" and sellers make public "asks to sell." Smith also repeated the trading round multiple times with stationary supply and demand parameters to allow markets sufficient time to approach the equilibrium prediction from price theory.

In January 1956, Smith conducted his first experimental market at Purdue. As he describes in his memoirs (Smith 2018a, 200), the results from his double-auction markets were dramatically different from Chamberlin's bilateral negotiation markets:

(T)o my amazement the experimental market converged quickly, at least relative to my expectations, to near the predicted equilibrium price and exchange volume, although there were "only" twenty-two buyers and sellers, none of whom had any information on supply or demand except their own private cost or value. I thought something must be wrong with the experiment, perhaps that it was an accident of symmetry in the buyer and seller surpluses. I shot that idea down with an experiment at the beginning of class the following fall, using a design in which the seller surplus was much greater than that of the buyers. Had I somehow stumbled upon an engine for testing ideas inside and outside the prescriptions of traditional economic theory?

Smith continued to alter the perimeters of his double-auction markets over the next five years and published the results of his experiments in the *Journal of Political Economy* in 1962. The publication process was long and brutal, including an initial rejection, four negative referee reports, and multiple revisions. During a visit at Stanford University in the fall of 1961, Smith met Sidney Siegel, a psychology professor who had published an economics-related experiment with Lawrence Fouraker (Siegel and Fouraker 1960). "Sid was far more than a master experimentalist; he also used theory and statistics with great skill in the design and analysis of experiments" (Smith 2018a, 201).[8] Smith's visit increased his interest in experimental economics and his contributions to the field led to his Nobel Prize in Economic Sciences "for having established laboratory experiments as a tool in empirical analysis, especially in the study of alternative market mechanisms."

After twenty fruitful years at Purdue, where he was promoted to associate professor in 1957 and full professor in 1961, Smith moved back out west to the University of Arizona in 1975. One of his Ph.D. students at Arizona, Arlington Williams, programmed Smith's market

---

[8] Siegel's unexpected death at the end of 1961 likely lengthened the timetable for the recognition of experimental economics as a valid research methodology. For a detailed description of the development of experimental methods in economics, see *Experimental Methods: A Primer for Economists* by Daniel Friedman and Shyam Sunder (Friedman and Sunder 1994).

experiments in PLATO. Smith and his associates soon developed techniques for running experiments that distinguished experimental economics from experimental psychology: (1) incentive payments to participants for profits earned as a consequence of their decisions, (2) no deception so that participants could believe and act on whatever the instructions specified, and (3) clear and simple instructions that were printed out and/ or presented on the computer screen. A fundamental characteristic of their experimental research was an underlying respect for lab results and the rationality of human participants. In contrast to psychologists and behavioral economists, who characterized behavior inconsistent with traditional economic theory as "irrational," Smith and his colleagues began to ask, "What are the subjects trying to tell us about the world as they see it?" (Smith 2018b, 46).[9]

While at Arizona, Smith recruited like-minded economists who understood the importance of testing key assumptions and predictions of neoclassical theory in the lab, including Jim Cox in 1977, Mark Isaac in 1980, and Stan Reynolds and Kevin McCabe in 1982. Smith and his associates continued to examine the veracity of the strong market efficiency results emerging in double-auction markets. Going back to W. S. Jevons in 1871, neoclassical economics believed that the equilibrium price prediction could only be reached if all traders had complete information regarding conditions of supply and demand. All that was required to achieve the equilibrium price prediction in these experimental studies, however, was a market institution that reflected the way capital markets had evolved in market economies.[10] To demonstrate the power of this emergent market institution, Dhananjay Gode and Shyam Sunder (1993) ran double-auction markets that included some computerized traders who chose bids and asks randomly subject to a no-loss constraint. Surprisingly, they found that highly efficient market outcomes were still achieved in the presence of these "zero intelligence" traders.

It wasn't until Smith, Suchanek, and Williams (1988) incorporated long-lived assets in the lab that the market results varied wildly from neoclassical price theory as in Chamberlin's experiments. Smith (2018b, 64) describes the new experimental setup in his memoirs:

---

[9] As Smith (2018b, 46) states in his memoirs, "So, I tended to be at odds with both the profession and the behavioral economic psychologists.... The subjects had it right; consequently, when they appeared to be getting it 'wrong,' some interpretive caution was in order."

[10] Surprisingly, convergence to the competitive equilibrium prediction under the double-auction market institution was only slowed by complete information (Smith 1976).

The experimental setup was simple: Each subject received an up-front endowment of shares and cash. Trading took place in a sequence of 15 periods. At the end of each period, each share would receive a dividend with expected value specified by a dividend distribution, e.g., o, 8, 28, 60 cents, with equal probability yielding a mean of 24 cents per share. Consequently, the fundamental dividend ("rational expectations") value of a share was 15 × 24 = 360 in period 1, 336 in period 2, and so on down to 24 in period 15 as the inventory of dividend drawing rights expired. In each period, the future expected dividend value of a share was well defined by theory, and a price below that value would provide a profitable opportunity for anyone to buy, a price above that value an opportunity to sell profitably.

The plan was to begin with a fully transparent environment to observe the rational expectations market price and then incorporate private supply and demand information as in prior double-auction markets. The fully transparent market setting, however, yielded large price deviations from the declining path of fundamental asset value. Market prices bubbled up above fundamental value in the early periods before crashing down just before the final period. This bubble-crash behavior was replicated at experimental labs across the nation with alternative participants, including corporate middle-level executives as well as graduate and undergraduate students. Researchers soon discovered that the opportunity for short-term capital gains drove this behavior. The bubble depended vitally on the inflow of cash, and the crash occurred after the inflow stopped and the opportunity for short-term gains dried up. In the wake of the 2007–08 mortgage market crash, Gjerstad and Smith (2014) used the results from these experiments to derive a unique explanation of the crash based upon house price declines and fixed mortgage debt that froze liquidity.[11]

Smith and his associates at Arizona began conducting experimental tests of two-person interactive games in the 1990s. For example, McCabe, Rassenti, and Smith (1996) examined a two-stage trust game where the first-mover, Player 1, can choose Payoffs of $10 for herself and $10 for her paired counterpart, Player 2. Alternatively, Player 1 can choose to pass her turn to Player 2; if she does, the original $20 pie grows to $40, and Player 2 chooses to return $15 to Player 1 and keep $25 or

[11] At the time of the final editing of this book in the fall of 2022, house prices had bubbled up to historic highs in America after the economic stimulus of near-zero interest rates by the Federal Reserve and trillions of dollars of spending by the US Congress to soften the blow of the COVID shutdowns. After the Fed's rapid increase in interest rates to curb runaway inflation, the scene has been set for another historic crash in the real estate market in 2023.

return zero and keep $40. In these two-person interactive games, Smith and his associates observed that the self-interested prediction from neo-classical economic theory was frequently violated in favor of norm-based behavior consistent with reciprocity and fairness norms. Again, these results have been repeated in multiple settings with multiple participant groups.[12]

In his memoirs, Vernon Smith (2018b, 200–201) describes how the experimental results in these two-person games led him back to Adam Smith's moral theory in *A Theory of Moral Sentiments*:

In "Sentiments," socialization is a process of maturation in which we learn to control our self-interested actions that are knowingly hurtful to others and to reward the intentionally beneficent actions of others; in this process, we follow rules or norms that define our group identity. The theory, based on the human capacity for moral sentiment, existed long before we started doing the experiments that falsified the model of strictly self-interested agents. We did not have to change the preference function to accommodate the experimental data. We had only to discover Adam Smith's theory and apply it to the experimental games to understand the results.... We see here how distorted and superficial is the popular image of Smith as a single-dimensional champion of individualism.

In his 2002 Nobel Prize lecture (Smith 2003), Smith highlighted the emerging results in experimental economics that had changed his mind regarding neoclassical economic theory. In particular, he explained how the results in the lab revealed two rational orders that were originally identified by Hayek. Results from impersonal market experiments revealed the robustness of neoclassical predictions based on *constructivist* rationality but highlighted the importance of market institutions that had emerged and proven their fitness in market economies. In contrast, results from two-person interactive games revealed *ecological* rationality based on humanity's social and cultural heritage and emerging social and moral norms. He would later write a larger work based on his Nobel lecture, *Rationality in Economics: Constructivist and Ecological Forms* (Smith 2008). I have used his book to teach experimental economics in my Ph.D. seminars at Florida State University and Georgia State University. I like to use Smith's book not only because of its rich theoretical and methodological insights, but also because the emerging results of his lab experiments have caused him to join the search for a moral foundation for capitalism.

---

[12] For a detailed review of the experimental literature in game theory, see Smith (2008).

6.3 MICHAEL JENSEN JOINS THE SEARCH

After assuming the presidency of Harvard in 1869, Charles W. Eliot (1834–1926) ignored repeated calls to establish a school of business, "arguing that such a project would be anathema to the university's educational purpose of teaching students how to live worthy lives" (Khurana 2007, 45). By the turn of the century, however, more than half of Harvard's graduates were going into business. When Eliot finally succumbed and established a graduate school of business administration at Harvard in 1908, he emphasized the importance of viewing the business profession as a "calling." In a speech before his fellow business school deans at the 1927 meeting of the AACSB, Wallace B. Donham (1877–1954) stated his perceived justification for founding a business school at Harvard (AACSB 1927, 1):

I have reached the conclusion that the greatest need of a civilization such as ours, if it is to progress in an orderly evolution, is for socially-minded business men. I am convinced that this social need is the sole basis which justified our ancient university and all of the institutions that are represented here today in entering upon business training.

Khurana (2007) documents how the vision of business education at the university-based business school was transformed from *higher aims* to *hired hands*. He identifies three historical phases in this transformation: (1) an early phase from the founding of the Wharton School through the 1940s where business management was viewed as "a profession" with broad social and moral responsibilities, (2) a second phase in the 1950s where business management was viewed as "management science" with an emphasis on technical training, and (3) a third phase beginning in the 1960s where business management became narrowly viewed as providing high returns to shareholders with a focus on "the maximization of stock price." Khurana identifies factors that contributed to this transformation, including the needs of national defense during two world wars and the Cold War, as well as foundation reports by Carnegie and Ford that were highly critical of business school education in the university (Pierson 1959; Gordon and Howell 1959).[13]

---

[13] Both foundations emphasized the need for Ph.D.-trained faculty and scholarly research befitting the business school's place in the university. The Ford Foundation followed up its report with nearly fifteen years of financial grants totaling $35 million that went to prominent business schools to supplement their recommendations for reform (Miles 2016).

The largest contributing factor to the narrowing view of business management at the university-based business school, according to Khurana, was the growing influence of neoclassical economists. Although the stock market collapse of 1929 and the ensuing Great Depression breathed life into the professionalism project of institutional economists, especially upon revelations of stock-swindling activities and financial abuses of many executives, the wider social and moral obligations of managers took a back seat in the eyes of neoclassical economists who were achieving growing status in the university. This trend found its apex during the economic distress of the 1970s when a "perfect storm of external economic shocks, compounded by a drop in productivity growth, cost-of-living adjustments built into union contracts, and an economy shifting toward services, dealt the final blows to the postwar managerialism" (Khurana 2007, 297).

In the course of the 1970s and early 1980s, the "relationship capitalism" that had developed during the postwar years became increasingly viewed as the source of the stagflation that plagued the economy. As a result, the regulatory policies and normative practices that had supported managerialism in America were rapidly dismantled. Neoclassical economists associated with the Chicago School, in particular, came to view any government involvement in the economy as inefficient and dysfunctional. Reflected in the writings of George Stigler (1971a, 1971b) from the School of Business at Chicago, government regulators were viewed as self-interested agents focused on expanding their power and influence. When accounting researchers applied Stigler's theory of regulation, they similarly characterized accounting regulators and policymakers as self-interested agents (Watts and Zimmerman 1986).

The growing influence of the Chicago School was especially felt in corporate finance, which shifted its focus from strategies to attract and allocate capital to a narrow focus on how financial decisions affected the market value of firms (Khurana 2007, 310):

These changes in the field of corporate finance, combined with the introduction of a variety of ideas developed in econometrics and accounting, eventually resulted in the positing of the Efficient Market Hypothesis, a theory that came to represent "the cornerstone of modern academic finance." The theory is built on the assumption of John Stuart Mill's "homo economicus," a rational economic man "characterized by perfect self-interest, perfect rationality and free access to perfect information regarding a specific condition." According to this theory, if markets are efficient it is not possible for investors to make profits by trading on already-available information. In other words, it is not possible for investors to consistently earn above-market returns on the basis of publicly available information. As a result, market prices ... are the best reflectors of the fundamental economic value of the firm.

The emboldened neoclassical economic theory out of Chicago created a new logic of shareholder primacy that limited the responsibility of management to obtaining high stock prices for the shareholders of the firm. Neoclassical economists initially modeled the firm simply as a production function with no role for management. "(B)ecause it was assumed in the neoclassical view, for example, that market processes ensure unanimity of responses, the issue of ownership and control (which had provided a critical underpinning of managerialism) was deemed irrelevant. Competition in the marketplace was assumed to solve any and all problems arising from, say, the separation of ownership and control" (Khurana 2007, 314–315).

It wasn't until the 1970s that Michael C. Jensen (1939–), William H. Meckling (1922–98), and Eugene F. Fama (1939–) developed a neoclassical theory of the firm that took the management of the firm seriously. Consistent with the Chicago School view of managers as self-interested agents, however, their theory focused on the agency conflict between managers and owners of the firm. The theory identified three mechanisms for managing this agency conflict: (1) monitoring managerial performance, (2) providing economic incentives, and (3) promoting an active market for corporate control. The first mechanism incorporated accounting disclosures, internal control systems, and a professional board of directors. The second mechanism incorporated powerful financial incentives that aligned the financial interests of managers with shareholders. The third mechanism incorporated the threat that poorly performing management "insiders" would be replaced by efficiency- and profit-oriented "outsiders." Agency theory soon became the dominant theoretical framework in finance, accounting, and organizational behavior (Khurana 2007, 318):

In contrast to earlier business school scholarship grounded in inductive observation, and with no overarching conceptual framework, agency theory brought a deductive and generalizable approach to business school research – the lack of which had haunted business education from the start, and had particularly concerned the Ford Foundation – and progressively applied it to a widening variety of corporate phenomena. Drawing on the legitimacy of the economics discipline, agency theory in the business school had the academic authority to classify managerial action and managerial character in decisive ways.

The academic authority of agency theory found its way into the elite business school at Harvard through the influence of Michael Jensen. After completing his Ph.D. in 1968 at the University of Chicago under the supervision of Merton Miller, Jensen joined Meckling at the University of Rochester where they further developed their neoclassical theory of the firm (Jensen and Meckling 1976). In 1988, however, Jensen was hired by Harvard's increasingly prestigious business school. While at Harvard, Jensen and several of his colleagues developed a popular MBA course entitled, "Coordination, Control, and the Management of Organizations" (CCMO). Grounded thoroughly in agency theory, the course addressed "issues of motivation, information and decision-making, the allocation of decision rights, performance measurement systems, organizational and personal rewards and punishments, corporate financial policy, and governance" (Khurana 2007, 322).[14]

Agency theory's emphasis on narrow self-interest with preferences only for wealth and leisure challenged the beliefs of MBA students who maintained a broader social and moral perspective (Khurana 2007, 322):

So powerful was the course in creating a particular point of view, Jensen said, that students found that the logic and outlook of CCMO challenged "some of their deeply felt beliefs." The course helped students, Jensen argued, to become more "tough-minded" and shifted them away from the "stakeholder model" of organizational purpose, which was "dear to the hearts of many of our students."

The underlying assumptions of narrow self-interest and efficient markets were counterintuitive to most business students. For example, the efficient market hypothesis threatened the traditional roles of accounting and finance in providing information relevant to firm valuation (Graham and Dodd 1934). Further, the Modigliani and Miller (1958) theorem, which stated that the market value of the firm was independent of the mix of debt and equity used to finance it, violated previous intuition in corporate finance. In time, the efficient market hypothesis became a victim of more detailed market analysis and worldwide market crashes, and the Modigliani–Miller theorem faded from view after the authors themselves acknowledged that it ignored the potential costs of bankruptcy.[15] Nevertheless, the neoclassical theory of the firm out of Chicago had a powerful influence on the management training that business students

---

[14] Similar agency-based courses soon appeared at Rochester, the University of Chicago, the University of Southern California, and other schools whose faculties were populated by Jensen's students.

[15] As Vernon Smith (2018a, 237–238) points out in describing the failure of the Modigliani–Miller theorem in his autobiography, "Full-blown bankruptcy isn't required, only risk of default on debt so that you don't recover all of the interest or principal on the bonds. This is not rocket science; it's just simple common sense."

received in America's business schools from the 1970s through the end of the twentieth century.

The growing influence of agency theory significantly altered the fields that MBA students went into upon graduation. Between 1965 and 1985, Harvard saw the number of students going into fields such as financial services and consulting skyrocket, whereas the number of students going into corporate and nonprofit management shrank considerably. As Stanford's Harold Leavitt would explain in an MBA publication in 1990 (Khurana 2007, 326):

> The new, professional MBA-type manager [in the 1980s] began to look more and more like the professional mercenary soldier – ready and willing to fight any war and to do so coolly and systematically, but without ever asking the tough pathfinding questions: Is this war worth fighting? Is it the right war? Is the cause just? Do I believe in it?

For a case study of the type of manager who came out of the elite MBA programs during this period, one need look no further than Jeffrey Skilling of Enron. Skilling earned his MBA from Harvard in 1979, graduating in the top 5 percent of his class as a Baker Scholar. As with other students at the top of his class, he pursued a high-paying career in consulting and eventually became one of the youngest partners in the history of McKinsey & Company. The conversion from relationship capitalism to investor capitalism in the 1980s hit the natural gas industry particularly hard. After years of cost-based price regulation that guaranteed profits to everyone in the industry, natural gas prices were deregulated and began to fluctuate wildly. Skilling encouraged one of his top clients, Enron, to take advantage of the new deregulatory environment by engaging in complex futures transactions and by creating new markets for natural gas based on its growing expertise in the futures markets (Fusaro and Miller 2002).

In 1990, CEO Kenneth Lay hired Skilling to direct Enron's futures markets and to groom him to be Lay's replacement. Skilling was promoted to chief operating officer of the company in 1997 and replaced Lay as CEO in 2001. He was known for hiring the best talent, recruiting only from top MBA programs and investment banks, and rewarding his new talent with merit-based bonuses that had no cap (Thomas 2002). Enron went through a period of rapid growth fueled by aggressive mergers and acquisitions and was named by Fortune as "America's Most Innovative Company" for six years in a row. However, it became increasingly difficult for Skilling to meet analysts' rising earnings expectations and the stock price of the firm began to plummet. The firm engaged in aggressive accounting practices to increase reported earnings and used special purpose entities (SPEs) to keep debt off its books. As predicted in an email to Lay by whistle-blower Sherron Watkins, Enron soon imploded in a wave of accounting scandals. The firm filed for bankruptcy in December 2001, and its auditor, Arthur Andersen, was forced to dissolve due to its role in enabling the accounting scandals. While denying all responsibility, Skilling was convicted of federal felony charges and sentenced to twenty-four years in prison (McLean and Elkind 2003).

By promoting a view of managers as self-interested agents, the Chicago School harkened back to an earlier era in America. As capital poured into US industries during the second industrial revolution, vast fortunes were made by "Robber Barons," who created their wealth through opaque public reporting, insider trading, and stock price manipulation. This self-interested culture was epitomized by J. P. Morgan in his famous quip in 1901, "I owe the public nothing" (Marchand 1998). In the same spirit, Milton Friedman published a famous article in the *New York Times Magazine* in 1970 trumpeting his view that "the social responsibility of business is to increase its profits" (Friedman 1970). Jensen viewed Friedman's article as "a sign of growing academic skepticism about managerialism and an important cultural event in its own right" (Khurana 2007, 317). Through Jensen's efforts, the Chicago view of business management came to dominate the university-based business school. Jensen's writings in the popular press also encouraged a large wave of merger, takeover, and restructuring activity in America in the 1980s as well as soaring executive compensation that has continued to this day (Holmstrom and Kaplan 2001).

Jensen published a comprehensive review of agency theory and its implications for management and public policy in 2000 in *A Theory of the Firm: Governance, Residual Claims, and Organizational Forms*. The book contained a spirited defense of agency theory and a frontal attack on stakeholder theory, which argued that the firm had an obligation to create value for all of the stakeholders of the firm including customers, employees, suppliers, and communities (Freeman 1984). Jensen (2000, 9) begins his review by arguing that the disciplining effect of the market for control in the 1980s was long overdue:

The takeover boom of the 1980s brought the subject of corporate governance to the front pages of newspapers as a revolution was mounted against the power complexes at corporate headquarters. The mergers, acquisitions, leveraged buyouts (LBOs), and other leveraged restructuring of the 1980s constituted an assault on entrenched authority that was long overdue. Control of the corporation was transformed from a means of perpetuating established arrangements into a marketplace where the highest bidder made certain that the owners' interests would prevail.

Jensen (2000, 16–17) draws direct parallels between the merger boom of the 1980s and the merger activity during the second industrial revolution. First, he argues that in both periods the capital markets played a major role in eliminating excess capacity and increasing profit for shareholders. Second, he argues that the takeover specialists in both periods were disparaged by managers, policy makers, and the press. In fact, he directly associates the takeover specialists of the 1980s with "the so-called Robber Barons" of the late nineteenth century. Third, he states that in both periods "the criticism was followed by public policy changes that restricted the capital markets: in the nineteenth century the passage of antitrust laws restricting combination, and in the late 1980s the renewed regulation of the credit markets, antitakeover legislation, and court decisions that restricted the market for corporate control." Jensen concludes that internal corporate control has failed to provide the same discipline and productivity as the market for corporate control.

In his review of agency theory, Jensen (2000, 59–60) makes recommendations for future research. He recommends that researchers examine further "how industry-wide excess capacity arises, how markets and firms respond to such market pressures, and why exit is so difficult for organizations to deal with." He also recommends that researchers examine "the weaknesses that cause internal corporate control systems to fail and how to correct them." Among his other recommendations, Jensen calls on researchers to examine "how capital budgeting decisions are actually made" and the nature of "implicit contracts" and how to "limit opportunistic behavior regarding those implicit contracts." He concludes: "(W)e have to understand even better than we do now the factors leading to organizational failures (and successes): we have to break open the black box called the 'firm,' and this means understanding how organizations and the people in them work. In short, we are facing the problem of developing a viable theory of organizations. To be successful we must continue to broaden our thinking to new topics and to learn and develop new analytical tools."

Jensen did not alter his neoclassical theory of the firm in response to the dot-com market crash in 2000 and the widespread corruption uncovered at Enron, Adelphia, Tyco, and Worldcom. In articles published over the following two years, Jensen criticized two management controls commonly used in practice: participative budgeting because it encouraged managers to lie and cheat (Jensen 2001) and the balanced scorecard because of its foundation in stakeholder theory (Jensen 2002). Over time, however, Jensen began to question the narrow assumptions of the neoclassical theory of the firm. The first signs of a change in his thinking appeared in 2004, when he partnered with Werner Erhard to develop a leadership course that emphasized *integrity* and *authenticity* as key conditions for individual thriving as well as institutional effectiveness. Together with Erhard, Jensen developed a positive economic model of integrity and began to circulate it as a working paper for further discussion (Erhard, Jensen, and Zaffron 2008).

It was not until the crisis of capitalism brought on by the global market crash of 2007–08, however, that Jensen challenged researchers to incorporate the role of values and integrity in their economic theory. This turn in his thinking is reflected in a foreword he wrote for Paul Zak's edited book, *Moral Markets: The Critical Role of Values in the Economy* (Jensen 2008, ix–x):

Economics, having traditionally focused on the positive analysis of alternative institutional structures, has far too long ignored the normative world. By the term "positive analysis," I mean, of course, the analysis of the way the world is, however it behaves, independent of any normative value judgments about its desirability or undesirability.... By "normative," I mean establishing, relating to, or deriving from a standard or norm that specifies desirable or undesirable conduct or behavior, that is, what ought to be.... I look forward to seeing the creation of an entirely new field of inquiry in economics, and in its sister social sciences, focused deeply on the positive analysis of the role of values in elevating the possible outcomes of human interaction.

Unlike Jensen, Friedman and Stigler did not live to see the severe market crash of 2007–08. One can only speculate whether they would have altered their neoclassical economic theory in the wake of this severe market crash and the near collapse of the global financial system. Once their neoclassical theory became the new paradigm in economics, finance, and accounting, they generally ignored new developments in economic theory or empirical evidence inconsistent with that paradigm. This latest crisis of capitalism, however, jarred Jensen's thinking so much that he significantly altered his views and joined the search for a moral foundation for capitalism (see Chapter 7).

6.4 INITIAL ATTEMPTS TO EXTEND
NEOCLASSICAL ECONOMIC THEORY

The dominance of the neoclassical theory of the firm and its emphasis on narrow self-interest can be traced to the growing influence of the Chicago School. When Friedman was hired to replace Jacob Viner in 1946, he took over Viner's microeconomics graduate course called "price theory." Stigler had been the Economics Department's first choice to replace Viner given that nine of his ten journal articles were on price theory and he had written two editions of a textbook on the subject. The university president at the time, however, vetoed Stigler's appointment, and Friedman was hired instead. Stigler had completed his Ph.D. at Chicago in 1938 under Knight's supervision and was a fellow Ph.D. student with Friedman and W. Allen Wallis (1912–98). Yet it was only through the efforts of Wallis, who had become the Dean of the Graduate School of Business (GSB), that Stigler was hired at the GSB and given the prestigious Walgreen Professorship. Upon Stigler's arrival in 1958, the three former classmates were rejoined at last (Hammond 2010).

As discussed in Chapter 5, Hayek and Simon included Friedman, Stigler, and Wallis in their original plan for developing a Free Market Study at Chicago with money from the Volker Fund. After Simon's untimely death, Hayek handpicked Wallis to replace him on the Managing Committee, and Wallis attended the first meeting of the Mont Pélerin Society in 1947. Rejoined at Chicago, Friedman, Stigler, and Wallis advanced Hayek's neoliberalism as well as their own neoclassical economic theory. As their efforts began to pay off and neoclassical theory became the dominant paradigm in economics, however, Hayek came to realize that they had gone too far. "Because he did not think neoclassical economics was especially useful for his project, Hayek ultimately left economics" (Nik-Khah 2011, 138). In turn, Friedman stopped using the label "neoliberalism" to describe his economic and political positions in favor of the more narrow label, "libertarianism."

Friedman wrote a memorandum in 1946 to explain the purpose of the Free Market Study at Chicago. It helps explain the motivation of the neoclassical economists who had congregated at Chicago by 1958 (Van Horn and Mirowski 2015, 152):

The free market [is] the most efficient organizer of economic activity – [the Study will] emphasize and explain that the free market is systemic, rational, not chaotic or disorderly.... [It will also] show how the free market performs some of the more difficult functions, such as allocating resources to their best use and distributing consumption through time.

In their quest to link free markets with political and personal freedom, they needed to demonstrate that capital markets were systematic, rational, and orderly. Friedman's memorandum also identified both private monopoly and public regulation as "The Menace to the Free Market," with the former being viewed as less dangerous. In time, however, the Chicago School went so far as to view private monopoly as acceptable in free markets. To Friedman and Stigler, government intervention became the ultimate threat to free-market capitalism. Friedman's solution was to popularize "the lessons of neoclassical economics for the purpose of appealing directly to the public through his bestselling books, his television series (*Free to Choose*), and his *Newsweek* column. Friedman's popularizations of neoclassical-libertarian ideas made him the public face of the Chicago School" (Nik-Khah 2011, 139).

While Friedman advised a Republican president (Reagan), Congress, and the public on important policy debates from monetary policy to minimum wages, Stigler focused on developing their neoclassical economic theory and applying it across an array of business and social settings in a form of "economics imperialism." Stigler's solution to the problem of government intervention was to apply the self-interested view of neoclassical economics to government agents involved in regulating business and markets. As Steven Medema (2011, 158) points out, Stigler made self-interest the center of his neoclassical theory and attributed his view to Adam Smith:

For Stigler, self-interested behavior was at the center of economic analysis and had been since the time of Smith, whose Wealth of Nations he described as "a stupendous palace erected upon the granite of self-interest".... Stigler's perception of the centrality of self-interested behavior in Smith here led him to label Smith "the premier scholar of self-interest" ... and to call this aspect of Smith's work "the crown jewel" of The Wealth of Nations.... Stigler even went so far as to link up Smith's approach with contemporary economics imperialism, characterizing Smith as giving us "a theorem of almost unlimited power on the behavior of man" that is "Newtonian in its universality".... This "always and everywhere" gravitational allusion is not accidental, but rather reflects what Stigler saw as the pervasiveness of self-interested behavior throughout human life.

Other leading economists at Chicago applied Stigler's neoclassical price theory to a host of social issues. For example, Gary S. Becker (1930–2014) used Stigler's rational choice approach to examine social issues such as discrimination, education, crime, the family, and politics. Becker won his Nobel Prize in Economic Sciences in 1992 for establishing an economic approach to all human behavior (Becker 1976b), which he emphasized was a method of analysis. Becker's method of analysis involved examining human behavior "as a result of individual choices characterized by utility maximization, forward-looking stance, consistent rationality and stable and persistent preferences" (Teixeira 2010, 256). Stigler's rational choice approach was also extended to the field of law by Richard A. Posner (1939–) and Eric A. Posner (1965–).

By focusing on the rational choices of individual actors and ignoring important social and moral issues, Becker's economic analysis of human behavior yielded counterintuitive results. For example, Becker's rational choice theory viewed discrimination as rational and yet viewed traditional forms of altruistic behavior in the family as irrational. While Becker's method of analysis mentioned social and moral issues in passing, it ultimately focused on the financial implications of behavior based on narrow self-interest. Other members of the Chicago School applied Becker's rational choice theory directly to social issues. In *Law and Social Norms*, for example, Eric Posner (2000, 46) acknowledged that social behaviors "bubble forth from a cauldron of instincts, passions, and deeply ingrained attitudes." He argued, however, "that rational choice theory can shed light on social norms by focusing on the reputational source of behavior regularities to the exclusion of their cognitive and emotional sources." Thus, Posner defined social norms narrowly as behavioral regularities that emerge as a consequence of people acting on their rational self-interest and their desire to reap the financial reward of such norm-based behavior.

Other prominent neoclassical economists have highlighted the shortcomings of this rational-choice approach. In *The Firm, the Market, and the Law*, for example, Ronald H. Coase (1910–2013) highlighted its inability to address important social and institutional aspects of organizations and markets (Coase 1988, 3):

This preoccupation of economists with the logic of choice, while it may ultimately rejuvenate the study of law, political science, and sociology, has nonetheless had, in my view, serious adverse effects on economics itself. One result of this divorce of the theory from its subject matter has been that the entities whose decisions economists are engaged in analyzing have not been made the subject of study and in consequence lack any substance. The consumer is not a human being but a consistent set of preferences. The firm to an economist as Slater has said, "is effectively defined as a cost curve and a demand curve, and the theory is simply the logic of optimal pricing and input combination." Exchange takes place without any specification of its institutional setting. We have consumers without humanity, firms without organization, and even exchange without markets.

Coase (1988, 9) pointed out that commodity and stock exchanges regulate in great detail the activities of those who trade in these markets – including the times at which transactions can be made, what can be traded, the responsibilities of the parties, and the terms of settlement – and impose sanctions upon those who violate these regulations. Yet these exchanges are often used as examples of perfect markets with perfect competition and no regulation. He concluded, "It suggests, I think correctly, that for anything approaching perfect competition to exist, an intricate system of rules and regulations would normally be needed. Economists observing the regulations of the exchanges often assume that they represent an attempt to exercise monopoly power and aim to restrain competition. They ignore or, at any rate, fail to emphasize an alternative explanation for these regulations: that they exist in order to reduce transaction costs."

Coase attacked Stigler's interpretation of his two seminal studies. In his early study, *The Nature of the Firm* (Coase 1937), Coase showed that in the absence of transaction costs there is no economic basis for the existence of the firm. In his later study, *The Problem of Social Cost* (Coase 1960), Coase showed that in the absence of transaction costs it does not matter what the law is, since people can always negotiate without cost to acquire, subdivide, and combine rights whenever this would increase the value of production. Coase's (1988, 14–15) own interpretation of his two seminal studies, which led to his Nobel Prize in Economic Sciences in 1991, was "the need to introduce positive transaction costs explicitly into economic analysis so that we can study the world that exists." In the third edition of his price theory textbook, however, Stigler interpreted what he labeled "the Coase Theorem" as follows: "under perfect competition private and social costs will be equal." Coase rejected this interpretation of his seminal work and identified it as an attempt to deflect criticism of the neoclassical theory of the firm out of Chicago:

The extensive discussion in the journals has concentrated almost entirely on the "Coase Theorem," a proposition about the world of zero transaction costs. This response, although disappointing, is understandable. The world of zero transaction costs, to which the Coase Theorem applies, is the world of modern economic analysis, and economists therefore feel quite comfortable handling the intellectual problems it poses, remote from the real world though they may be. That much of the discussion has been critical of my argument is also quite understandable since, if I am right, current economic analysis is incapable of handling many of the problems to which it purports to give answers. A conclusion so depressing is hardly likely to be welcomed, and the resistance that my analysis has encountered is therefore quite natural. It is my view that the objections raised to the Coase Theorem ... are invalid, unimportant, or irrelevant.

Similar to Stigler, Friedman was openly hostile toward attempts to extend the neoclassical theory of the firm out of Chicago. Oliver E. Williamson (1932–2020) analyzed Friedman's methodological essay in light of this hostility. In his article, *Friedman (1953) and the theory of the firm*, Williamson (2009, 241–242) begins by agreeing with the main message of Friedman's essay, "most economists are and should be engaged in the study of positive economics." Williamson takes issue, however, with Friedman's statement that "(t)ruly important and significant hypotheses will be found to have 'assumptions' that are *wildly inaccurate* descriptions of reality, and, in general, the more significant the theory, the *more unrealistic* the assumptions." He also takes issue with Friedman's statement that any criticism of the traditional theory of the firm and its assumptions "is largely beside the point unless supplemented by evidence that a hypothesis differing in one or another of these respects ... yields better predictions for as wide a range of phenomena."

As discussed in Chapter 5, Friedman developed his essay with significant input from Karl Popper. In addition to reflecting Popper's philosophy of science based on natural science (Popper 1934), however, Friedman's essay reflected a resistance toward extensions of neoclassical theory that was characteristic of Thomas S. Kuhn's (1922–96) philosophy of science based on community, culture, and social norms (Kuhn 1962/1996).

Kuhn argued that normal science functions within a scientific community's commitment to a *theoretical paradigm*. "In particular, normal science involves the laborious process of accumulating detail in accord with the established theory, without questioning or challenging the underlying assumptions of that theory. In essence, Friedman was concerned that critics had gone too far in questioning the underlying assumptions of the established neoclassical theory of the firm. Rather than question these assumptions, he argued for getting on with the task of accumulating more detail in accord with the established theory" (Stevens 2019, 8–9).

In contrast to Friedman, Williamson (2009) argued that unrealistic assumptions of a theory are fair game for its criticism. Further, he argued for pluralism rather than a single, all-purpose theory of the firm. To Williamson, Friedman's insistence that alternate theories must prove their ability to predict over as wide a range of phenomena privileged current neoclassical theory over promising upstart contenders that have not had the benefit of successive extensions, applications, and refinements. In his book, *The Economic Institutions of Capitalism*, Williamson (1985) described his large body of research incorporating transaction costs into the neoclassical theory of the firm. Williamson received the Nobel Prize in Economic Sciences in 2009 for his contributions to the field of transaction cost economics. His research approach expanded the neoclassical theory of the firm along the lines suggested by Coase and verified the fruitfulness of his approach. While Friedman and Stigler were very receptive to extending their neoclassical theory to government regulation and a host of other social issues, it appears that they were not receptive to obvious and useful extensions of their theory suggested by other leading economists.

6.5 CONCLUSION

The story of the victory of neoclassical economics over institutional economics is filled with intrigue and originates with the battle in Europe between the younger German Historical School of Schmoller and the neoclassical Austrian School of Menger. Due to Schmoller's powerful influence, economists associated with the Austrian School were shut out of German universities for decades. In the open exchange between German and American universities in the late nineteenth and early twentieth centuries, historical and institutional economists crossed the Atlantic and exerted a powerful influence on the development of economic theory in America. When Friedrich Hayek brought the neoclassical theory of the Austrian School to the University of Chicago in the 1940s, it was initially resisted by Frank Knight who had been heavily influenced by Max Weber's institutional economic theory. In time, however, the neoliberalism and free-market ideas of Hayek found fertile soil in the academic and political aspirations of Knight's two students at Chicago, Milton Friedman and George Stigler.

In their increasing emphasis on narrow self-interest and highly efficient markets, however, Friedman and Stigler eventually expunged the Economics Department at Chicago of their mentor Knight, their inspiration Hayek, and the talented neoclassical economists associated with the Cowles Commission for Research in Economics. In an effort to explain emerging results in experimental tests of neoclassical economic theory, neoclassical economist Vernon Smith has rediscovered Adam Smith's moral theory based on social norms and culture. The crisis of capitalism caused by the global market crash of 2007–08 has also caused neoclassical economist Michael Jensen to expand his theory of the firm by including the roles of values and integrity. As we will see in the following chapter, an economist associated with the Cowles Commission would become the youngest recipient of the Nobel Prize in Economic Sciences for his extensions of neoclassical economic theory. His theoretical advances in social choice theory would inspire another neoclassical economist from India to provide further theoretical advances that would earn him a Nobel Prize.

7

Rescuing Capitalism from the Capitalists

Amartya Sen

There are plenty of 'social choice problems' in all this, but in analyzing them we have to look not only for an appropriate reflection of *given* individual preferences, or for the most acceptable procedures for choices based on those preferences, but also to go beyond both these aspects to allow the possibility of value formation. We need to depart both from the assumption of unresponsive individual preferences and from the presumption that people are purely self-interested specimens of *homo economicus*. Useful insights on social choice come from many different sources, and we have to recognize that important fact.

Amartya Sen
Collective Choice and Social Welfare

Through the work of Milton Friedman in the public sphere and George Stigler in the academic sphere, the influence of the neoclassical economic theory out of Chicago grew rapidly and became associated with Adam Smith and free-market capitalism itself. In the continued narrowing of their discipline, Friedman and Stigler came to view government intervention as the ultimate threat to capitalism. Financial economists such as Michael Jensen (2000) applauded the deregulatory environment spawned by this view and the "third industrial revolution" it had brought to the West. Gone were the warnings expressed by early political economists regarding the vulnerabilities and excesses of unregulated markets. Consistent with Karl Polanyi's theory of the *double movement*, however, attempts to unleash the power of the market through deregulation exposed capitalist society to unparalleled risk. The emboldened neoclassical theory out of Chicago, with its logic of narrow self-interest and highly efficient markets, had set the stage for a return to the opportunism of the second industrial revolution. In the first decade of the twenty-first century, that opportunism would cause a major market crash that nearly collapsed the global financial system. In this chapter, I discuss the latest crisis of capitalism and Amartya Sen's journey from India to the West to rescue capitalism from the capitalists.[1]

7.1   THE INCREASING VULNERABILITY
OF CAPITALIST SOCIETIES

Despite the victory of the Austrian School over the German Historical School in the nineteenth-century "battle of the methods," historical analysis remained an important tool for the development of neoclassical economic theory. In his memoirs, transparently entitled *Memoirs of an Unregulated Economist*, Stigler (1988) describes the importance of historical analysis at the University of Chicago during his doctoral program in the 1930s. He emphasizes that both of his mentors, Frank Knight and Jacob Viner, were astute scholars of history as well as neoclassical price theory. Thus, it was not unusual for Stigler to choose a doctoral dissertation under Knight that involved a history of economic theory in the last third of the nineteenth century. He used this history to provide insights regarding the development of economic thought related to production and distribution.[2] Stigler won the Nobel Prize in Economic Sciences in 1982 for his seminal studies of industrial structures, functioning of markets, and causes and effects of public regulation.

As for Friedman, he conducted an important historical study of the monetary policy of the United States from 1857 to 1960 with Anna Schwartz to emphasize the role of banks, money, and the Federal Reserve in economic downturns (Friedman and Schwartz 1963). Public policy experts have argued that Friedman and Schwartz's historical study saved the global financial system in 2008 by convincing financial regulators "that monetary policy played a key role in the events of 1929–33, that the Fed failed to supply liquidity just at the time it was most needed, and in a real sense turned what would have been a severe depression into the cataclysm of the Great Depression" (Coleman 2019, 3). In his published comments at a celebration of Friedman's 90th birthday at the University of Chicago in 2002, Ben Bernanke, a current member and future director of the Federal

---

[1] As the epigraph to this chapter suggests (Sen 1970/2017, 41), Amartya Sen has played a major role in expanding neoclassical economic theory to incorporate important social and moral issues arising in capitalist society.

[2] Over the course of his career, Stigler published numerous articles on the history of economics and republished fourteen of them in 1965 (Stigler 1965).

Reserve's Board of Governors, stated, "I would like to say to Milton and Anna: Regarding the Great Depression. You're right, we did it. We're very sorry. But thanks to you, we won't do it again" (Bernanke 2002).

Friedman and Schwartz's (1963) historical study, however, did little to help the Fed avoid the mortgage market bubble and crash that gave rise to the financial crisis of 2007–08.[3] As discussed previously, Karl Polanyi's (1944/2001) historical study of England revealed the presence of a *double movement* whereby the movement to unleash the power of the market through deregulation leads to a countermovement to shield society from the vulnerabilities and excesses of unregulated markets. He argued that the first industrial revolution (1760–1840) brought with it social alienation and dislocation in addition to great economic growth, and that protective countermovements were soon put in place to shield society through England's Poor Laws and the so-called "Speenhamland Law." Polanyi also attributed the "dismal science" of the classical economists to the economic and moral climate generated by these protective countermovements. Polanyi's thesis of the double movement can be used to explain the rise of the Chicago School and the deregulatory movement it unleashed, as well as the increasing vulnerability it created for capitalist societies around the world.

Polanyi (1944/2001) placed part of the blame for World War I on the utopian idea of the self-regulating market. Consistent with his countermovement theory, governments went into action after the war to protect society from the vulnerabilities of the unregulated market. In addition to these governmental efforts, nonprofit organizations were established to provide research on market downturns and business cycles. In 1920, for example, institutional economist Wesley Mitchell (1874–1948) helped found the National Bureau of Economic Research (NBER). Friedman's study of income within the medical profession from 1937 to 1941 with Simon Kuznets, which led to Friedman's Ph.D. from Columbia in 1946, was conducted at NBER. While NBER director Reynold Noyes wanted the researchers to apply a theory of imperfect competition (Robinson 1933) and allow for differences in abilities and equipment, Friedman and Kuznets assumed perfect competition and used Marshallian price theory in their analysis (Cherrier 2011).

---

[3] As discussed below, Bernanke and the Federal Reserve took actions that encouraged the binge of borrowing that led to the mortgage-backed security bubble and crash of 2007–08. That did not stop Bernanke from receiving the Nobel Prize in Economic Sciences along with economists Douglas Diamond and Philip Dybvig in October 2022 for their ground-breaking research on bank runs and measures to prevent them.

The institutional economists at NBER were highly critical of the growing theoretical abstraction of their discipline. Some neoclassical economists associated with the Economics Department at Chicago, however, were highly critical of NBER for minimizing the importance of positive analysis and violating the rigorous canons of science. For example, Tjalling C. Koopmans (1910–1985) excoriated the institutional research at NBER in a published paper in the prestigious *Review of Economics and Statistics* in 1947. Koopmans had fled to the United States after Germany invaded the Netherlands in 1940 and joined the Cowles Commission for Research in Economics at Chicago in 1946. Two years later, Koopmans became the director of the research group, which focused on expanding economic theory through mathematical modeling and statistical analysis. Friedman took the side of the institutional economists at NBER in their criticism of the Cowles Commission. Given the increasingly hostile environment at Chicago, Koopmans convinced the Cowles family to move the Cowles Commission to Yale University in 1955 where it was renamed the Cowles Foundation.[4]

Michael Bernstein has written a history of the early struggles of the economics profession to form an effective public policy in America entitled, *A Perilous Progress: Economists and Public Purpose in Twentieth-Century America* (Bernstein 2001). Bernstein highlights attempts by Herbert Hoover (1874–1964) to establish a body of expertise in economics to help guide America and the world through World War I and the interwar period. After graduating from Stanford University as a mining engineer, Hoover found himself in London in 1914 helping organize food relief for the people of Belgium suffering under the Kaiser's "Schlieffen Plan." Bernstein (2001, 54) describes Hoover's meteoric rise during his goodwill mission to Europe:

So successful was Hoover in this widely admired (and publicized) activity that President Wilson charged him with responsibility to organize the nation's agricultural sectors for war mobilization in the spring of 1917. Actively courted by the Democrats to run for the presidency, Hoover remained nonetheless a loyal Republican. When Warren Harding took office in March 1921, Hoover assumed the Commerce portfolio; in the words of one of his less ardent admirers, he became "secretary of Commerce and assistant secretary of everything else."

---

[4] The heavy mathematical and statistical approach of the Cowles Commission belied the belief among many of its neoclassical economists in active government management of the economy, which was another source of conflict between the Cowles Commission and the other neoclassical economists at Chicago (Cherrier 2011).

Hoover enjoyed close personal and professional ties with many of the leading economists of his day, especially institutional economists such as Wesley Mitchell. When he took the oath of office as the thirty-first president of the United States in March 1929, Hoover had a detailed conception of what he wanted to accomplish in economic policy and how to go about it. "Yet it was the cruel irony of history that Hoover, who as commerce secretary had done more than any other cabinet officer to utilize the skills of professional economists in the work of government, would be so ill served by the very experts whom he had cultivated with such zeal. None of his economic advisors forewarned him of the devastating collapse in financial markets that would occur a half year after his inauguration; only a few would provide him with compelling and practical ideas to attempt a resolution of the crisis once it took hold" (Bernstein 2001, 60–61).

On October 24, 1929, the New York Stock Exchange (NYSE) experienced a large sell-off that quickly spread across world markets. Over the next five days, the NYSE lost more than 30 percent of its value. In an economic conference at the University of Chicago in the fall of 1931, the nation's leading economists passed a general resolution calling upon the federal government to avoid any reduction in annual spending targets with a view toward maintaining what little stimulus for demand existed in the nation's markets. In direct violation of this resolution, however, both President Hoover and his Democratic challenger Franklin D. Roosevelt (1882–1945) made the reduction of fiscal spending a centerpiece of their presidential campaigns. After his loss at the polls, Hoover wrote to colleagues, expressing his belief that capitalism could not survive unless "there are real restraints upon unbridled greed," and that "the Great Depression was, at its root, the result of a betrayal of capitalism by some of its most fortunate beneficiaries" (Bernstein 2001, 63).

Despite the best efforts of the Roosevelt administration and the large government spending of the New Deal, the economic crisis continued unabated. By 1933, stock prices had dropped 89 percent, wiping out millions of investors. At its lowest point, gross domestic product had dropped 30 percent, 9,000 banks had failed, and unemployment had reached 25.3 percent, representing 15 million unemployed Americans. Prior to the 1930s, capital markets in America had been highly unregulated with few controls for opportunistic financial reporting or trading behavior. During the Great Depression, however, the US government swiftly increased regulation and oversight. In 1933, for example, Congress enacted the Glass–Steagall Act to create bank deposit insurance and build an impregnable wall between the activities of investment banks and commercial banks. In 1934, the Roosevelt administration established the Securities and Exchange Commission (SEC) to standardize accounting and financial reporting for publicly traded companies.[5]

The double-digit unemployment of the Great Depression, however, was only cured by the economic stimulus generated by the demands of World War II. By the time of the Japanese naval offensive in the Hawaiian and Aleutian Islands, America's unemployment rate had fallen to 7 percent. In what leading MIT economist Paul Samuelson (1915–2009) called "the economist's war," neoclassical economists proved their ability to help mobilize and successfully execute the war. For example, Koopmans developed a mathematical model that aided decision makers in establishing transport routes, schedules, and tonnage objectives in both Asian and European theaters of military operations. He was awarded the Nobel Prize in Economic Sciences in 1975 for his theory of the optimum allocation of resources. "It is one of the great ironies of this history that a discipline renowned for its systematic portrayals of the benefits of unfettered, competitive markets would first demonstrate its unique operability in the completely regulated and controlled economy of total war" (Bernstein 2001, 89).

After proving their worth during World War II and the victory over fascism, neoclassical economists were called upon once again to win the Cold War. A vigorous national economy was needed to meet the needs of national defense as well as to demonstrate the virtues of American capitalism to the world. Unlike other major industrial nations, however, the United States entered the postwar period with its economy essentially intact and its organizational and technological assets preserved. While the labor market faced the normal challenges of demobilization, domestic production was buoyed by foreign demand from those regions devastated by the war. Further, the United States stood as the world's creditor, and the dollar, both by default and by the multilateral agreements at Bretton Woods, had become the world's currency. These strong economic tailwinds aided the United States in achieving unparalleled economic growth throughout the 1950s and 1960s.

The strong economic tailwinds that helped fuel the postwar prosperity of the US economy, however, soon reversed and became strong headwinds. The Bretton Woods international monetary agreements

---

[5] The task of standardizing accounting and reporting for publicly traded companies, however, was delegated to members of the accounting profession (Stevens 2019).

were abandoned as recovering industrial nations began to meet their own industrial needs and compete with the United States on world markets. American industry was further hampered by drops in productivity growth, cost-of-living adjustments built into union contracts, and an economy shifting away from manufacturing toward services. When combined with economic shocks such as the 1973 oil embargo by the Organization of the Petroleum Exporting Countries (OPEC), these trends led to an extended period of economic distress in America. The postwar confidence in Keynesian economics was severely shaken as the accelerated inflation of the late 1960s and 1970s was blamed on fiscal interventionism and big government. The combination of economic stagnation and high inflation gave birth to a new economic malady called "stagflation," and the sum of the rates of inflation and unemployment became a new measure called the "misery index." A growing chorus of voices from across the political spectrum now called for the dismantling of the regulatory environment that seemed to have hobbled the economy (Khurana 2007).

Béatrice Cherrier (2011, 343–344) has written about the "lucky consistency" of Friedman's neoclassical economic theory and his politics. She argues that his libertarianism "gradually reinforced itself as Friedman shifted his attention back and forth between scientific and non-scientific spheres," and "created lenses through which he interpreted new evidence, which he therefore saw as supporting his beliefs." Friedman's libertarian beliefs were also a product of "the protective and united Chicago intellectual environment." Friedman's closest colleagues, including his wife Rose, exhibited similar scientific backgrounds (Chicago training with a NBER-style empirical practice)."[6] Friedman's view of the capitalist system as comprised of narrowly self-interested agents coordinated through competitive markets with no role for government can be seen in his famous 1970 article in the *New York Times* Magazine entitled, *The Social Responsibility of Business Is to Increase Its Profits*. In the article, Friedman argued that incorporating any notion of social responsibility in business was a "fundamentally subversive doctrine" in a free society. In particular, Friedman asserted that the claim that business is responsible

---

[6] Rose's influence was especially significant, as she provided editorial input for *Capitalism and Freedom* in 1962 (Friedman 1962), coauthored the bestseller *Free to Choose: A Personal Statement* in 1980 (Friedman and Friedman 1980), and insisted that her husband accept the invitation to write articles for *Newsweek*. She also co-wrote their joint memoirs entitled, *Two Lucky People: Milton and Rose D. Friedman Memoirs* (Friedman and Friedman 1998).

for promoting desirable "social" ends such as "providing employment, eliminating discrimination, avoiding pollution and whatever else may be the catchwords of the contemporary crop of reformers ... (is) preaching pure and unadulterated socialism" (Friedman 1970, 1).

Critics of Friedman's controversial article have concluded that it "fails to prove that the exercise of social responsibility in business is by nature an unfair and socialist practice" (Mulligan 1986, 265). More recently, however, some researchers have viewed his article more positively as containing useful warnings against the inefficient use of investor funds and the intrusion of big business in the arena of public politics.[7] In an article celebrating its fifty-year anniversary, for example, Ramanna (2020, 33) argues that "Friedman was responding to what he saw as a deteriorating competitive environment in the United States, where major corporations were becoming, so to speak, fat and happy." In little more than a decade, Friedman's economic views became the dominant public policy in the West through the "Reagan Revolution" in America and "Thatcherism" in Great Britain. As it was designed to do, the new deregulatory environment unleashed the power of the market and reawakened economic growth. Consistent with Polanyi's double movement, however, the new deregulatory environment also increased the vulnerability of capitalist societies to opportunistic self-interest. This increased vulnerability would cause a crisis of capitalism within the first decade of the twenty-first century.

7.2 THE NEAR COLLAPSE OF THE GLOBAL FINANCIAL SYSTEM

The continuing economic malaise in America during the 1960s and 1970s supported the Chicago School view of government regulation as inept and inefficient. Thus, Friedman and Stigler found their intellectual and political agenda in harmony with the needs and ambitions of the largest capitalist country in the world. To support their deregulatory movement, Stigler developed a theory of government regulation that attributed such regulation to narrow self-interest on the part of special interest groups and regulators themselves. Because neoclassical economists had provided no better explanation for regulation, his theory became the "perceived wisdom" at the time (Moore 1986, xxiv). By the end of the 1980s,

---

[7] As discussed in Chapter 8, Friedman's (1970) warnings appear prescient in view of rising corporate activism in the post-pandemic world.

Friedman and Stigler's view of government regulation had thoroughly captured the discipline of economics as well as the related disciplines of finance and accounting.[8]

Inspired by Friedman's (1953) *Essays on Positive Economics*, researchers in finance and accounting began to discount the importance of unrealistic assumptions in their economic theory. In addition to the assumption of narrow self-interest, these researchers readily accepted the assumption of efficient capital markets (Fama 1970). The latter assumption was the natural extension of the assumption of perfect competition in price theory.[9] The broad acceptance of the simplified assumptions of neoclassical economic theory had a dramatic effect on academic research in finance and accounting. In finance, for example, these simplified assumptions led to Modigliani and Miller's (1958) theorem on the independence of firm value, leverage, and payout policy. Their theorem was valid given its simplified assumptions (including perfect capital markets, no transaction costs, and the ability of investors to borrow without restriction at the same terms as the firm), but the implication that capital structure had no effect on firm value turned out to be empirically incorrect (Jensen 2000). In accounting, these simplified assumptions reduced research in financial reporting and corporate governance to studies of stock price reactions to accounting information and control settings.

The neoclassical economic theory out of Chicago, however, made capitalist economies vulnerable by maximizing the role of narrow self-interest and minimizing the role of financial regulation in the economy. Historical studies by Chandler (1977) and Johnson and Kaplan (1987) revealed the importance of advances in accounting and financial control in the development of capitalism and the firm. Similarly, Douglass North (1991) documented the importance of formal contracting as well as informal rules and norms in the rise of capitalism. According to Jacob Soll's (2014) work of historical economics, *The Reckoning*, double-entry accounting and a culture of transparency and accountability allowed free-market capitalism to arise first in northern Italy and then spread to the Netherlands, Britain, and the United States In my book, *Social Norms and the Theory of the Firm* (Stevens 2019), I devote a chapter to

---

[8] Applying Stigler's theory of economic regulation, the only rationale for regulation in finance and accounting became the self-interested concerns of special interest groups and regulators (Watts and Zimmerman 1986).

[9] The Efficient Market Hypothesis was so readily accepted by 1978 that researchers in finance and accounting were already labeling contrary evidence an "anomaly" (Jensen 1978).

the importance of social and moral norms in the development of capitalism and the firm. These historical studies suggest that the Chicago School ignored important economic and social institutions that were critical to the survival of capitalism.[10]

The unregulated environment of the second industrial revolution left the door wide open for Robber Barons in banking and industry to use opaque financial reporting, insider trading, and stock price manipulation to amass huge fortunes. These riches, however, were soon dwarfed by the wealth of investment bankers and hedge fund managers under the new deregulatory environment encouraged by the Chicago School. From the mid-1960s to the mid-1980s, the prevailing view was that market prices followed a random walk and investors could only earn above-average risk-adjusted returns by being lucky. By the 1990s, however, leading researchers in economics and finance were joining forces with hedge fund managers to get in on the great wealth being made on Wall Street. These hedge fund managers created special investment vehicles to avoid government regulation, use huge amounts of leverage, and allow their partners and private investors to earn "more money than God" (Mallaby 2010).

The most famous example of the involvement of leading market researchers in hedge funds is Long-Term Capital Management (LTCM). John W. Meriwether, a successful Wall Street broker and Chicago MBA, left the Arbitrage Group at Salomon Brothers in 1994 to start his own hedge fund. While at Salomon, he had accumulated a group of talented academics from leading Ph.D. programs, including Eric Rosenfeld and Lawrence Hilibrand from MIT. In launching his new hedge fund, however, Meriwether decided to go for "the leading scholar in finance, and considered a genius by many in his field" (Lowenstein 2000, 28). After completing his Ph.D. in economics at MIT in 1970 under Paul Samuelson, Robert C. Merton had improved upon the formula for deriving the price of stock options developed by Fischer Black and Myron S. Scholes (Black and Scholes 1973). He had also trained several generations of Wall Street traders, including Eric Rosenfeld. Merton jumped at the opportunity to join LTCM, named after its investment strategies based on long-term bond arbitrage. To help sell the fund, Meriwether also recruited Myron Scholes who was better known on Wall Street and had also worked at Salomon Brothers.

---

[10] North (1991, 97) defines institutions as "humanly devised constraints that structure political, economic and social interactions." In sociology, Richard Scott (1995, 33) defines institutions as "cognitive, normative, and regulative structures and activities that provide stability and meaning to social behavior."

Meriwether and his academic partners at LTCM were strong proponents of the efficient market hypothesis out of Chicago, and their investment strategies took advantage of temporary market anomalies that occurred due to tax rules, government regulation, or the idiosyncratic needs of large financial institutions. Merton, in particular, was eager to showcase his financial theories on Wall Street. As explained by Roger Lowenstein (2000, 30) in his book, *When Genius Failed: The Rise and Fall of Long-Term Capital Management*:

> Derivatives (contracts that derived their value from stocks, bonds, or other assets) ... had blurred the lines between investment firms, banks, and other financial institutions. In the seamless world of derivatives, a world that Merton had helped to invent, anyone could assume the risk of loaning money, or of providing equity, simply by structuring an appropriate contract. It was function that mattered, not form. This had already been proved in the world of mortgages, once supplied exclusively by local banks and now largely funded by countless disparate investors who bought tiny pieces of securitized mortgage pools.

The price anomalies identified by LTCM were far too small to profit from without the multiplier of borrowed money. Thus, their investment strategies required huge amounts of leverage. LTCM's highly leveraged arbitrage strategy was initially highly profitable. "Even after subtracting its 2 percent management fee and its 25 percent performance fee, LTCM returned 19.9 percent in its ten months of trading in 1994, followed by 42.8 percent in 1995 and 40.8 percent the year after.... The gains from its convergence trades were not correlated with any stock or bond index. Small wonder that LTCM had no difficulty raising capital" (Mallaby 2010, 226).

As their fund balance increased and more investment banks were needed to execute their trades, however, LTCM's investment strategies were copied by competitors. LTCM's profit shrank to only 17.1 percent in 1997, and the partners returned $2.7 billion of outsiders' capital to ensure that nearly a third of the remaining fund was from their own capital. In October 1997, Merton and Scholes received the heady news that they had won the Nobel Prize in Economic Sciences for the new finance spawned by their options-pricing models. In 1998, however, LTCM lost $4.6 billion in less than four months following the Russian bond crisis. This loss represented more than 80 percent of the fund's nearly $5 billion in remaining capital, but the partners had further leveraged the fund by entering into $1 trillion in derivatives contracts with the nation's largest investment banks. By August 21, the stock market had begun to tumble, and there were rumors that Lehman Brothers in particular might go under. To avoid a wider market collapse, the Federal Reserve negotiated an orderly liquidation of LTCM's securities and derivatives with eleven banks agreeing to contribute $300 million each. Due to its weakened financial condition, however, Lehman Brothers contributed much less to the bailout. As for the LTCM partners, "The wizards of Wall Street personally lost $1.9 billion" (Lowenstein 2000, 219).

The clear takeaway from the blowup of LTCM should have been greater humility regarding modern finance theory and the need for greater government regulation in the hedge fund industry. The message that many Wall Street firms appeared to receive, however, was that financial firms deemed "too big to fail" could expect a bailout from the Fed. The deregulatory environment encouraged by the Chicago School would continue unabated. In 1999, the US Congress repealed the Glass–Steagall Act and replaced it with the Gramm–Leach–Bliley Act. The new legislation removed the wall of separation between investment and commercial banks, allowing commercial banks to underwrite and sell securities as well as take deposits and make loans. As part of the New Deal in 1938, Congress had established the Federal National Mortgage Association (Fannie Mae) to purchase certain mortgages from originators and securitize them for resale to investors. Fannie Mae went public in 1970, the same year that the federal government allowed it to purchase conventional mortgages, and issued its first mortgage-backed security in 1981. In response to the Clinton administration's (1993–2001) push to extend mortgages to low-income borrowers, Fannie Mae and the more recently formed Federal Home Loan Mortgage Corporation (Freddie Mac) became increasingly active in the mortgage-backed security business.

Seeing the opportunity for profits, Wall Street investment banks began to securitize the higher-yield mortgage loans that were either "subprime" or "Alt-A" (between prime and subprime). By 2005 and 2006, Wall Street was securitizing one-third more loans than Fannie Mae and Freddie Mac, and more than 70 percent of those loans were subprime or Alt-A. Rapidly losing market share to Wall Street, Fannie Mae and Freddie Mac loosened their underwriting standards. From 2005 to 2008, they not only purchased riskier loans for securitization, but they also began to purchase subprime and Alt-A mortgage-backed securities from investment banks. The resulting torrent of liquidity and profits generated a moral hazard all along the mortgage securitization chain. Mortgage brokers were compensated based on the volume of loans they generated, while mortgage securitizers were compensated based on the number of new mortgage-backed securities created and sold. Thus, agents up and down the mortgage chain reaped enormous profits by keeping the gravy train going despite the potential for huge losses for investors and taxpayers.

The outcome of this moral hazard should have been foreseeable. By the third quarter of 2006, home prices were falling and mortgage delinquencies were on the rise. Despite these warning signs, investment banks such as Bear Stearns and Lehman Brothers kept ordering up mortgage loans, packaging them into securities, and taking huge profits. By the end of 2007, however, subprime mortgage lenders and investment banks began to fail. In January 2008, Bank of America announced that it would be acquiring the ailing subprime lender Countrywide. Bear Stearns was bought by J. P. Morgan with government assistance later in the spring, and Fannie Mae and Freddie Mac were in conservatorship by the end of the summer. In September, Lehman Brothers filed for bankruptcy after it failed to receive a bailout from the government. American International Group (AIG), however, was eventually bailed out due to its massive credit default swap portfolio. Before the carnage was over, the US government had initiated its fourth bailout of a major financial institution and was on the hook for trillions of dollars through more than two dozen programs aimed at stabilizing the financial system.

In addition to encouraging the deregulatory environment, the Chicago School promoted strong financial incentives for top executives. For example, Jensen and Murphy (1990) argued that executive compensation was not sufficiently "high-powered." To better align the self-interest of top executives with the owners of the firm, they argued, their compensation should be tied substantially to the stock price. In response, corporate boards increased the financial incentives of top executives. Between 1992 and 2000, the average inflation-adjusted pay of CEOs at S&P 500 firms climbed from $3.5 million to $14.7 million (Bebchuk and Fried 2004). This increase in CEO pay, which included shares of stock granted as part of stock options, far outpaced the growth in average employee pay. As a result, the ratio of average CEO pay to average worker pay at these large firms grew from 140:1 to 500:1 (Revell 2003). Compensation consultants and corporate boards frequently used the writings of Jensen to justify high-powered financial incentives (Bebchuk and Fried 2003). Jensen's writings had similarly encouraged the widespread use of Leveraged Buyouts (LBOs) by corporate raiders in the 1980s to discipline the self-interested behavior of managers.

The deregulatory environment encouraged by the Chicago School, combined with the reduced lending standards encouraged by government policy, created a house of cards that would soon topple. The actions of top executives at Fannie Mae and Freddie Mac demonstrate the effects of this perfect storm of deregulation and greed. When Franklin Raines accepted the CEO position at Fannie Mae in 1999, he had an impressive resume as a partner at investment bank Lazard Freres and budget director under President Clinton. Based on Jensen's finance theory, Congress had mandated in 1992 that "pay for performance" be a substantial component of top executives' total compensation at Fannie Mae (Emmons and Sierra 2004). In an effort to turbocharge Raines's financial incentives, Fannie Mae's board tied his annual bonus to annual earnings goals. During the four-year period from 2000 to 2003, Fannie Mae reported increased earnings each year that surpassed the annual earnings goal. During this period, Raines amassed $13 million in annual cash bonuses and almost $30 million worth of Fannie Mae shares under his lucrative compensation package (Bebchuk and Fried 2005).

In December 2004, however, the same board that granted Raines his high-powered compensation package demanded his resignation. This action followed the determination by the SEC that Fannie Mae had used accounting manipulation to increase its earnings over the previous four years by at least $10 billion, wiping out a large portion of the company's total reported profits during those years (Bebchuk and Fried 2005). Fannie Mae's regulator, the Office of Federal Housing Enterprise Oversight (OFHEO), determined that the company's hedging activities and derivative transactions violated Generally Accepted Accounting Principles (GAAP). Also in violation of GAAP, Fannie Mae had used a "cookie jar" reserve for its portfolio of mortgage-backed securities to smooth its quarterly earnings. OFHEO concluded that Raines had created a toxic culture that encouraged lax internal controls and inaccurate financial reporting (Fannie Uncovered 2004). The accounting scandal at Fannie Mae in 2004 and a similar accounting scandal at Freddie Mac generated widespread calls for increased government regulation. However, the opportunistic culture at the two government-sponsored enterprises (GSEs) continued. The results would be disastrous for investors and taxpayers. Fannie Mae and Freddie Mac were completely wiped out by the mortgage market crash in 2008. From January 2008 through the third quarter of 2010, the two GSEs lost $229 billion, requiring a bailout from the US Treasury of $151 billion (FCIC 2011).

In 2009, the US Congress created the Financial Crisis Inquiry Commission (FCIC) to investigate the causes of the great market collapse of 2007–08. The FCIC report, published in 2011, concluded that the collapse was fully avoidable. The Fed responded to the dot-com crash in

2000 and the resulting recession by cutting interest rates, and the low rates on bank deposits caused investors to look for higher returns. At the same time, government policies encouraged weaker mortgage lending standards. The Fed took little action, however, to stem the tide of subprime mortgage lending and securitization these policies encouraged. Bond rating agencies used outdated risk models and not only rated packaged securities with high-risk mortgages as top quality (AAA), but they also earned record profits by instructing banks how to package the mortgage-backed securities. For their part, accounting firms were ineffective at stopping the accounting manipulation used to conceal the true financial condition of financial institutions up and down the mortgage chain.[11]

As for the major financial firms, the FCIC (2011, xviii–xix) concluded that a key cause of the crisis was their dramatic failures of corporate governance and risk management:

There was a view that instincts for self-preservation inside major financial firms would shield them from fatal risk-taking without the need for a steady regulatory hand, which, the firms argued, would stifle innovation. Too many of these institutions acted recklessly, taking on too much risk, with too little capital, and with too much dependence on short-term funding. In many respects, this reflected a fundamental change in these institutions, particularly the large investment banks and bank holding companies, which focused their activities increasingly on risky trading activities that produced hefty profits. They took on enormous exposures in acquiring and supporting subprime lenders and creating, packaging, repackaging, and selling trillions of dollars in mortgage-related securities, including synthetic financial products. Like Icarus, they never feared flying ever closer to the sun.

The Commission singled out the role of corporate governance failures at Lehman Brothers. As described in an inside account by Lawrence G. McDonald (McDonald and Robinson 2009), Lehman's chairman and CEO, Richard S. Fuld Jr., was an aloof leader who ignored the warnings of his top-level managing directors and executive committee. Fuld and his president and chief operating officer, Joe Gregory, had large offices on the thirty-first floor of their office building, and they were rarely seen by the rank-and-file on the lower floors. Like the other investment banks, Fuld and Gregory had developed a culture of big rewards and huge bonuses at Lehman, and they made sure that they received the lion's share. As the firm teetered on the verge of collapse at the end of 2007, with bond

---

[11] Auditing researchers have documented that it is very difficult to uncover financial manipulation in an opportunistic environment where management is determined to profit from such manipulation (see Ege, Knechel, Lamoreaux, and Maksymov 2020).

prices crashing and the stock market beginning its deep descent, Fuld and Gregory paid themselves huge stock bonuses valued at $35 million for Fuld and $29 million for Gregory.

At the time of LTCM's collapse in 1998, Lehman had similarly been at death's door. Rather than strengthen its capital and liquidity position, however, Lehman hit the gas pedal. Fuld and Gregory acted like they could spend their way out of trouble or "had decided to make themselves so rich that it wouldn't matter to them whether the ship survived or not" (McDonald and Robinson 2009, 274). By the time the ship finally went down on September 15, 2008, the firm had $82 billion in leveraged mortgages, $30 billion in Leveraged Buyouts (LBOs), $40 billion in Collateralized Mortgage-Backed Securities (CMBSs), $5 billion in the oil industry, and $20 billion in hedge funds. These purchases were funded by over $700 billion in debt, as Lehman's leverage approached forty-four times its equity capital.

Lehman Brothers focused on investments in unregulated industries including shadow banks (mortgage lenders who borrowed their funds), LBOs, CMBSs, and hedge funds. Its major source of short-term funding was also in an unregulated market. The commercial paper market was the quickest, cheapest, and easiest way to get funding, and it was not regulated by the SEC. As trust and confidence in investment banks such as Bear Stearns and Lehman Brothers broke down, however, the commercial paper market froze up. This precipitated a run on Bear Stearns first and then Lehman. The Federal Reserve worked with JPMorgan Chase to arrange a bailout of Bear Stearns. When the Bank of America and Barclays looked over Lehman's books to consider a similar bailout, however, it became clear that Fuld had thoroughly "cooked the books" by significantly overstating assets and understating liabilities. Thus, Bank of America and Barclays refused to acquire Lehman without significant funding guarantees from the Fed.

On September 15, 2008, the secretary of the US Treasury, Henry Paulson, announced that he had elected to allow the 158-year-old investment bank to fail. Valued at about $660 billion, Lehman's Chapter 11 bankruptcy would be six times larger than any previous bankruptcy. Lehman's irresponsible behavior included peddling its toxic mortgage-backed securities to governments and financial institutions around the globe, including those in the United Kingdom, Continental Europe, Iceland, and throughout Asia. The collapse of Lehman Brothers and other major financial institutions was precipitated by another act of Congress in 2000, the Commodity Futures Modernization Act (CFMA).

The CFMA deregulated the entire business of trading a credit default swap (CDS) and unleashed a weapon of mass destruction: the ability of anyone to take out insurance and bet against the survival of financial institutions and major corporations. "In times to come, hedge funds and investors, even banks, would start betting against these big mortgage corporations' survival, against corporations with big debts, and against corporations that were just plain inefficient" (McDonald and Robinson 2009, 61). As the FCIC (2011) report concluded, the deregulatory environment encouraged by the Chicago School played a key role in the most devastating crisis of capitalism since the Great Depression.

7.3 AMARTYA SEN'S JOURNEY TO RESCUE CAPITALISM FROM THE CAPITALISTS

The Ganges River and the Brahmaputra River originate in the same frozen lake high up in the western Himalayas, and they both empty into the Bay of Bengal. The great Ganges, however, runs quickly south through the steep mountains before wandering southeast through the plains of northern India, whereas the Brahmaputra flows east across the slowly flattening Himalayas before jogging south to join the Ganges. The Ganges-Brahmaputra delta system is the largest river delta in the world, more than twice the size of the river delta of the Nile, and it played a major role in the explosion of international trade in the seventeenth century (Sudipta Sen 2019). In 1871, the Eastern Bengal Railway opened a new line from Calcutta northeastward to where the two great rivers meet. Because of the wide expanse of the two rivers – the Brahmaputra is five to eight miles (eight to thirteen km) across during the rainy season – the only way to cross over to the other side is by boat. The small town of Goalando (also spelled Goalundo or Gaolondo), on the southern bank, instantly became a major transportation hub for travel to eastern parts of Bengal. Travelers making the long journey from Calcutta to the major Bengal city of Dhaka could now take a train to Goalando, board a steamboat for an overnight ferry east to the port town of Narayanganj on the northern bank, and then take another train north into Dhaka.[12]

In 1941, an eight-year-old boy and his father would leave Dhaka and take the historic steamboat ferry west on their way to his new primary

---

[12] The overnight steamboat ferry became famous for the chicken curry the Muslim boatmen served over rice to the passengers. For more information on the Ganges River and its role in the religions and cultures of India, see Sudipta Sen's (2019) book, *Ganges: The Many Pasts of an Indian River*.

school. The father, a chemistry professor at Dhaka University, had originally placed his son in the local missionary school at St. Gregory's. After the Japanese occupation of Burma, however, he became concerned that the rapidly expanding city might become the next victim of India's alliance with the Allies in World War II. The boy's maternal grandfather was a well-known Sanskrit scholar who taught at the progressive Indian school in Santiniketan. Due to his father's wartime concerns, Amartya Sen moved from his traditional western school in the city to a remote Indian school with open classrooms. The move meant that Sen would learn the ancient Hindu language of Sanskrit under the loving influence of his grandfather, Kshita Mohan Sen. It also meant that he would meet the famous founder of the progressive school, the Nobel-prize-winning poet Rabindranath Tagore. The move would also bring the young student in contact with leading dignitaries of state such as Mahatma Gandhi and Eleanor Roosevelt. Before leaving Santiniketan to attend college in Calcutta ten years later, Sen would witness firsthand the futile attempts of India's Hindu and Muslim leaders to form a united, secular state after independence from Britain in 1947.

As he had done on previous steamboat trips, Sen asked his father to take him below deck to view the pumping steel rods of the engine amid the distinctive aroma of hot oil and grease. Back on deck, he observed the constantly varying riverbank, alternating between thick marshes, wooded canopies, and busy villages teaming with curious little children who would never cross the threshold of a school. Sen enjoyed attempting to identify the many varieties of exotic plants and flowers on the riverbank or just below the surface of the water as well as the various species of birds circling overhead. Shiny black river dolphins would occasionally appear beside the boat along with teams of flying fish skimming over the water. Sen noted the shifting sandbars and retreating soil suggesting that the powerful river had overflowed its banks during the rainy season, submerging towns and villages and threatening human life. He would later view the ambivalent nature of the river as "a captivating analogy for the struggle for a secure role in society – a society that can both help and decimate the human beings relying on it" (Sen 2022, 23).

The Japanese threat would soon subside, but a new threat would rise up to make it impossible for Sen to return to his beloved city of Dhaka. As independence from Britain approached, the formerly peaceful region of Bengal erupted in violence as Hindus and Muslims clashed in bloody riots and their leaders agitated for separate statehood. In the partition of India in 1947, the predominantly Muslim regions in the northeast and northwest were formed into East Pakistan and West Pakistan before further conflict in 1971 led to the formation of two independent Muslim states: Bangladesh and Pakistan. Meanwhile, the Hindu region of West Bengal remained a part of India with its capital in Calcutta (now Kolkata). Founded as an East India Company trading post in the early eighteenth century, Calcutta was chosen as India's original capital when the British government replaced the company rulership of India with the British Raj in 1773.[13]

After completing his broad primary education at Santiniketan in 1951, Sen entered the same Indian college where Charles Henry Tawney had learned Sanskrit, translated and cataloged many ancient Hindu writings, and served as Principal from 1876 to 1892. At Presidency College in Calcutta, Sen began to read the writings of a Scottish Enlightenment philosopher named Adam Smith. In *The Wealth of Nations*, Sen came across Smith's analysis of the role of rivers in the development of the market economy. Smith attributed the booming trade in Bengal during the seventeenth and eighteenth centuries to its highly navigable network of rivers and streams. Smith's insightful analysis of Bengal and the history of the East India Company, although he had never actually visited the South Asian colony, impressed Sen so much that he decided to major in economics with a minor in mathematics. Writing in his memoir, Sen (2022, 32) recalls his instant connection with Smith in his early years at Presidency College:

Adam Smith's speculation, I could happily note, on the relation between the presence of navigable rivers and the flourishing of civilizations offered more substance to think about. Given the traditionally river-centered life of the Bengalis, it is quite natural that social and cultural issues are frequently given some kind of a river-based analogy. The river supports human life, sustains it, destroys it and can kill it. The society that has grown up around it can do the same to individual human beings.

Sen also came across Smith's moral theory in *A Theory of Moral Sentiments* and found it particularly interesting. It was only later, as a Ph.D. student in economics at Trinity College in Cambridge, that Sen was introduced to the narrow version of Adam Smith created by classical and neoclassical economists. Shortly after Keynes's departure, the Economics Department at Cambridge had splintered into two warring

---

[13] India is the birthplace of four of the world's major religions – Hinduism, Buddhism, Jainism, and Sikhism – and is home to over 170 million Muslims and almost 30 million Christians. Nevertheless, its constitution states that it is a secular nation.

camps: the neoclassical economists represented by A. C. Pigou and Dennis Robertson and the neo-Keynesian economists represented by Joan Robinson and Richard Kahn. While the Economics Department had a reputation for being "left-wing" and even had a leading Marxist on the faculty named Maurice Dobb, Sen found the faculty to be generally unconcerned with issues of inequality, poverty, and exploitation that had become important to him in India. Sen would later reflect that among the faculty at Cambridge, it was the "right-wing" neoclassical economist A. C. Pigou who seemed to take the greatest interest in such issues (Sen, Deaton, and Besley 2020).

When Sen suggested a dissertation topic in welfare economics to Joan Robinson, he was unsuccessful in persuading her that it was a topic worth pursuing. Robinson urged Sen to focus on research related to "imperfect competition" and help her "put the last nail in the coffin of neoclassical economics." In his memoir, Sen (2022, 288) admits that he had never heard of neoclassical economics before arriving at Cambridge and that he soon learned that it was simply "mainstream economics, with a cluster of maximizing agents – capitalists, labourers, consumers and so on – who follow mechanical rules of maximization by equating marginal this with marginal that." Rather than join Robinson in her quest to destroy neoclassical economic theory, however, Sen determined to enhance the theory by incorporating important social and moral factors. Given what he had learned about political economy from the "real" Adam Smith, Sen was convinced that he could be successful.

Sen found an unlikely ally in the Economics Department at the University of Chicago. During his time at the Cowles Commission from 1946 to 1949, Kenneth J. Arrow (1921–2017) had identified a conceptual problem in the concept of "social choice" (Maskin 2019).[14] Arrow set up the problem as follows: a group of individuals (i.e., a society) must choose from a set of social alternatives, and individual preferences must be combined using a *social welfare function* (SWF) to determine the socially preferred alternative. One commonly used SWF, he argued, was majority rule. In examining the majority rule SWF, however, Arrow discovered that allowing more than two alternatives in the set of alternatives could lead to suboptimal social choices. This led him to wonder if there was some other reasonable way of determining social preferences from individual preferences. Given three natural and reasonable conditions, Arrow

---

[14] Arrow later discovered that the French philosopher and mathematician Condorcet had originally discovered the problem in the late eighteenth century.

demonstrated that the only SWF satisfying all three conditions is a *dictatorship*.[15] In his famous "impossibility theorem," Arrow proved that no other SWF could satisfy all three conditions given his general setup.

Arrow published his theoretical results, which became his Ph.D. dissertation at Columbia, in a book entitled *Social Choice and Individual Values* (Arrow 1951). While the significance of Arrow's theoretical results was initially lost on the economics faculty at both Chicago and Cambridge, the book drew the attention of two talented undergraduate students at Presidency College. Sukhamoy Chakravarty had come across the book in a local bookstore and borrowed it to share with his classmate, Amartya Sen (Sen 1970/2017, xiv):

In long sessions sitting in the Coffee House on College Street, across the road from our college, Sukhamoy and I discussed Arrow's formal results and informal insights, including the significance of the "impossibility theorem." That was the beginning of my life-long interest in the subject. The book fitted in very well with my already developing interest in democracy and justice. I took an immediate liking to social choice theory as a deeply engaging subject, even though I realized that using a mixture of mathematical and non-mathematical reasoning to address very basic social problems of the world appeared rather eccentric to most of my classmates and teachers.

Arrow's social choice theory and other breakthroughs in general equilibrium theory would earn him the Nobel Prize in Economic Sciences in 1972.[16] Arrow's theoretical breakthroughs supplemented Sen's growing interest in political economy, which at the time included the writings of Adam Smith and Karl Marx. Sen and his fellow classmates at Presidency College were heavily influenced by the Marxian line of thinking that was popular at the time in Calcutta. However, another book soon arrived in the Calcutta bookstores, written by Harvard economist John Kenneth Galbraith and entitled, *American Capitalism: The Concept of Countervailing Power* (Galbraith 1952). While neoclassical economists panned the book for coming from an institutional economist, and its impact was generally limited to the public sphere, Sen found Galbraith's book a refreshing and important counterbalance to some of Marx's views (Sen, Deaton, and Besley 2020, 3–4):

[15] The three "reasonable" conditions provided by Arrow included that the SWF should always work no matter what preferences individuals happen to have (the Unrestricted Domain condition), the SWF should always select the alternative that individuals prefer (the Pareto condition), and the SWF should ignore irrelevant alternatives (the Independence of Irrelevant Alternatives condition).

[16] Arrow was only fifty-one years old at the time he received his Nobel Prize, and he remains the youngest economist to ever win the award.

If Arrow filled a big gap in my naive thinking, Galbraith filled another, in particular how to keep in check privileged people with their particular social ambitions through a system of countervailing powers ... (Galbraith's new book was) a denial of Marx's temptation to rely on his favored set of values, which he saw as good for society. Even if the idea of the "dictatorship of the proletariat" may sound attractive in an egalitarian way, it can play havoc with building a pluralist society.... Marx shared the common illusion that if somehow you get dedicated people to take charge of the government, they are going to govern things well. Ken Galbraith's "American Capitalism," which in a sense is a praise of capitalism (one aspect of it), helped to shatter the illusion. He presented quite a profound understanding of the corruption of power and the need to restrain even dedicated people, including those dedicated to high political objectives.

Prior to leaving India for Cambridge in 1953, therefore, Sen had come under the influence of a highly mathematical neoclassical economist from Chicago (Arrow), an institutional economist from Harvard (Galbraith), and a moral economist from the Scottish Enlightenment (Adam Smith). He had also lived through a very traumatic period of Indian history. Sen had lived under the worrying developments of World War II and the Bengal famine in 1943. He had also witnessed the communal violence leading up to the 1947 partition of India, including the widespread rioting and murdering throughout the formerly peaceful region of Bengal. Like the son of Charles Henry Tawney, Sen's early life experiences in India would forever color his perspective.

Sen found a dissertation topic that was acceptable to Joan Robinson involving how to choose appropriate techniques of production in a cheap-labor economy. He received a coveted Prize Fellowship at Cambridge for his topic that included four years of funding. After completing his dissertation research in about a year, Sen used the extra time "to learn some serious philosophy" (Sen 2022, 336). He had become a member of the elite philosophical discussion group called "the Apostles," which counted Charles Henry Tawney and John Maynard Keynes among its former members. Thus, he began to study the philosophical work of leading Apostles including Henry Sidgwick and G. E. Moore, who viewed the question of what ends and goals to pursue in life as a moral question that must be answered before political or economic issues are addressed. After completing his Ph.D. in 1959 and spending several years researching and teaching at American universities (including MIT and Stanford), Sen returned to India to take a chaired position at the Delhi School of Economics from 1963 to 1971.

Upon his return to India, it was impossible for Sen to overlook the widespread poverty and lack of crucial public services such as public education and basic health care. Yet it was in his home country that Sen found Adam

Smith's writings particularly useful. He contrasted the popular concept of the "social contract" view of morality, whereby people undertake moral actions only in the expectation that others will reciprocate, with Smith's notion of moral obligations that people accept as their responsibility or duty. In contrast to Marx's deep skepticism of capitalism, "Smith had a serious interest in supplementing market processes through the use of non-market institutions, for example by state intervention to expand public services such as government-supported education and health care. It was helpful to discuss in class how a combination of institutions might have clear advantages in overcoming divisiveness and deficiencies, especially for the seriously deprived parts of the population" (Sen 2022, 405–406):

A powerful component of Smithian moral reasoning is the use of what he called "the impartial spectator": paying attention to the lack of bias and divisiveness that we should try to utilize by imagining how someone from outside, devoid of personal or local prejudices, would assess a particular situation, including ongoing inequalities…. Our class discussions also included the fact that Smith – with his deep sympathy for the poor and the disadvantaged – always stood up against the claimed "superiority" of the better placed … (Smith) was resolutely firm in his total hatred of racism and in declaring the complete unacceptability of slavery in any form. He was furious about the slave-owners' attribution of a lower form of life to the slaves.

Sen used the example of increased educational opportunities and inequality reduction in post-war Britain, which R. H. Tawney and others had worked so hard to achieve, as something India should strive for in its own governmental policy. When talking about political and economic policy, Sen also contrasted Smith's views with that of Marx. He found that his teaching on Adam Smith was met with widespread agreement, sympathy, and pride from his students. Sen would eventually bring his unifying message of prosperity and social justice back to Britain and America through various visiting positions at Oxford and Cambridge as well as at California Berkeley and Cornell. He penned his magnum opus, *Collective Choice and Social Welfare*, in 1969 and received the Nobel Prize in Economic Sciences in 1998 for his contributions to economic theory. Sen is currently a professor of economics and philosophy at Harvard University.

7.4 SEN'S CRITIQUE OF CAPITALISM

In a published discussion of welfare economics with Angus Deaton and Tim Besley (Sen, Deaton, and Besley 2020, 7), Amartya Sen describes his combustible relationship with Joan Robinson, who became his dissertation supervisor at Cambridge in his second year. At their first meeting, Robinson told Sen she had just finished writing a book entitled *The Accumulation of Capital* (Robinson 1956) and that instead of writing essays for the two of them to discuss, he could read one chapter of her book each week and discuss it with her. Sen recalled enjoying discussing Robinson's book with the author but finding it a "politically inspired book, of an apparently left-wing kind." In one of their many confrontations, Sen recalled siding with A. C. Pigou (1920) in arguing that "if there is a downfall of capitalism, it won't be because of some subtle mistake in capital theory; it will be because of the 'mean streets' and 'withered lives' that capitalism makes many people have. And that relates to welfare economics and social choice. This upset her very much.... I don't think she understood my take on capitalism at all."

In her quest to put the last nail in the coffin of neoclassical economic theory, Robinson could not free herself from the narrow utilitarianism of that theory. Similar to Milton Friedman, she believed that economists and politicians should focus on simply maximizing economic growth. Once a county had grown rich, it could begin to think about addressing inequities and providing health care, education, and other basic needs to its poorest citizens. After his own trip to India in the 1950s, Friedman had concluded "that economic development must rest primarily on the aspirations and actions of millions of individuals risking their own capital and seeking their own fortunes" (Cherrier 2011, 343). In contrast to Robinson and Friedman, Sen saw the traditional utilitarian approach as "one of the more profound errors that you can make in development planning" (Sen, Deaton, and Besley 2020, 7).[17]

In his influential book, *On Ethics and Economics*, Sen (1987) attempts to break his discipline free of the arbitrary constraints imposed by neoclassical economists. He argues that there is no basis for disassociating the study of economics from that of ethics and political philosophy. After reminding the reader that Adam Smith was a Professor of Moral Philosophy at the University of Glasgow and the subject of economics was for a long time seen as a branch of ethics, Sen (1987, 3–4) identifies two central issues where economics needs to incorporate ethics:

---

[17] Wherever this narrow utilitarian approach has been implemented in a developing country, it has typically resulted in disaster. The involvement of Milton Friedman, Arnold Harberger, and former Ph.D. students at Chicago (the "Chicago Boys") in the economic policy of Chile has remained highly controversial. Their "value-free" approach to economic development was unsuccessful and led to accusations of putting economic growth above democratic ideals (see Hammond 2011).

First, there is the problem of human motivation related to the broadly ethical question of "How should one live?" To emphasize this connection is not the same as asserting that people will always act in ways they will themselves morally defend, but only to recognize that ethical deliberations cannot be totally inconsequential to actual human behavior. I shall call this "the ethics-related view of motivation." The second issue concerns the judgement of social achievement ... (the) "ethics-related view of social achievement" cannot stop the evaluation short at some arbitrary point like satisfying "efficiency." The assessment has to be more fully ethical, and take a broader view of "the good." This is a point of some importance again in the context of modern economics, especially modern welfare economics.

Sen is particularly critical of Friedman's arbitrary emphasis on positive theory and Stigler's arbitrary emphasis on narrow self-interest. Regarding the former, Sen (1987, 7) argues that "(t)he methodology of so-called 'positive economics' has not only shunned normative analysis in economics, it has also had the effect of ignoring a variety of complex ethical considerations which affect actual human behavior and which, from the point of view of the economists studying such behaviour, are primarily matters of fact rather than of normative judgement." Regarding the latter, Sen notes that there is neither evidence for the claim that self-interest maximization provides the best approximation to actual human behavior nor that it leads necessarily to optimum economic outcomes. He asserts that an unbiased reading of Adam Smith's writings does not lend support to a narrow interpretation of self-interested behavior either in his moral philosophy or his political economy (Sen 1987, 28):

The support that believers in, and advocates of, self-interested behavior have sought in Adam Smith is, in fact, hard to find on a wider and less biased reading of Smith. The professor of moral philosophy and the pioneer economist did not, in fact, lead a life of spectacular schizophrenia. Indeed, it is precisely the narrowing of the broad Smithian view of human beings, in modern economies, that can be seen as one of the major deficiencies of contemporary economic theory. This impoverishment is closely related to the distancing of economics from ethics.

Sen (1987, 14–15) is highly critical of arbitrarily narrow views of economic rationality. Neoclassical economists typically characterize rationality as (1) internal *consistency* of choice and (2) the *maximization of self-interest*. Sen criticizes the first characterization by arguing that "even the very idea of purely *internal consistency* is not cogent, since what we regard as consistent in a set of observed choices must depend on the interpretation of those choices and on some features *external* to choice as such (e.g., the nature of our preferences, aims, values, motivations)." Sen criticizes the second by arguing that "(t)he self-interest view of rationality involves a firm rejection of the 'ethics-related' view of motivation.... To see any departure from self-interest maximization as evidence of irrationality must imply a rejection of the role of ethics in actual decision making (other than some variant or other of that exotic moral view known as 'ethical egoism')"

Sen's response to Arrow's stunning "impossibility theorem" is a powerful example of how economists can incorporate social and moral issues of importance to capitalist societies in their theory. Condorcet had already shown in the eighteenth century that majority rule decisions can be inconsistent with individual preferences and in some voting situations can lead to no winner at all (generally beginning with more than two options). Arrow (1951) showed that Condorcet's pessimistic result applied to *all* social choice rules that satisfy some minimal conditions of apparent reasonableness. Further, Arrow's impossibility theorem showed that when the unattractive rule of dictatorial choice is eliminated from consideration with these minimal conditions present, *no* social choice rule works effectively and consistently in combining individual preferences.

Sen and his fellow schoolmate at Presidency College, Sukhamoy Chakravarty, found Arrow's result challenging on several fronts. First, the proof of his impossibility theorem was quite complicated and it applied a different kind of mathematical logic than the young students had confronted in their college courses. Second, moving away from the mathematical logic and underlying proof, there was the question of how significant the result was and its implications for economic and political policy. In the Marxist climate of Calcutta at the time, some commentators interpreted Arrow's result as an excuse for authoritarianism. Sen and Chakravarty spent long hours debating the significance of Arrow's impossibility theorem (Sen 2022, 205):

> I particularly remember one long afternoon sitting next to a window in the coffee house, as Sukhamoy talked about alternative interpretations of Arrow's result.... He felt that it was not immediately clear what the implications of Arrow's theorem were for political democracy and for integrated social judgements, and there was a lot to be done to work out how to proceed from Arrow's stunning mathematical result to the practical world of social choice and of political and economic decisions.

Friedman was in the process of completing his methodological essay at around this same time, and he and many other neoclassical economists in the West simply discounted the underlying assumptions of Arrow's social choice theory or rejected the popular interpretation of his impossibility theorem on purely ideological grounds. Sen and Chakravarty recognized, however, that Arrow's theorem had particular significance to the newly independent state of India. Many of India's leaders and fellow citizens were wondering if they could have democracy in their young country or if it was all a pipe dream (Sen 2022, 206):

> In many academic discussions in Calcutta at the time, Arrow's ideas got a good deal of airing. A common interpretation was that you simply couldn't have democratic consistency. In particular we needed to scrutinize the apparent conditions of reasonableness of the conditions – or axioms – that Arrow tended to impose. I was not at all convinced that we could not choose other axioms that were also reasonable and which permitted non-dictatorial social choice.... Social choice problems, as investigated by Arrow, became critically important parts of my long-term intellectual engagement.

James M. Buchanan (1919–2013), another Ph.D. student of Frank Knight who would receive the Nobel Prize in Economic Sciences in 1986, was particularly dismissive of Arrow's impossibility theorem. Buchanan (1954) asked whether it made sense to talk about consistency properties of social choice (i.e., "collective rationality") since a society could not engage in integrated reflections like an individual can. It wasn't until Sen's year at MIT in 1960–61 that he was able to address Buchanan's objections. He concluded that they were likely valid when it came to voting outcomes, but that did not exclude the theorem's significance for social choice in general (Sen 2022, 377):

> If, for example, social policy a would yield more social welfare than policy b, and policy b more social welfare than policy c, then we should be able to presume that policy a would offer more social welfare than policy c, because of valuational congruity. In that case, ideas of collective rationality should make sense for social welfare judgements in a way that they would not for purely institutional outcomes. Thus, in the case of welfare judgements, demands such as transitivity of social preference would make sense.

During one of his semesters at MIT, Sen taught Paul Samuelson's two-hour lecture on welfare economics. In the process, he realized that Samuelson had not considered how to capture the idea of interpersonal comparisons of different people's preferences. Thereafter, Sen had many discussions with Samuelson about the potential of such an approach. "He remained entirely focused on the truth that could emerge from the argument, rather than being concerned with winning the debate, which he could have done easily enough, given his dominant standing in economics" (Sen 2022, 364). When Sen returned to Cambridge in the fall of 1961, however, Joan Robinson and other members of the economics faculty were hesitant in letting Sen teach his new specialty area of welfare economics and social choice theory. It was not until his return to India in 1963 that Sen was able to teach these subjects and make steady progress on his theoretical research.

In 1970, Sen published his seminal work on welfare economics and social choice theory. He expanded Arrow's original social choice framework, consolidated his key insights, extended some of his results, questioned and relaxed some of the restrictions imposed by him, and proposed some modification of how to think about social choice. His major innovations were that (1) Arrow's impossibility result no longer holds once interpersonal comparisons are admitted for use in the social choice framework, (2) interpersonal comparisons allow considerations of personal liberties and individual rights within the axiomatic system of social choice, and (3) interpersonal comparisons allow the theory of social choice to address the legitimacy of the very idea of "social preference" as raised by James Buchanan and others (Sen 1970/2017, xix–xx).

At Cambridge, Joan Robinson had urged Sen to abandon his interests in welfare economics and social choice theory and join her in extracting the "neoclassical poison" from economics (Sen 2022, 368). The promising young scholar, however, was adamant about building upon the rigorous foundation laid by neoclassical economists rather than destroying it. Following in Sen's footsteps, researchers have continued to push the boundaries of neoclassical theory by re-examining its underlying assumptions and predictions. In particular, researchers in experimental economics, game theory, and agency theory have found that expanding the narrow assumptions of neoclassical theory has revealed the importance of Adam Smith's moral foundation for capitalism. This fruitful area of research is of critical importance for both developed and developing countries that would like to provide their citizens with the prosperity and freedom that only capitalism can provide.

7.5 CONCLUSION

The deregulatory environment encouraged by the Chicago School unleashed the power of the market but also increased the exposure of capitalist societies around the world to the vulnerabilities and excesses of unregulated markets. The inevitable result of that deregulatory environment was a severe market crash and the near collapse of the global financial system in 2007–08. This latest market crash uncovered widespread corruption and opportunism up and down the mortgage security chain and required immediate taxpayer-funded bailouts of major financial institutions, many of which benefited handsomely from the deregulatory environment. Polanyi's theory of the double movement helps explain the movement to deregulate markets after the highly regulated postwar period, the inevitable crisis of capitalism this movement caused, and the resulting countermovement of increased regulation in its aftermath. The presence of unregulated markets continues to be a feature of modern capitalism, including the latest financial securities related to the crypto-currency markets. Thus, the interplay between Polanyi's two movements will continue into the foreseeable future and will require a wise public policy. That public policy will require an economic theory that encourages moral responsibility and grants the government a role in the proper functioning of the economy.

This chapter tells the story of Amartya Sen's attempt to rescue capitalism from the capitalists by extending neoclassical economic theory. He developed a powerful and thoughtful critique of capitalism from his early life experiences in Colonial India during World War II and postwar independent India. Sen argued that the field of economics could learn from the field of ethics, and vice versa. In particular, Sen (1987, 3–4) argued that human motivation could not be separated from the broadly ethical question of "How should one live?" He also argued that to emphasize this connection "is not the same as asserting that people will always act in ways they will themselves morally defend, but only to recognize that ethical deliberations cannot be totally inconsequential to actual human behavior." Sen found the origins of his ethics-related view of economics in Adam Smith, which he discovered reading Smith's major works prior to his exposure to the biased interpretations provided by classical and neoclassical economists. Sen's extensive knowledge of neoclassical theory, in addition to his understanding of historical and cultural realities, suggests that reintroducing Smith's moral foundation to neoclassical economic theory is both possible and desirable. The opportunities and challenges of such an approach are the topic of the final chapter.

8

The Promise of Capitalism

Joining the Search

But apart from this contemporary mood, the ideas of economists and political philosophers, both when they are right and when they are wrong, are more powerful than is commonly understood. Indeed, the world is ruled by little else. Practical men, who believe themselves to be quite exempt from any intellectual influence, are usually the slaves of some defunct economist. Madmen in authority, who hear voices in the air, are distilling their frenzy from some academic scribbler from a few years ago. I am sure that the power of vested interests is vastly exaggerated compared with the gradual encroachment of ideas.

John Maynard Keynes
The General Theory of Employment, Interest and Money

In his memoirs published in 1988, George Stigler described the essential three approaches of the Chicago School of Economics as "the shift to studies of market efficiency, the pervasiveness of competitive pressures, and the application of economics to the causes and effects of public regulation." Stigler argued that the neoclassical theory out of Chicago had "conquered the field" of economic theory that existed in the postwar period, including the historical and institutional theory that had crossed the Atlantic from Germany to the United States. He also celebrated the Chicago School's victory over all forms of neo-Keynesian economic theory, such as Joan Robinson's theory of imperfect competition (Robinson 1933) and Edward Chamberlin's theory of monopolistic competition (Chamberlin 1933). Finally, Stigler argued that "(t)he Austrian School persisted from 1870 to 1930," whereas the Chicago School had survived "for forty-odd years" from its founding at the first Mont Pélerin Society meeting in 1947 to the time of his writing (Stigler 1988, 165–167).

At the time he published his memoirs, Stigler was quite confident in the ongoing dominance of the Chicago School. I would argue, however, that 1988 was the height of its influence. The previous year, I had entered a rigorous MBA program at the Krannert School of Management at Purdue University. In my first semester, I was exposed to the new finance theory out of Chicago. As with the Harvard MBAs under Michael Jensen, I found that the theory challenged my deepest held beliefs. My first hint that the theory was incomplete was the stock market crash of October 19, 1987, which shook the confidence of my young finance professor. The combined assumptions of efficient markets, perfect competition, and narrow self-interest challenged the traditional roles of finance and accounting, and yet these two disciplines were fully captured by the new finance theory. My initial reaction to the neoclassical economic theory out of Chicago motivated me to pursue a Ph.D. degree in accounting at Indiana University. I didn't realize it at the time, but I had joined the age-old search for a moral foundation for capitalism. In this concluding chapter, I address the promise of capitalism from the perspective of those who have joined the search.[1]

8.1 THE INCOMPLETENESS OF CLASSICAL AND NEOCLASSICAL ECONOMIC THEORY

Polanyi (1944/2001) provided historical evidence that classical economic theory was heavily influenced by Darwinian Theory and unintended consequences of the early Poor Laws in England. To explain the reality of abject poverty for some members of capitalist society in the midst of abundant wealth for others, Thomas Malthus (1766–1834) developed a model of economic growth that earned political economy its reputation as "the dismal science."[2] Malthus assumed that mankind was subject to natural selection and overpopulation similar to the rest of the animal kingdom. His Darwinian logic linked a nation's standard of living to the death rate. In particular, the "Malthusian Trap" assumed that short-term gains in income through technological advances were inevitably lost through population growth. Further, anything that reduced the death

---

[1] As the epigraph to this chapter suggests (Keynes 1936, 382), the influence of "defunct economists" and "academic scribblers of some years back" is underestimated by modern-day economists and policymakers.

[2] The use of this label to describe the classical economic theory of Malthus and Ricardo has been credited to the Scottish essayist, historian and philosopher Thomas Carlyle (1795–1881).

rate – including advances in medical care, personal hygiene, and public sanitation, as well as peace and harmony – only reduced living standards for the average person. Finally, workers could not profit from superior skill or effort but were inevitably doomed to receive a minimal subsistence income.

As Gregory Clark (2007) documents in his book, *A Farewell to Alms: A Brief Economic History of the World*, classical economic theory was a brilliantly successful description of the world that existed before 1800. Consistent with Maddison (1995), Clark finds a general lack of real economic growth from 1000 BC to 1800 AD as measured in income (gross domestic product) per person. Thereafter, however, he finds that the average income per person underwent strong and sustained growth in a favored group of countries including the Netherlands, Britain, and the United States. Advances in technology, trade, and capitalist institutions allowed people in these countries to become ten to twenty times wealthier on average in 2000 than they were in 1800. At the precise moment these countries had broken out of the Malthusian Trap, however, classical economists such as Malthus and Ricardo developed the theory that economic growth – if it did occur – would inevitably produce only a larger population living at the subsistence level.

According to Clark (2007, 33), "the Industrial Revolution after 1800 represented the first break of human society from the constraints of nature, the first break of the human economy from the natural economy." Yet classical economists and their neoclassical descendants continued to equate humanity with the animal kingdom and apply theory from the expanding physical sciences to the economic sciences. Clark argues that while our knowledge of the physical sciences has dramatically increased over time, our knowledge of the economic sciences has been stymied due to the modernist link between the physical and economic sciences (Clark 2007, 15):

In most areas of inquiry ... knowledge declines as we move away from our time.... But in economics the Malthusian era, however odd, is the known world.... Differences in social energy across societies were muted by the Malthusian constraints. They had minimal impacts on living conditions. Since the Industrial Revolution, however, we have entered a strange new world in which economic theory is of little use in understanding differences in income across societies, or the future income in any specific society. Wealth and poverty are a matter of differences in local social interactions that are magnified, not dampened, by the economic system, to produce feast or famine.

Classical economists could not grasp the inability of their theory to explain economic growth after 1800 because of a lack of data or, as

Polanyi (1944/2001) has suggested, because their experience of the first industrial revolution in England seemed to support their dismal theory.[3] This may help explain why the broad, optimistic political economy of Adam Smith was lost on the classical economists who followed him. In time, however, the incompleteness of classical economic theory became apparent. As Milgate and Stimson (2009, 259) argue in their review of the nineteenth-century transformation in political economy, there were two responses to the incompleteness of classical economic theory. One was the critique embarked upon by the early marginalist writers, including Carl Menger in Austria, William Stanley Jevons in England, and Léon Walras in France. The other was the critique embarked upon by Karl Marx.[4]

In the case of Menger, Jevons, and Walras, they and others who followed them were to engineer a new conceptual understanding of the operation of the market mechanism and its implications for the efficacy of political action as well as individual welfare and freedom that within a generation of the first appearance of their critiques, had become the conventional wisdom of the discipline of economics – and it has remained so ever since. In the case of Marx, he and those who followed him generated a repository of ideas and arguments concerning the alienating and exploitative character of capitalism, and the limited efficacy of social and political reform, that inspired revolutionaries and radical critics alike.

The two critiques identified the same fundamental error in Ricardo's theory of value. His simple equation for the value of production, "produce = profit + wages," involved the attempt to determine two unknown quantities from one equation. To determine the value of the product it was necessary to know the rate of profit, but to determine the rate of profit it was necessary to know the value of the product. "Although the language of Marx (and his method of proceeding) was very different from anything to be found in Jevons or Walras, the analytical problem identified by Marx was much the same" (Milgate and Stimson 2009, 261). Ultimately, the Marxian approach was deemed "analytically unsound and unscientific economics" and the marginalist approach became mainstream theory in what we now call neoclassical economics. After the victory of the marginalist approach over the Marxian approach, the value of production was no longer examined in the context of the "objective

---

[3] The grave conditions of the general populace in England during the first industrial revolution are reflected in the novels, short stories, and social commentary of Charles Dickens (1812–70).

[4] Marx has been credited with coining the term "classical political economy" in the first chapter of *Das Kapital* (Milgate and Stimson 2009, 3).

conditions of production" but in the context of "subjective conditions of consumption" in perfectly competitive markets (Milgate and Stimson 2009, 264).

The focus on supply and demand conditions in perfectly competitive markets, as systemized by Alfred Marshall at Cambridge, emptied political economy of its political and social content. Milgate and Stimson (2009, 266) conclude that Marx sacrificed theoretical and scientific soundness to promote what he viewed as critical political and social issues, whereas neoclassical economists sacrificed political and social relevance to promote increasing theoretical and scientific soundness in economics:

(T)he narrowing of the conceptual focus of neoclassical economics to the question of how the market mechanism resolves problems of allocating given resources between competing ends within its abstract model of perfect competition effectively distanced the understanding of economic life from political life. Yet it did so at the cost of producing a science that tended to adopt a certain studied indifference towards the political and social institutions and structures within which markets function. Furthermore, while diverging the understanding of the market mechanism from either its historical or social context, it made possible an economic science claiming to offer valid truths irrespective of the constraints of time or location.

Inevitably, this focus on theoretical and scientific soundness led classical and neoclassical economists to build their economic theory on Bentham's utilitarianism and J. S. Mill's behavioral assumption of narrow self-interest. Yet Marx suffered the same malady in his quest to supplant classical economic theory as Joan Robinson did in her quest to supplant neoclassical economic theory. In his determination to overthrow classical economic theory, Marx was unable to think outside of the utilitarianism and narrow self-interest of that theory. His theory of class conflict and historical materialism simply replaced the self-interest of the owners (bourgeoisie) with the self-interest of the workers (proletariat). This explains why he predicted the overthrow of capitalism by violent revolution and the rise of the dictatorship of the proletariat. Marx's theory of economics and history, however, was flawed as evidenced by the growing dominance of capitalism in the contemporary world and the "ever-dwindling ranks of Marxist historians" (Milgate and Stimson 2009, 5). As Griswold (1999, 2) has concluded, "The march of the liberal Enlightenment has all but destroyed its fraternal enemy, the illiberal Enlightenment fathered by Marx."

A detailed analysis of Marx's flawed theory can be found in Joseph A. Schumpeter's (1883–1950) seminal work, *Capitalism, Socialism, and Democracy* (Schumpeter 1942/1950). An Austrian-born political economist who emigrated to America in 1932 to teach at Harvard, Schumpeter attempted to bridge insights from the German Historical School with the neoclassical theory of the Austrian School. He identified four shortcomings of Marx's approach: (1) the narrowness of his underlying assumptions, (2) his lack of economic sophistication, (3) his lack of historical perspective, and (4) his lack of insight regarding the economic system that would replace capitalism after its collapse. In Schumpeter's criticism of Marx, however, he was also heavily influenced by the narrow utilitarianism of neoclassical economic theory. His belief in "creative destruction" or the dwindling sustainability of economic profit, along with the other underlying assumptions of neoclassical theory, led him to also conclude that capitalism could not survive as an economic system. In his critique of Marx's highly flawed theory, therefore, Schumpeter revealed the inability of traditional neoclassical theory to support capitalism.[5]

One potential threat to capitalism is the dark and shadowy world of hedge funds. In his book, *More Money Than God: Hedge Funds and the Making of a New Elite*, Sebastian Mallaby (2010) argues that the first hedge fund was created by Alfred Winslow Jones (1900–89).[6] Born the son of an affluent business executive who ran General Electric's Australian operations, Jones moved with his family back to GE headquarters at Schenectady, New York where he received his secondary education. After graduating from Harvard in 1923, Jones toured the world before joining the US State Department. In 1930, he was stationed in Berlin where he witnessed firsthand the devastating effects of Germany's soaring inflation and high unemployment. After conducting several studies on the conditions of Germany's industrial workers, Jones became romantically involved with a young socialite and left-wing activist. When his embassy colleagues discovered that the couple had secretly married and attended a Marxist Workers School together in Berlin, Jones was forced to resign from the State Department in May 1932. After returning to New York in 1934, Jones enrolled in a Ph.D. program in sociology at Columbia University. He remarried in 1937 and took his new wife hitch-hiking

---

[5] This inconvenient aspect of Schumpeter's (1942/1950) seminal work is often ignored by economists and policymakers seeking to use his scathing critique of Marx in their support of capitalism.

[6] Leading financial investors such as Warren Buffett and John Templeton credit the creation of the hedge fund to Benjamin Graham, co-author of the value investor's handbook *Security Analysis* (Graham and Dodd 1934).

to war-torn Spain with writer Dorothy Parker where he met and drank Scotch with Ernest Hemingway.

Jones had seen Germany torn apart by the Marxist revolution after World War I and the fascist counter-revolution leading to Hitler and World War II. For his doctoral thesis at Columbia, therefore, he was motivated to examine whether the same calamity he witnessed in Germany could befall his own country. In 1938 and 1939, he conducted a study of industrial conflict in Akron, Ohio to tease out the links between Americans' economic conditions and their attitudes toward class conflict and leftist politics. Based on 1,700 field interviews, Jones concluded that "acute economic division did not actually carry over into polarized worldviews. It was a repudiation of the socialist assumptions of his youth and a testimony to the vitality of American democracy" (Mallaby 2010, 19). In 1941, Jones published his findings in a book entitled *Life, Liberty and Property*. It became a popular sociology textbook in America.

As Weber had discovered in his voyage to America in 1904, Jones's research uncovered a different view of capitalist society than that promoted by Marxist revolutionaries. The publication of his book led to a career as a journalist at *Fortune* magazine. In his research for an article published in 1949 on predicting the direction of the stock market, Jones came across the 1933 and 1944 market studies of Alfred Cowles. Reviewing thousands of investment recommendations issued by financial practitioners, Cowles had concluded that the very act of publicly forecasting a trend was likely to destroy it. By the time his article appeared in *Fortune*, Jones had launched a private investment fund with $60,000 from four friends and $40,000 of his own money. To magnify his returns, he added borrowed money to his original capital. Rather than converting to cash when his market research signaled trouble ahead, as with other investment funds, Jones reduced his exposure by selling stocks short.[7] Jones would soon leave his journalism career behind to manage his hedge fund full time.

The knowledge of the market gained from reading Cowles, and his clandestine activities in Europe, taught Jones the value of keeping all aspects of his investing activities secret. Jones had also learned to charge his investors 20 percent of the hedge fund's investment profits rather than a flat management fee to save on taxes. In addition to staving off competitors,

---

[7] Both leverage and short selling had been used in the 1920s, but the trauma of the 1929 market crash had caused these investing techniques to fall out of favor and they were tightly regulated in public investment funds.

Jones stayed private to avoid intrusive and costly government regulation. As a private investment fund, he was able to avoid regulations designed to protect the average investor, such as the Securities Act of 1933, the Investment Company Act of 1940, and the Investment Advisors Act of 1940, which restricted investment funds from borrowing or selling short. In essence, Jones established his hedge fund to avoid the kind of transparency and accountability that capitalist society requires. "(T)hanks to the pattern that he established in those early years, hedge funds have been forever mysterious, shadowy, and resented" (Mallaby 2010, 31).

The story of Alfred Winslow Jones reveals that the hedge fund industry was launched by a bohemian drifter who studied at the Marxist Workers School in Berlin, ran secret missions for a clandestine ani-Nazi group called the Leninist Organization, and honeymooned on the front line of the civil war in Spain. As Mallaby (2010, 391) notes, the structure of the hedge fund industry allows partners and their private investors to use high leverage to "earn more money than God." As we have seen, however, this industry poses a potential threat to capitalism itself. "Today, hedge funds are the new merchant banks – the Goldmans and Morgans of half a century ago. Their focus on risk is equally ferocious, and they are equally lightly regulated.... The wheel of Wall Street turns. Greed and risk are always with us."

The risk posed by the hedge fund industry is well known by hedge fund managers themselves. After his hedge fund earned nearly $1 billion profit by shorting $10 billion worth of British sterling in 1992 and another small fortune in 1997 shorting $2 billion worth of the Thai baht, George Soros stated in an address to the 1997 meeting of the World Bank and International Monetary Fund that "(t)he laissez-faire idea that markets should be left to their own devices remains very influential.... I consider it a dangerous idea." Soros's shorting activities in 1992 collapsed the initial currency agreement of the newly formed European Union and his shorting activities in 1997 worsened Asia's currency crisis that contributed to the collapse of LTCM and the near collapse of Lehman Brothers. At the same meeting, Soros also stated that he believed the main enemy of the open society "is no longer the communist but the capitalist threat" (Mallaby 2010, 207).[8]

The birth of free-market capitalism, as has been shown, coincided with the discovery of double-entry accounting and the culture of transparency

---

[8] As discussed below, Soros (2009) would later claim that the worldwide financial collapse of 2007–08 was the final blow for the neoclassical economic theory out of Chicago.

and accountability that followed that key discovery in northern Italy (Soll 2014). The birth of Marxist socialism, on the other hand, coincided with the collapse of agrarian economies that had been controlled by monarchs and greedy absentee landlords in Russia and Germany. In contrast to capitalist economies, socialist regimes hold on to power by avoiding transparency and accountability and by feeding their population a constant diet of propaganda. A major theme of this book is the importance of responsibility, transparency, and accountability to capitalist economies. By encouraging narrow self-interest and ignoring the vulnerabilities and excesses of unregulated markets, therefore, neoclassical economists associated with the Chicago School have put capitalism at risk. This has been acknowledged by one of the main architects of the theory of the firm after the severe market crash and near collapse of the global financial system in 2007–08. Michael Jensen has placed much of the blame for the recent crisis of capitalism on the neoclassical theory of the firm out of Chicago (Dierksmeier 2020).

8.2 THREE RESPONSES TO THE RECENT CRISIS OF CAPITALISM

We will never know how George Stigler and Milton Friedman would have responded to the severe market crash that nearly collapsed the global financial system in 2007–08. Stigler died in December 1991 and Friedman passed away in November 2006. Given Cherrier's (2011) thesis of the lucky consistency of Friedman's views on economic theory and politics, the crash represented a very unlucky event for his views. It certainly jolted Alan Greenspan, the chair of the US Federal Reserve from 1987 to 2006 who was a public follower of Ayn Rand's moral philosophy. Many economists had already abandoned the efficient market hypothesis based on empirical evidence and previous market crashes in 1987, 1998, and 2000. Yet the market crash of 2007–08 was so severe, and its global impact so great that even prominent members of the Chicago School such as Michael Jensen moderated their views in its wake. The latest crisis of capitalism, therefore, has opened wide the door for innovations in neoclassical economic theory.

I identify three different responses to the market crash of 2007–08 based on books published shortly after the crash. Richard Posner's (2009, 235–236) book, *A Failure of Capitalism: The Crisis of '08 and the Descent into Depression*, provides an example of a "minimalist" approach to the market crash and the severe recession that followed, which he called a depression:

As far as one can judge on the basis of what is known today (obviously an important qualification), the depression is the result of normal business activity in a laissez-faire economic regime – more precisely, it is an event consistent with the normal operation of economic markets. Bankers and consumers alike seem on the whole to have been acting in conformity with their rational self-interest throughout the period that saw the increase in risky banking practices, the swelling and bursting of the housing bubble, and a reduction in the rate of personal savings combined with an increase in the riskiness of those savings. The market participants made plenty of mistakes, but that is par for the course. Whenever has it been different? Economic life is permeated with uncertainty.

Posner's book reflects what I call the "double-down" approach to the crisis. He states, "Laissez-faire capitalism failed us, but government allowed the preconditions of depression to develop and wreak havoc with the economy. And its responses to the crisis were late, slow, indecisive, and poorly articulated. The responses also created 'moral hazard' (the tendency to engage in risky behavior if one is insured against the consequences of the risks' materializing)." Posner shared a weekly blog on issues of economic policy with Gary Becker, so his views reflect the views of the Chicago School. I heartily concur with Posner's (2009, 266) honest admission that "(e)conomic understanding of the causes and cures of depressions has not progressed to the point at which ideology no longer influences analysis," and that "this depression, like the last, is likely to stimulate fresh thinking by economists, as well as to provide new data for empirical analysis." Nevertheless, I take issue with Posner's (2009, 284–285) Darwinian view of capitalism:

But although the financiers bear the primary "responsibility" for the depression, I do not think they can be "blamed" for it – implying moral censure – any more than one can blame a lion for eating a zebra. Capitalism is Darwinian. Businessmen take risks (mostly within the law) that promote their financial interest; it would make no more sense for an individual businessman to worry that because of the instability of the banking industry his decisions and those of his competitors might trigger a depression than for a lion to spare a zebra out of concern that lions are eating zebras faster that the zebras can reproduce. To tell banks not to make risky loans – to upbraid them for "an unquenchable thirst for easy profits" or for taking "unjustifiable risks for their own gain, and in so doing jeopardizing the future of the nation's credit system and now the economy itself – or to upbraid a homebuyer for taking out a mortgage loan that he may be unable to repay, is like telling lions and zebras to build a fence between them.

Posner's views reflect Gary Becker's broad application of the Chicago School's neoclassical economic theory based on natural science. Both Stigler and Friedman were highly supportive of Becker's application of their neoclassical theory to all of life, including his forays into crime and punishment, discrimination, and family relations (Becker 1993). Again, this does not mean that Stigler or Friedman would similarly double-down on their neoclassical theory after the crisis of capitalism in 2007–08. We must allow for the possibility that they would have taken advantage of the opportunity to moderate their views as Michael Jensen did. There is no evidence, however, that Posner or Becker ever did.

A second type of response to the crisis of capitalism in 2007–08 is reflected in the book published by George Soros (2009, vii), *The Crash of 2008 and What it Means: The New Paradigm for Financial Markets*. Soros's book provides an example of what I call a "scorched-earth" approach to the market crash and the severe recession that followed:

> We are in the midst of the worst financial crisis since the 1930s. In some ways it resembles other crises that have occurred in the last twenty-five years, but there is a profound difference: the current crisis marks the end of an era of credit expansion based on the dollar as the international reserve currency. The periodic crises were part of a larger boom-bust process; the current crisis is the culmination of a super-boom that has lasted for more than twenty-five years. To understand what is going on we need a new paradigm. The currently prevailing paradigm, namely that financial markets tend towards equilibrium, is both false and misleading; our current troubles can be largely attributed to the fact that the international financial system has been developed on the basis of that paradigm.

Soros's book reflects his rejection of traditional economic theory in favor of his general theory called *reflexivity*. His theory emphasizes that, inconsistent with natural science, reality in economic science is reflected in people's thinking about that reality. Further, people make economic decisions based on their thinking about that reality. Thus, people serve both a "cognitive" function in thinking about economic reality and a "participating" function in forming that reality. "The two functions work in opposite directions and in certain circumstances they can interfere with each other. The interaction between them takes the form of a two-way reflexive mechanism" (Soros 1995, 66). Soros states that he wrote his book "because I thought the unfolding financial crisis would offer an excellent opportunity to demonstrate the validity and relevance of my conceptual framework" (Soros 2009, 215–216):

> The prevailing interpretation of financial markets – the Efficient Market Hypothesis (EMH) – has been well and truly discredited by the Crash of 2008. The current financial crisis was not caused by some exogenous factor – like the formation or dissolution of an oil cartel – but by the financial system itself. This puts the lie to the assertion that financial markets tend towards equilibrium and deviations are caused by external shocks. But the alternative theory of how markets work that I am proposing – the theory of reflexivity – has not taken its place. It has not

even received serious consideration by the economics profession.... Those who are most sympathetic to my views explain to me that my theory is not getting more attention because it cannot be formalized and modeled. But that is exactly the point I am trying to make: Reflexivity gives rise to uncertainties that cannot be quantified and probabilities that cannot be calculated. Frank Knight made that point a century ago ... and John Maynard Keynes recognized it too. Yet market participants, rating agencies, and regulators alike came to depend on quantitative models in calculating risks.

Soros would concur with Posner that economic understanding of the causes and cures of depressions has not progressed to the point at which ideology no longer influences analysis. In contrast to Posner, however, the ideology that he applies in his analysis comes from the political left.[9] As with many behavioral researchers in economics, finance, and accounting, Soros sees evidence inconsistent with neoclassical theory as an opportunity to adopt alternative theories based on irrationality or bias. Such bias frequently calls for government intervention consistent with the desires of progressives on the left.

A third type of response to the crisis of capitalism in 2007–08 is reflected in the book published by Colin Mayer (2013), *Firm Commitment: Why the Corporation is Failing Us and How to Restore Trust in It*. Mayer's book provides an insightful critique of the corporate governance literature launched by Michael Jensen and offers practical ways to build upon the traditional theory of the firm to maximize the promise of capitalism. Mayer writes from the perspective of a leading researcher, administrator, and entrepreneur in corporate finance. After his Ph.D. in economics from Oxford University in 1981, Mayer returned to Oxford University in 1994 as the first professor in the newly formed School of Management Studies. In the year that he was due to deliver the manuscript for his book to Oxford University Press in 2006, Mayer was chosen to serve as Dean of what by then had become the Saïd Business School at Oxford. While his administrative duties delayed the delivery of his manuscript by five years, he was able to incorporate valuable insights gleaned by the market crash of 2007–08 and his exposure to world leaders in business, finance, and government. His book also reflects over three decades of research and consulting in corporate governance and organizational control.

---

[9] Soros (1995, 196) is fully transparent about his political bias: "I don't consider the survival of the fittest the most desirable outcome. I believe we must strive for certain fundamental values, such as social justice, which cannot be attained by unrestricted competition. It is exactly because I have been successful in the marketplace that I can afford to advocate these values. I am the classic limousine liberal."

Mayer (2013, 22–23) marvels at the potential of the business corporation to support capitalist society:

The corporation is a legal entity that has an existence in law that is not dissimilar
to you and me. It is a legal personality that is distinct from the people who own
it, and those who run it. It can undertake activities, raise finance, open bank
accounts, and pay others under its own name. It can sue and be sued, employ and
be employed. It can be dormant at some times and active at others. It has been the
source of some of the most important inventions and innovations in the world,
brought modern technology to people's homes, created communities, and built
cities. It is the producer of power and life-saving medicines.... Far from being on
its last legs, the corporation is seen as being a form of commercial creativity, a
solution to the inefficiency of the public sector, and a way of delivering goods and
services around the world.

Mayer argues, however, that we have reached a crisis point in the very
institution that has helped deliver the great prosperity of capitalism – a
collapse of trust in the corporation prompting extensive, intrusive regulation. As Mayer (2013, 23–24) points out, over the last few decades
corporate mistakes have caused environmental catastrophes that have
threatened towns, oceans, and animal species. "It is only over the last few
years that the activities of corporations have brought financial systems to
a point of collapse and national governments to a state of bankruptcy....
The change which is occurring is that whereas previously the actions
of companies could have devastating consequences for their customers,
suppliers, and investors, now they can destroy economies, communities,
and species. It is not an exaggeration to say that through their negligence,
incompetence, greed, or fraud, corporations are a threat to our livelihood
and the world we live in."

Mayer (2013, 144) argues that by focusing on the agency problem
between management and owners, the traditional theory of the firm has
undermined the position of other stakeholders who have significant interests in the corporation. Further, the assumption of narrow self-interest
has encouraged solutions to the agency problem that are detrimental to
trust and commitment, such as hostile takeovers, shareholder activism,
and powerful economic incentives that drain the resources of the firm.
In particular, the traditional theory of the firm "does not recognize the
fundamental role of commitment in all aspects of our commercial as well
as social lives and the way in which institutions contribute to the creation and preservation of commitment." He argues, however, that the
corporation is one institution that is especially capable of supporting
trust and commitment and spreading the benefits of capitalism (Mayer
2013, 149–150):

What (business corporations) do is to allow people to escape from economic exclusion. They achieve this by enhancing the potential of those working for them, supplying them, or purchasing from them to make credible commitments through restricting their future range of options. They are control devices that limit the possible courses of conduct that can be undertaken and without which people would be incapable of restraining themselves from pursuing activities that are to the detriment of others. Institutions do this by constraining the ways in which people act and disengage, imposing rules and conventions that limit their choice, alternatives, and liquidity. By restricting behavior in this way, they encourage other people to make commitments to them that otherwise would not be forthcoming and thereby enhance rather than diminish the current capabilities of those whose actions they constrain.

Mayer (2013, 2) argues that the corporation "offers the opportunity to provide a means of extracting ourselves out of poverty, inequality, and environmental destruction." He turns agency theory on its head by arguing that the separation of ownership from control is the very vehicle by which the corporation can uphold obligations to other stakeholders of the firm. Thus, the traditional emphasis on "agency costs" due to the separation of ownership from control is misplaced. To Mayer (2013, 6), the miracle of the corporation "derives from its ability to combine and balance the traditional perspective on incentives, ownership, and control with the alterative view presented here of obligations, responsibilities, and commitment." In his book, Mayer provides many powerful and practical solutions to creating the "moral firm" based on trust and commitment.

As discussed in Chapter 6, Michael Jensen was one of the main architects of the theory of the firm that Mayer criticizes in his book (Jensen and Meckling 1976; Jensen 2000). Jensen and his fellow neoclassical economists addressed the agency problem identified by Berle and Means (1932) within their theoretical framework of narrow self-interest, perfect competition, and highly efficient markets. Their theory of the firm focused on the problem of getting self-interested managers to act in the interest of shareholders and led to the shareholder primacy view of the firm based on distrust and the maximization of stock price. Jensen formerly repudiated other motivations besides narrow self-interest and broader views of the responsibility of the firm such as stakeholder theory (Freeman 1984). In the wake of the severe market crash and near collapse of the global financial system in 2007–08, however, Jensen has moderated his views. Similar to Mayer, Jensen has placed much of the blame for the recent crisis of capitalism on the neoclassical theory of the firm out of Chicago. He has extended his theoretical framework to incorporate values and integrity as well as responsibilities to other stakeholders of the firm besides shareholders. As discussed below, however, Jensen's continuing emphasis on positive economic theory (Friedman 1953) has hindered his attempt to add values and integrity to the traditional theory of the firm.

8.3 KEY INSIGHTS FROM THE SEARCH FOR A MORAL FOUNDATION

In this book, I have used a group of leading characters to tell the continuing story of the search for a moral foundation for capitalism. I now summarize some of the key insights that can be gleaned by their lives and writings. As we have seen, Adam Smith provided a well-developed moral theory to explain the conscience as well as the social and moral norms that arise in society to control narrow self-interest. That moral theory is based on the ability of humans to "sympathize" (empathize) with each other and develop standards of right and wrong behavior based on the "impartial spectator" of social experience. Smith articulated his moral theory in his seminal work of moral philosophy, which he then used as the moral foundation for his seminal work of political economy. His moral foundation for capitalism, therefore, relies on social norms and culture as well as the ability of commerce, religion, education, and government to maintain high moral character. Consistent with Stoic philosophy, Smith viewed the practice of virtue as the ultimate good rather than seeking maximum pleasure or minimum pain. He also viewed the pursuit of virtue as fully rational and consistent with one's responsibility as a member of society. Smith's moral foundation for capitalism was heavily influenced by John Locke's theory of natural law, which required that all humans be free and equal. Locke's theory supported capitalist institutions by providing a moral argument for private property as well as laws to protect that property.

Max Weber and R. H. Tawney wrote seminal works attributing the development of capitalism to religion. As such, their writings support a moral foundation for capitalism based on religion. Weber rejected Marx's theory of historical materialism which emphasized class conflict and minimized the role of religion in society. Weber not only acknowledged the role of religion in capitalist society, he also foresaw that issues of alienation and exploitation would become less of a concern as workers began to own shares of public corporations and view their labor as a freely chosen activity based on material interest. Weber's historical development attributed capitalism to the sixteenth-century Protestant Reformation, which provided a culture of asceticism, frugality, and hard work consistent with the bourgeois virtues of the rising middle class. As a scholar of the German language, Frank Knight studied Weber and translated some of his early writings into English. Knight shared Weber's dynamic view of capitalism, which led him to conclude that it was a flexible economic system that would evolve to meet the wider needs of society as they evolved. Both Weber and Knight expressed deep concerns regarding the continued narrowing of economic theory by neoclassical economists. Weber's close association with the German Historical School, however, blinded them both to the moral foundation for capitalism provided by Adam Smith.

R. H. Tawney's concern for the inhumane conditions of the working class during the first industrial revolution reflected the indigenous British socialism of the period based on a Christian worldview. Despite his tendency to associate with the political left, Tawney also rejected Marx's historical materialism and his rationalization of all statements into expressions of class interest. He was good friends with Beatrice and Sidney Webb, co-founders of the Fabian Society and the London School of Economics (LSE), but he rejected their leftist arguments for state control of important industries. Tawney's close association with Anglo-Catholic theologian Charles Gore influenced his history of capitalism and led him to support efforts to revive a Christian social ethic that could address the needs of capitalist society. His seminal work of economic history complemented Weber's history by emphasizing the influence of the Catholic religion in the development of capitalism. In contrast to Weber, however, Tawney's economic history was critical of some of the changes to society that had been brought by the new economic system of the Protestant Reformation. Tawney was teaching at LSE when Lionel Robbins assumed leadership in 1929 and began to move the school away from its leftist founding, which included inviting Friedrich Hayek from the Austrian School to join the faculty in 1931.

Karl Polanyi and John Maynard Keynes wrote seminal works supporting a moral foundation for capitalism based on humanism. Polanyi shared Tawney's deep Christian faith but became convinced that it was necessary to provide a secular moral foundation for capitalism. His search for a moral foundation based on humanism initially led him to the early writings of Marx, who had argued that the rising capitalist system corroded all traditional values and institutions. As Polanyi analyzed Marx's later writings, however, he realized that Marx had incorporated the same narrow utilitarianism that plagued the classical economic theory that he detested. By the time Polanyi published his seminal critique of capitalism, it encompassed a direct attack on Marxism. His search for a moral foundation for capitalism led Polanyi to rediscover the moral foundation provided by Adam Smith, which had been lost due to the German Historical School and the classical and neoclassical economists' association of humanity with the animal kingdom. In his history of capitalism, Polanyi demonstrated the workings of two movements – the movement to release the power of the market through deregulation and the countermovement to protect society from the vulnerabilities and excesses of unregulated markets. He attributed the "dismal science" view of classical economic theory to the unintended consequences of Britain's Poor Laws. Thus, his seminal work exposed the ever-present need for a wise and effective public policy to support capitalist society.

Keynes initially shared the radical humanism of his elite friends associated with the Apostles at Cambridge and the Bloomsbury group. After two world wars and the Great Depression, however, an older and wiser Keynes rejected the utopian hedonism of his youth and embraced a more traditional humanism based on responsibility and duty. Of particular importance for the world economy, he took on the challenges of industrial capitalism during the volatile period of the early twentieth century. Like Tawney and Polanyi before him, Keynes rejected the narrow utilitarianism of classical and neoclassical economists. He also believed that his general theory had knocked away the Ricardian foundations of Marxism, and he felt no need to revisit Marx's theory after it had already been debunked. Despite their public debates, Keynes was highly supportive of Friedrich Hayek's classic book attacking socialism, *The Road to Serfdom*. He wrote Hayek expressing his deep moral and philosophical agreement with the book, but he challenged him to provide guidance as to where to draw the line regarding government involvement in the economy. Against the advice of Frank Knight, Hayek's book was published by the University of Chicago and was used by Milton Friedman and George Stigler to support their increasingly narrow neoclassical economic theory. While Friedman admitted in his memoirs that he was thoroughly "Keynesian" in his early years, he came to associate the evoking of any role for government in the economy with socialism. The increasingly narrow neoclassical theory of Friedman and Stigler eventually pushed both Hayek and Knight out of the Economics Department at Chicago.

The Chicago School of Economics eventually "conquered the field" of economic theory that existed in the postwar period. In particular, the Chicago School went further than the Austrian School in minimizing the social and moral emphasis of historical and institutional economists.

This does not suggest, however, that the neoclassical economists associated with the Chicago School provided no moral foundation for capitalism. The Chicago School's emphasis on narrow self-interest introduced
ethical egoism as the new moral foundation for capitalism. In contrast to
the moral foundations provided by Polanyi and Keynes based on humanism, the Chicago School's emphasis on narrow self-interest left no room
for social and moral responsibility. Similarly, Ayn Rand's moral foundation for capitalism based on rational egoism provided no motivation
to protect society against the vulnerabilities and excesses of unrestricted
markets. Rand's moral philosophy rejected the controlling power of both
religion and the state. Although her political views often conflicted with
members of the Chicago School, her glorification of self-interest was a
natural extension of their neoclassical economic theory.

Vernon Smith and Michael Jensen provide examples of prominent
neoclassical economists who have joined the search for a moral foundation for capitalism. After witnessing Edward Chamberlin's use of
experiments in his graduate course at Harvard, Vernon Smith found the
methodology useful to test the assumptions and predictions of neoclassical economic theory. Consistent with the neoclassical price theory out
of Chicago, he initially documented rapid convergence to the competitive equilibrium prediction using repeating single-period markets formed
as double-auctions. When Smith and his colleagues examined markets
with multi-period assets, however, they documented systematic bubble-
crash behavior in the lab. In experimental tests of two-person interactive games, they also documented norm-based behavior consistent with
preferences for fairness, trust, and reciprocity. Instead of labeling this
norm-based behavior irrational, as psychology-based behavioral economists had done, Smith associated this behavior with Hayek's notion
of *ecological* rationality emerging from humanity's social and cultural
heritage. Vernon Smith's attempt to explain the norm-based behavior
emerging in the lab eventually led him to rediscover Adam Smith's moral
theory and incorporate insights from that theory into his research (see
Smith and Wilson 2019).

Financial economist Michael Jensen was the most visible and committed promoter of the neoclassical theory of the firm. For example, he was
chosen to represent the Chicago School in a 1984 debate with Warren
Buffett at Columbia commemorating the fiftieth anniversary of Benjamin
Graham and David Dodd's (1934) landmark book on securities analysis. In the debate, Warren Buffett supported Graham and Dodd's value-
investing approach based on detailed financial analysis, whereas Jensen

supported the efficient market hypothesis suggesting that above-average returns could not be systematically earned from analyzing publicly available information. Jensen also played a leading role in introducing his neoclassical theory of the firm, called *agency theory*, into the university-based business school. Through his efforts, the neoclassical theory of the firm out of Chicago captured the mother discipline of economics as well as the sister disciplines of finance and accounting. Through his interactions with the financial press, he encouraged an active market for corporate control and powerful financial incentives to align the interests of managers with the owners of the firm. The severe market crash and near collapse of the global financial system in 2007–08, however, shook Jensen's confidence in his neoclassical theory and caused him to promote integrity and values in his MBA courses and consulting.

Amartya Sen's story bridges the development of capitalism in the West with its development in the East. Sen's search for a moral foundation for capitalism was shaped by his unique experience growing up in the Bengal region of Colonial India during World War II and the postwar struggle for independence between the Hindus and Muslims in Postcolonial India. That struggle generated deep ethnic conflict that resulted in widespread rioting and murdering throughout the formerly peaceful region and split the region into Hindu-dominated West Bengal and Muslim-dominated East Bengal (Bangladesh). At Presidency College in Calcutta and later at Cambridge University, Sen experienced the strong Marxist sympathies of the period as well as the neo-Keynesianism of Joan Robinson. He eventually rejected both attacks on neoclassical economic theory and elected instead to expand the theory by incorporating Adam Smith's moral theory. While Jensen found that teaching the traditional theory of the firm challenged the deepest held beliefs of his MBA students, Sen found that incorporating Smith's moral foundation into that theory gave his Indian students great pride and dignity. He found Smith's moral foundation particularly useful to address the vulnerabilities and excesses of free-market capitalism, including issues of poverty, inequality, and exploitation.

While Michael Jensen played a major role in introducing his neoclassical theory of the firm into the university-based business school, he has spent the end of his career promoting integrity and values in business education. In particular, he has moved away from promoting a mechanistic "value-free" approach to business education to a humanistic "value-rich" approach that encourages business students and executives to give authentic expression to their personal values in their professional lives. As Dierksmeier (2020) argues, however, Jensen's continuing commitment to Milton Friedman's positive theory of economics (Friedman 1953) has impeded the kind of progress he envisions for business education. In his "positive model of integrity," for example, he ignores more traditional definitions of integrity with normative implications and uses a definition from the materialistic world of engineering: *"the state of being whole, complete, unbroken, unimpaired, sound, perfect condition"* (Jensen and Erhard 2011, 26). Thus, Jensen seeks to bring back values into management and business education while keeping a safe distance from all normative talk (Dierksmeier 2020, 81):

> His positivist commitments make for an unusual take on morality, though. According to Jensen, individuals and societies simply "have" certain values – and these they should enact then with integrity and authenticity. This view overlooks not only the dynamic interplay between individuals and institutions, persons and cultures in the generation of norms, suggesting an oddly solipsistic view of the rise of personal values. What is more, it also conflates a distinction fundamental to all moral philosophy, i.e., that between the "genesis" and the "validity" of moral norms (Dodd and Stern-Gillet 1995).

The leading characters in this book provide valuable insights regarding the values that business leaders and educators should promote to support capitalist society. For example, Adam Smith argued that middle class values such as honesty were preferred for success in commerce and market economies. He also maintained the importance of religion and other sources of traditional values such as the Stoic virtues.[10] Smith joined his friend David Hume in believing that reason was and should be the slave of the passions, and he was passionate about social and moral issues as well as economic self-interest. In particular, he took sides against the injustice of slavery and the inhumane treatment of many of those under British colonial rule, including members of the British empire in North America and India. Max Weber believed it was "not only possible, but obligatory to engage in controversy about normative standards" in science (Löwith 1993, 124). In particular, he argued that "scientific judgement cannot really be categorically *severed* from value judgement, though the two must be distinguished" (Löwith 1993, 53, italics in the original). In contrast to Friedman, Stigler, and Jensen, therefore, Weber believed that there could be no value-free economics just as there could be no value-free science. The broad view of economics and capitalism

---

[10] I refer the reader to another well-known economist from the Chicago School, Deirdre McCloskey (2006) and her writings supporting the importance of the "bourgeois virtues" to capitalist society.

reflected in this book, therefore, supports the recent trend in business education to return to the "professionalism project" of the founders of the university-based business school.

8.4 JOINING THE SEARCH

As with the leading characters of this book, my search for a moral foundation for capitalism has been heavily influenced by my own times and life experiences. When I arrived on the campus of Indiana University to begin my Ph.D. program in 1989, I had already been indoctrinated into the Chicago School of Economics from my MBA program at Purdue University. In contrast to Purdue, however, Indiana had a group of accounting researchers who were trained in psychology and sociology and conducted experimental research from a theoretical perspective that included limited rationality, decision bias, and inefficient markets. Given the unnerving experience during my MBA of the stock market crash on October 19, 1987, I was initially drawn to the behavioral research being conducted by these accounting researchers. In addition to attending their doctoral seminars, I began to read the behavioral research of Richard Thaler (Thaler 1992) and other economists challenging the underlying assumptions of neoclassical economic theory.

Although I majored in music and minored in philosophy/religion during my undergraduate degree at Spring Arbor College, my father taught business management at the small liberal arts college. I also had six years of work experience that included various banking and investment jobs, including a job driving the corn fields of Iowa and Illinois selling commodities hedging programs to farmers. Therefore, I remained deeply interested in the neoclassical economic theory out of Chicago. When I learned that a group of economists at Indiana were conducting experimental tests of that economic theory, I eagerly signed up for a doctoral seminar taught by one of those economists, Arlington Williams. Arlie was Vernon Smith's former Ph.D. student at Arizona who had programmed his market experiments in a computer language called Plato. Arlie taught me that it was not necessary to abandon neoclassical economic theory in my experimental research. I was hooked. I spent more and more time in the Economics Department at Indiana honing my new research specialty in experimental economics.

Similar to Amartya Sen at Cambridge, however, I had a hard time finding a senior accounting professor who would supervise a dissertation in my specialty area of experimental economics. The only experimental economist in the accounting department at the time was an untenured assistant professor, Susan Watts. With her help, I developed a dissertation topic that utilized an experimental market to test price and volume reactions to public information signals. However, none of the senior faculty in accounting felt comfortable signing off on that dissertation topic. I also began working with another assistant professor in accounting who had research interests in investor disagreement and trading volume, Orie Barron. He taught me the trading volume theory of Oliver Kim and Ro Verrecchia based on noisy rational expectations models. Of course, the Chicago School's assumption of highly efficient markets left little room for investor disagreement or trading volume. Thus, my research in trading volume also conflicted with the neoclassical economic theory out of Chicago. Orie and I began to develop a noisy rational expectations model that analyzed the disagreement reflected in analysts' forecasts of earnings announcements.

My original dissertation topic became an experimental market study with Anne Gillette, Susan Watts, and Arlie Williams. We found that market price underreacted to pubic information signals and that, in violation of Milgrom and Stokey's (1982) "no-trade theorem," significant investor disagreement and trading volume occurred in an experimental market with all public information. That study was eventually published in *Contemporary Accounting Research* (*CAR*) and has been widely cited (Gillette, Stevens, Watts, and Williams 1999). After adding Oliver Kim and Steve Lim, the noisy rational expectations model I began with Orie Barron was eventually published in *The Accounting Review* (*TAR*). By modeling common properties of analysts' forecasts of earnings – including forecast error and dispersion – in terms of the quality of analysts' public and private information, our model provided useful economic intuition and empirical proxies for capital markets researchers in economics, finance, and accounting (Barron, Kim, Lim, and Stevens 1998). It would become one of the most heavily cited papers in *TAR*.

Despite my research productivity at Indiana, I still needed a dissertation topic approved by a senior accounting professor to complete my Ph.D. My research interests in experimental economics and investor disagreement conflicted with the neoclassical economic theory out of Chicago. Therefore, it was natural for me to select a research topic that directly challenged Michael Jensen's theory of the firm. Mark Young (1985) had recently published a budgeting experiment in one of the top accounting journals out of Chicago, the *Journal of Accounting Research*. His experiment showed that student subjects who participated in the formation of their production budget built budgetary slack that was correlated with their risk preferences. I thought that I could use a similar experiment to show that budgetary slack (understating one's productive capacity in the budget to achieve a higher bonus) was reduced by one's ethical and reputation concerns regarding honest reporting. Senior accounting faculty Joe Fisher and Mike Tiller conducted experimental studies related to budgetary slack from a behavioral perspective, and they generously agreed to co-chair my dissertation.

I completed my Ph.D. from Indiana in 1996 after taking an assistant professor position at the University of New Hampshire in 1995. Because UNH did not have an experimental lab, I took a visiting assistant professor position at the University of Arizona in 1998. This gave me the opportunity to conduct experiments with Jeff Schatzberg and attend research workshops with other leading experimental economists including Vernon Smith and Kevin McCabe. After taking an assistant professor position at Syracuse University in 1999, I began to conduct capital market research examining trading volume reactions to earnings announcements with Anwer Ahmed and Richard Schneible, Jr. We published a study in *CAR* demonstrating that the advent of online trading significantly altered price and volume reactions to earnings announcement (Ahmed, Schneible, and Stevens 2003). While at Syracuse, I also began to study Jensen's theory of the firm more formally with theorist Alex Thevaranjan. We eventually published a principal-agent model in the journal *Accounting, Organizations and Society* demonstrating a moral solution to the moral hazard problem based on a promise-keeping norm (Stevens and Thevaranjan 2010).[11]

My dissertation experiment documented that budgetary slack was negatively associated with a measure of moral responsibility and the moral judgement that building excessive slack into the budget was unethical. My dissertation was eventually published in the *Journal of Management Accounting Research* (Stevens 2002) and has been heavily cited in both the accounting and business ethics literatures. Although I continued my experimental research with Arlie Williams at Indiana and Jeff Schatzberg at Arizona, I missed not having an experimental lab while at Syracuse. When a faculty position opened up at Florida State University in 2005, therefore, I jumped at the opportunity. Mark Isaac had left Arizona for FSU in 2001 and had recruited a talented group of

[11] See the discussion of the results and implications of my principal-agent model with Alex Thevaranjan in Chapter 2.

experimental economists with a strong reputation for research in game theory, auctions, and public goods. While at FSU, I continued my trading volume research and eventually published the first detailed review of the literature with Linda Bamber and Orie Barron in *CAR* (Bamber, Barron, and Stevens 2011). Due to the experimental lab and the talented Ph.D. students I had the opportunity to work with at FSU (including Alisa Brink, Bruce Davidson, Jeremy Douthit, Eric Gooden, and Mark Mellon), my experimental economics research in accounting became particularly productive.

From my graduate education at Purdue and Indiana, I held the Chicago view of Adam Smith as the source of the straightjacket of self-interest in economics, finance, and accounting. I also held the Chicago view of neoclassical economic theory promoted by Milton Friedman in his methodological essays on "positive economic theory" (Friedman 1953). After attending research workshops and presenting my research before the experimental economics group at FSU, however, it became clear to me that their knowledge of Adam Smith and neoclassical economic theory had advanced far beyond my own. I felt like a new Ph.D. student learning economic theory all over again. As a result of my interaction with the FSU experimental economics group, I reached out to Christopher Berry at Glasgow University and arranged a semester as a Visiting Fellow at the Adam Smith Research Foundation in the spring of 2011. That semester in Glasgow I was introduced to the real Adam Smith.

After the loss of my first wife to breast cancer, I remarried and moved to Atlanta in 2013, where I took a faculty position at the Robinson College of Business at Georgia State University. Similar to FSU, GSU had an experimental lab with a distinguished group of experimental economists and talented Ph.D. students to work with. While at GSU I have had the opportunity to work with Jim Cox and Susan Laury in economics (Andrew Young School of Public Policy), Ivo Tafkov and Michael Majerczyk in accounting, and Glenn Harrison in risk management. As a fellow at the Center for the Economic Analysis of Risk (CEAR), I have also organized research conferences related to the effects of social norms on organizational and market risk (October 2015), the effects of formal and informal controls on organizational and market risk (March 2017), and the Chicago School (April 2019). These research conferences have given me an opportunity to interact with leading researchers from the United States and across the globe at my home institution in Atlanta. Interactions with CEAR director Glenn Harrison as well as conference participants Paul Fischer at Wharton, Mark Penno at Iowa, Shyam

Sunder at Yale, and Greg Waymire at Emory led to my first book on social norms and the theory of the firm (Stevens 2019).

In summary, my academic training and life experiences have given me a unique perspective regarding the search for a moral foundation for capitalism. I have discussed elsewhere my early challenges getting my research published in top academic journals (Stevens 2019). Those challenges included the powerful influence of the Chicago School, but they also included the difficulty of finding a useful theoretical foundation for my research. After applying theoretical frameworks in psychology and moral philosophy, I discovered Adam Smith's moral theory based on social norms. Beginning with my experimental study in *TAR* examining the effectiveness of a code of ethics for controlling opportunistic self-interest (Davidson and Stevens 2013), I have also applied insights from Cristina Bicchieri's (2006) model of social norm activation.[12] Her formal model explains how situational cues and information can activate normative expectations leading to norm-based behavior, which I have found useful in my experimental research (Douthit and Stevens 2015; Abdel-Rahim and Stevens 2018; Abdel-Rahim, Hales, and Stevens 2022; and Abdel-Rahim, Liu, and Stevens 2022). I have recently published a review paper with my co-authors from FSU in the *Journal of Business Ethics* explaining the usefulness of social norm theory for empirical research in business ethics (Blay, Gooden, Mellon, and Stevens 2018). That paper introduced Smith's moral theory based on social norms and Bicchieri's complementary model of social norm activation to the business ethics literature. As such, it has been heavily cited.

At the time I am writing this final chapter, it has been over twelve years since the three-day conference at Koch Industries referenced in Chapter 1. Over those years, Charles Koch has continued to write about his unique success at one of the largest private companies in the world. He has followed up his book on Market-Based Management (Koch 2007) with a book about how creating value for others led to the success of his company (Koch 2015). His latest book, co-written with Brian Hooks, explains the lessons that he has learned over the years and his perspective given the latest challenges facing capitalist society (Koch and Hooks 2020, xvi). In particular, Koch criticizes the one-size-fits-all approach to the recent pandemic and calls "for all of us to move away from a top-down approach to solving the really big problems in society toward an

---

[12] See the discussion of the challenges getting my experimental paper with Bruce Davidson accepted in *TAR* in Chapter 1.

approach that focuses on empowering people from the bottom up to act on their unique gifts and contribute to the lives of others." He describes his continuing quest for scientific and social progress and those "principles proven throughout history to bring about progress, prosperity, and peace" (Koch 2020, 3). In essence, Koch has continued to follow his own search for a moral foundation for capitalism.

As reflected in the Business Roundtable's release of its new Statement on the Purpose of a Corporation in August 2019, corporations have moved on from the shareholder primacy view of the firm. Milton Friedman's (1970) article arguing that the social responsibility of business is to increase its profits reflected the inefficiency of big business and big government in America at the time and was consistent with the narrow view promoted by the Chicago School. Over fifty years later, that view has fallen out of favor. For example, the British Academy Future of the Corporation program was launched in 2017 to help support new research and engagement to uncover why purpose is crucial to business success and how policy and practice could support business to be more purposeful. Led by Colin Mayer at the University of Oxford's Saïd School of Business, that program has confirmed that it has only been over the last half century that corporate purpose has come to be equated solely with profits earned for shareholders. Its landmark reports in 2018, 2019, and 2021 set out a framework of principles, practices and policies that support a new way of defining the purpose of business: "to profitably solve the problems of people and planet, and not to profit from creating problems" (British Academy 2023). Given its straightjacket of self-interest and general lack of support for government involvement in the economy, modern-day supporters of capitalism often ignore the Chicago School altogether and return to earlier insights from John Maynard Keynes, Friedrich Hayek, or the Austrian School.

Nevertheless, a major theme of Friedman's 1970 article remains valid. "In a competitive environment, corporations distracted away from profit are doomed to fail. As the world gets more competitive, as more countries seek to be net suppliers to global consumer demand, perhaps Friedman's message is only more relevant" (Ramanna 2020, 33). Mayer (2013, 152–153) points out the opportunity and risks of having corporations promote other social responsibilities and commitments besides increasing profits for shareholders:

Societies can choose the companies that they wish to support and those they wish to restrain. If we can choose to abide by the restrictions imposed by the corporation then we can enhance our commitment to the welfare of others while avoiding the curtailment of liberties that other institutions impose. It is a distinction between voluntarily agreeing to restrict our freedom to achieve desired outcomes in the future and having our liberty involuntarily curtailed to no benefit to us now or in the future. It is an important distinction and it means that the corporation holds out greater potential than other institutions, such as government, for establishing the commitment that we are individually unable to demonstrate. However, for it to be accepted in this role, then it must expound and uphold values with which we feel much more comfortable than we have to date.

The recent emphasis on Environmental, Social, and Governance (ESG) in finance and accounting is a case in point. As a type of expanded financial disclosure, ESG reporting is a useful way for corporations to fulfill their commitments to the environment and other stakeholders of the firm. As a type of government control, however, ESG reporting can curtail fundamental liberties and push unproven and expensive forms of energy. The science behind global warming and the significance of our carbon footprint, as with all science, remains uncertain. Further, neoclassical economists have left us with little understanding of the "social" or "governance" aspects of ESG. ESG hurdles imposed upon developing economies by the International Monetary Fund to qualify for loans have decimated local farmers and critical industries, putting those economies at risk. A more balanced approach will be required in the future. Too often, the current emphasis on environmental activism to the detriment of economic growth and human thriving resembles the Malthusian Trap of the classical economists.

Polanyi's (1944/2001) theory of the double movement remains relevant for public policy today. Writing shortly after the crisis of capitalism in 2007–08, Colin Mayer (2013, 68) argued that we had reached a crisis point in the very institution that has helped deliver the great prosperity of capitalism – a collapse of trust in the corporation prompting extensive, intrusive regulation. "We are therefore entering a cycle of the pursuit of ever-narrower shareholder interests moderated by steadily more intrusive but ineffective regulation. It is unsustainable and we need to break away from it." History suggests that we cannot completely break away from Polanyi's double movement, but we can reduce its severity by promoting his middle way. That middle way will require a move away from the two polar positions that have evolved based on narrow self-interest and utilitarianism: the Chicago School on the political Right and Marxist socialism on the Left. As long as these two polar positions remain the only options for public policy, the distrust and divisions that have emerged in the wake of the pandemic will only deepen.

The latest intrusion of big government in response to the pandemic has been devastating for prosperity, security, and individual liberties. Given the current return to the painful stagflation of the 1970s, we are likely to see a strong countermovement to reduce the long arm of government and unleash the power of the market to restore economic growth. That countermovement, however, will need to be supported by a commitment to important values and norms that have been missing in the past. Among the critical values that have created and supported capitalism in the past are responsibility, transparency, and accountability (Soll 2014; Stevens 2019). As this final chapter has highlighted, we have placed far too little emphasis on these three pillars of capitalism and democracy. This book has focused on the distortion and eventual abandonment of Adam Smith's moral foundation for capitalism by classical and neoclassical economics. It has also described, however, how prominent neoclassical economists have recently rediscovered that moral foundation. As such, this book provides initial guidance on how neoclassical economists can join the search for a moral foundation for capitalism and help develop a New Chicago School of Economics.[13]

8.5 FINAL CONCLUSION: THE IMPORTANCE OF THE SEARCH

The call for papers intrigued me from the start. Having organized international research conferences myself, I was impressed by the clarity and urgency of the call. The *International Consortium for Values-based Governance* (ICVG) was hosting its first annual conference at the Centre for Global Business at Monash University, Australia. The organizers had decided to make the topic of their inaugural conference "governance in its institutional context" and had enlisted the co-sponsorship of a prestigious international academic journal, *Management Accounting Research* (*MAR*). In addition to co-sponsoring the conference, *MAR* was promoting the conference to gather papers for a special issue of the journal on the relation between corporate governance and management control. The call for papers made clear that the organizers of the conference saw the need to extend the tradition boundaries of corporate governance to include institutional context:

---

[13] The author plans a future book describing the work that has already been done to recover Adam Smith's moral foundation for capitalism and providing a roadmap for future research in support of a New Chicago School.

A rich literature on corporate governance has highlighted the need for, and some-times also the reasons for the failure of, a range of ostensibly well-designed gover-nance mechanisms in organizations. Whether for designing effective governance or for understanding plausible causes of concern, context always matters. Indeed, organizations that weathered quite well the financial crisis and economic reces-sion of the prior decade, as well as the current pandemic, weren't always known for having the best governance as conventionally defined. Conversely, other organizations that performed worse were sometimes believed to be paragons of good governance. Clearly, context matters and understanding how governance interacts with any of several relevant situational factors, including other organi-zational design features such as management control systems, is crucial.

The call for papers also made clear that the organizers of the confer-ence saw the need to incorporate intangible social mechanisms related to values, norms, and culture:

We see governance broadly to include board monitoring and other forms of mon-itoring external and internal to the organization, as well as managerial incentives and managerial compensation, which tend to connect with management control systems, including performance measurement and risk management systems. But governance can also include more intangible mechanisms stemming from shared values and norms, common purpose, and reputations, as well as organizational and national cultures. We are also interested in the relationship between gover-nance and strategy and/or management control in different contexts and in the ways in which governance systems interact with organizational values, beliefs, norms, and purpose to affect performance and behaviors inside the organization.

Given the direction of my research and my interest in revising the tra-ditional theory of the firm out of Chicago, I developed a working paper and submitted it to the conference. I titled the paper, "In Search of a New Chicago School: Revising the Theory Behind Corporate Governance and Management Control" (Stevens 2022). In my new working paper, I described recent attempts by neoclassical economists to revise the theory of the firm to increase its usefulness. Consistent with this book, I argued that these attempts have been hampered by a flawed view of Adam Smith and the economic sciences as well as a lingering commitment to Friedman's (1953) positive economic theory. I also discussed the impli-cations of these flaws for the theory of the firm, including its inability to address common management controls such as participative budget-ing and the balanced scorecard (Kaplan and Norton 1996) in addition to emerging controls related to Diversity, Equity, and Inclusion (DEI) and Environmental, Social, and Governance (ESG). Finally, I described recent efforts by neoclassical economists to revise the theory by relax-ing the assumption of narrow self-interest, incorporating insights from stakeholder theory, and returning economics to a social science dealing with individual and societal diversity. I concluded my paper by arguing that these revisions made the theory of the firm more useful to researchers, practitioners, and policymakers.

I received a rapid and positive response from the conference organizers. Although the conference was face-to-face, the organizers had also set up online capabilities so that speakers and participants could attend the conference online. Could I possibly fly out from Atlanta to present my paper in person? Christo Karuna at Monash University encouraged me to attend in person, stating that he thought my paper would generate much interest and discussion. Not knowing the final schedule or who else would be at the conference, I agreed. I would later learn that the main speakers would include the current editor of *MAR*, Wim Van der Stede, and a list of prominent researchers at top US business schools including Columbia, Harvard, and Wharton. The organizers of the conference put my paper presentation first on the schedule after opening remarks by Karuna, the Dean of the Business School, the Head of the Department of Accounting at Monash University, and the opening keynote speech by the *MAR* editor entitled, "Values Alignment: Management Control beyond Purpose Washing."

I still had the nagging fatigue and headache of jet lag when I was introduced and invited to the podium. My PowerPoint slides had been dutifully uploaded for my presentation. I began by thanking my hosts for organizing such an interesting conference. Glancing down I noticed a plaque on the podium with a statement which read, "I wish to acknowledge the people of the Kulin Nations, on whose land we are gathered today. I pay my respects to their Elders, past and present." Each speaker from Monash University had repeated this statement at the beginning of their remarks as part of the University's efforts to formally recognize the Aboriginal and Torres Strait Islander people and the ancient cultures of Australia. The speakers before me had clearly set the stage for my frank and open discussion of the current state of neoclassical economic theory and the need for a "New Chicago School." The two other speakers included in my opening session, one from the University of Delhi and one from the University of Adelaide, would present papers related to the economic theory behind corporate governance and management control. One would focus on issues of concern to small, family-owned businesses in India and the other would focus on the ability of stakeholder theory (Freeman 1984) to address "the tragedy of the commons" in large corporations.

It was only when I looked up that I fully realized the diverse make-up of the audience. I was speaking before a truly international group of scholars, business professionals, and policymakers. In addition to nearby universities in Australia and New Zealand, there were conference participants from China, India, Indonesia, and Malaysia as well as England, France, Germany, Italy, and the United States. There were also conference participants from countries in Africa and the Middle East. Although I couldn't see them, there were an equal number of attendees who were viewing the conference online. I would later receive emails and invitations to connect via social media from many of them. Each individual represented a different set of values based on their country culture, religion, and life experiences. I was very familiar with this international diversity at my own academic institution in Atlanta, Georgia. Yet the dominant economic theory used to research and teach corporate governance and management control didn't reflect that diversity.

I decided to use the occasion to call on neoclassical economists to join me in revising the powerful theory of the firm out of Chicago. After providing some background on the founding of the Chicago School of Economics and its victory over competing schools, I argued that it had lasted from the founding of the Mont Pélerin Society in 1947 to the severe market crash and near collapse of the global financial system in 2007–08. I described how one of the main architects of the theory of the firm, Michael Jensen, had recanted many of his views after the latest crisis of capitalism. I also described how the theory had proven increasingly incapable of explaining organizational behavior and controls. Finally, I described how the search for a New Chicago School had already begun and was yielding fruitful results. I concluded that we were in an exciting but uncertain state where the old theoretical paradigm had ceased to be useful but no new paradigm had risen to take its place. To provide some caution and comic relief, I reminded the audience that I had been given many opportunities to ruin my career over my lifetime – and had taken advantage of every one of them (in a private conversion in Atlanta, the *MAR* editor recalled that comment).

As often happens, I didn't get through all of my slides. I had planned to conclude by discussing the sudden collapse of FTX and the investor fraud perpetuated by its young founder and CEO, Sam Bankman-Fried (SBF). SBF had become a media darling for promoting business ethics and a unique moral theory called "effective altruism." That moral theory encouraged people to aspire to amass great wealth to give it away for progressive moral causes. In a text interview with Vox, however, SBF admitted that his preaching of business ethics was merely "a shibboleth" or *virtue signaling* meant to impress people and win over potential investors and politicians. In the same interview, he disparaged government regulation as only making things worse. Thus, it appears his emphasis on business ethics, DEI, and ESG was only a ruse to mislead investors, regulators, and the media. His influence peddling and investor fraud is exactly what Milton Friedman warned about in his famous article regarding the purpose of the corporation in 1970.

My presentation did generate much discussion at the conference, which continued throughout the next few days in many private conversations. I was able to raise the example of FTX and its young CEO in several other sessions dealing with corporate governance in the new post-pandemic environment. I asked the presenter from Harvard Business School what lessons we could learn from the recent investor fraud at FTX and whether it would make a good business case. He stated that it was a simple case of poor corporate governance and management controls. Thus, he felt that there was not enough tension there to make a good business case out of FTX for presentation to MBAs. I disagreed. I said that I felt the FTX case could be used to emphasize the continuing need for responsibility, transparency, and accountability in both business and government. The FTX case had exposed the unholy alliance that had developed between big tech, big government, and big media in America. The fact that SBF latched on to a unique moral theory to justify his actions also reflected the ongoing demand for a moral foundation for capitalism. The presenter finally agreed that it may be an interesting business case for MBAs, and told me that he looked forward to seeing someone develop it in the future.

It became clear that the organizers and international participants at the conference possessed a greater sense of urgency to expand the traditional theory of the firm than the presenters who had been invited from top business schools in America. One presenter, for example, expressed the opinion that the shareholder primacy view of the Chicago School was really not that different from the increasingly popular stakeholder view. In a private conversation, however, the young professor in my session from the University of Adelaide agreed that the two views were incompatible. She had spent the summer studying the latest developments in stakeholder theory at the Darden School of Business at the University of Virginia. She confirmed that Michael Jensen had largely abandoned the narrow shareholder primacy view of the firm and moved over to the broader stakeholder view. However, she also informed me that Jensen's advancing age and struggles with dementia were making it increasingly difficult for him to actively participate in scholarship or academic debate. After raising the curtain on the New Chicago School, therefore, he was being forced to leave the stage. I was saddened by the news of Jensen's untimely health issues and determined that I would work that much harder to continue his efforts to reform the theory that he had spent his life developing and promoting.

The straight-jacket of self-interest has been particularly devastating to my own discipline of accounting. In addition to the investor fraud at FTX, estimated to be in the tens of billions of dollars, 2022 has been a record year for accounting scandals. One Big Four firm was fined a record $100 million by the SEC for its role in a cheating scandal on the CPA exam (SEC 2022). The SEC Division of Enforcement brought in a record $6.44 billion in fines from auditing firms in 2022, up from $3.85 billion in fiscal year 2021 (Going Concern 2022). The new watchdog of the accounting profession created by SOX, the Public Company Accounting Oversight Board (PCAOB), imposed the largest civil money penalty in its history when it hit a former audit partner with a $150,000 fine and barred him from public accounting for life (PCAOB 2022). The PCAOB levied a record $11 million in fines against accounting firms in 2022 (Foley 2023). The PCAOB announced that it would use the record fines to fund a large expansion of a scholarship program intended to lure students to the accounting profession. If those students are trained under the moral foundation of narrow self-interest provided by the Chicago School, however, we can expect more accounting scandals in the future.

The continuing investor fraud and accounting scandals, as well as the growing polarization of capitalist society after the pandemic, have convinced me that the search for a moral foundation for capitalism may be the critical challenge of our age. There is a growing sense that something has gone seriously wrong with capitalist society, and the current environment calls out for change. But who will lead that change? Given the importance of economic theory in business and capital markets, neoclassical economists have an important role to play in extending the traditional theory of the firm. Given the importance of public policy in protecting capitalist society, however, government leaders also have an important role to play. Finally, given the important of religion in the birth and development of capitalism, communities of faith also have an important role to play. As the epigraph to this chapter suggests (Keynes 1936, 382), the influence of "defunct economists" and "academic scribblers of some years back" is underestimated by modern-day economists and policymakers. It is time to reexamine the powerful but narrow economic theory left by neoclassical economists of the past.

One of the conference participants who reached out to me after my presentation was a young administrator at Australian Catholic University. He emailed me to say that he had watched my presentation virtually from his office in Sydney and was interested in discussing some of the issues I had raised. As the chief of staff to the Deputy Vice Chancellor, he had met with leaders in Australia, the United States and the United Kingdom to discuss the rise of corporate social activism and the deep polarization it had created. He perceived a growing interest in a more measured and depolarizing approach than that unfolding in the United States. I responded that I would be happy to meet with him during my stay in Australia. We met in a posh Italian Restaurant in the outskirts of Sydney for a beer and some pizza. I told him that any economic system based on utilitarianism and narrow self-interest was doomed to create social division, including both the Chicago system and the Marxist system. I also told him that I thought the lack of a clear moral foundation for capitalism had contributed to the rising polarization. Finally, I told him about my upcoming book on the subject and my belief that faith communities had an important role to play in helping capitalist society overcome the current corruption and polarization. That private conversation in Sydney is among a growing number of conversations I have had that have given me great hope for the future of capitalism.

References

Abdel-Rahim, H., and D. Stevens. 2018. The effect of information system precision on honesty in managerial reporting: A re-examination of information asymmetry effects. *Accounting, Organizations and Society*, 64(1): 31–43.

Abdel-Rahim, H., J. Hales, and D. Stevens. 2022. How far will managers go to look like a good steward? An examination of preferences for trustworthiness and honesty in managerial reporting. *Contemporary Accounting Research*, 39(2): 1023–1053.

Abdel-Rahim, H., J. Liu, and D. Stevens. 2022. *What Participative Budgeting Experiments Reveal about Agency Theory: Responsibility, Transparency, and Accountability*. Georgia State University Working Paper.

Addison, W. 1901. *The Snell Exhibitions: From the University of Glasgow to Balliol College, Oxford*. Glasgow, UK: James MacLehose & Sons.

Ahmed, A., R. Schneible, and D. Stevens. 2003. An empirical analysis of the effects of online trading on stock price and trading volume reactions to earnings announcements. *Contemporary Accounting Research*, 20(3): 413–439.

American Associate of Collegiate Schools of Business. 1927. *Proceedings of the Ninth Annual Meeting*. Ninth Annual Meeting of the AACSB, Cambridge, MA, May 5, 6, and 7.

American Associate of Collegiate Schools of Business. 1933. *Proceedings of the Fifteenth Annual Meeting*. Fifteenth Annual Meeting of the AACSB, Lexington, KY, Summer.

American Associate of Collegiate Schools of Business. 1936. *Proceedings of the Eighteenth Annual Meeting*. Eighteenth Annual Meeting of the AACSB, Boston, MA, April 22, 23, 24, and 25.

Andrews, D. 2010. *Keynes and the British Humanist Tradition: The Moral Purpose of the Market*. London, UK: Routledge.

Andrews, D. 2017. Keynes and Christian socialism: Religion and the economic problem. *The European Journal of the History of Economic Thought*, 24(4): 958–977.

Arrow, K. 1951. *Social Choice and Individual Values*. New York, NY: Wiley & Sons.

Arrow, K. 1985. The economics of agency. In *Principals and Agents: The Structure of Business.* J. W. Pratt and R. J. Zeckhause (Eds.). Boston, MA: Harvard Business School Press, 37–51.

Baehr, P., and G. Wells. 2002. Introduction. In *The Protestant Ethic and the "Spirit" of Capitalism and Other Writings.* Edited, translated and with an introduction by Peter Baehr and Gordon C. Wells. New York, NY: Penguin Books.

Bamber, L., O. Barron, and D. Stevens. 2011. Trading volume around earnings announcements and other financial reports: Theory, research design, empirical evidence, and directions for future research. *Contemporary Accounting Research*, 28(2): 431–471.

Barron, O., O. Kim, S. Lim, and D. Stevens. 1998. Using analysts' forecasts to measure properties of analysts' information environment. *The Accounting Review*, 73(4): 421–433.

Baumol, W., R. Litan, and C. Schramm. 2007. *Good Capitalism, Bad Capitalism, and the Economics of Growth and Prosperity.* New Haven, CT: Yale University Press.

Bebchuk, L., and J. Fried. 2003. Executive compensation as an agency problem. *Journal of Economic Perspectives*, 17(3): 71–92.

Bebchuk, L., and J. Fried. 2004. *Pay without Performance: The Unfulfilled Promise of Executive Compensation.* Cambridge, MA: Harvard University Press.

Bebchuk, L., and J. Fried. 2005. Executive compensation at Fannie Mae: A case study of perverse incentives, nonperformance pay, and camouflage. *Journal of Corporate Law*, 30(4): 807–822.

Becker, G. 1976a. Altruism, egoism, and genetic fitness: Economics and sociobiology. *Journal of Economic Literature*, 14(3): 817–826.

Becker, G. 1976b. *The Economic Approach to Human Behavior.* Chicago, IL: University of Chicago Press.

Becker, G. 1993. Milton Friedman. In *The Legacy of Milton Friedman as a Teacher.* J. Daniel Hammond (Ed.). Cheltenham, UK: Edward Elgar.

Beets, S. D. 2015. BB&T, Atlas Shrugged, and the ethics of corporation influence on college curricula. *Journal of Academic Ethics*, 13(4): 311–344.

Berg, J., J. Dickhaut, and J. McCabe. 1995. Trust, reciprocity, and social history. *Games and Economic Behavior*, 10(1): 122–142.

Berle, A., and G. Means. 1932. *The Modern Corporation and Private Property.* New York, NY: Harcourt, Brace & World.

Bernanke, B. 2002. *On Milton Friedman's Ninetieth Birthday: Remarks before the Conference to Honor Milton Friedman.* Chicago, IL: University of Chicago Press. www.federalreserve.gov/BOARDDOCS/SPEECHES/2002/20021108/.

Bernstein, M. 2001. *A Perilous Progress: Economists and Public Purpose in Twentieth-Century America.* Princeton, NJ: Princeton University Press.

Berry, C. 2006. Smith and science. In *The Cambridge Companion to Adam Smith.* K. Haakonssen (Ed.). New York, NY: Cambridge University Press, 112–135.

Bicchieri, C. 2006. *The Grammar of Society: The Nature and Dynamics of Social Norms.* New York, NY: Cambridge University Press.

Black, F., and M. Scholes. 1973. The pricing of options and corporate liabilities. *Journal of Political Economy*, 81(3): 637–654.

Blay, A., E. Gooden, M. Mellon, and D. Stevens. 2018. The usefulness of social norm theory in empirical business ethics research: A review and suggestions for future research. *Journal of Business Ethics*, 152(1): 191–206.

Block, F. 2001. Introduction. In *The Great Transformation: The Political and Economic Origins of Our Time*. Foreword by Joseph E. Stiglitz with a New Introduction by Fred Block. Boston, MA: Beacon Press, xviii–xxxviii.

Bowie, N., and R. Freeman. 1992. Ethics and agency theory: An introduction. In *Ethics and Agency Theory: An Introduction*. N. E. Bowie and R. E. Freeman (Eds.). New York, NY: Oxford University Press, 3–22.

Boyd, R. 1976. Introduction to the transaction edition. In *The Ethics of Competition/Frank Hyneman Knight*, with a new introduction by Richard Boyd. Chicago, IL: University of Chicago Press, vii–xxxii.

British Academy. 2023. *Policy and Research: Future of the Corporation*. www.thebritishacademy.ac.uk/programmes/future-of-the-corporation/about/, Accessed January 10, 2023.

Buchanan, J. 1954. Social choice, democracy, and free markets. *Journal of Political Economy*, 62(2): 114–123.

Burk, K. 2007. *Old World, New World: Great Britain and American from the Beginning*. New York, NY: Atlantic Monthly Press.

Burns, J. 2009. *Goddess of the Market: Ayn Rand and the American Right*. Oxford, UK: Oxford University Press.

Business Roundtable. 2019. *Statement on the Purpose of a Corporation* (August 19, 2019). https://opportunity.businessroundtable.org/wp-content/uploads/2020/08/BRT-Statement-on-the-Purpose-of-a-Corporation-August-2020.pdf

Caldwell, B. 2007. Introduction. In *The Road to Serfdom: Text and Documents, The Definitive Edition*. Bruce Caldwell (Ed.). London: Routledge, 1–33.

Chamberlin, E. 1933. *The Theory of Monopolistic Competition*. Oxford, UK: Oxford University Press.

Chandler, A. Jr. 1977. *The Visible Hand: The Managerial Revolution in American Business*. Cambridge, MA: Belknap Press.

Cherrier, B. 2011. The lucky consistency of Milton Friedman's science and politics, 1933–1963. In *Building Chicago Economics: New Perspectives on the History of America's Most Powerful Economics Program*. Robert Van Horn, Philip Mirowski, and Thomas Stapleford (Eds.). Cambridge, UK: Cambridge University Press, 335–367.

Clark, G. 2007. *A Farewell to Alms: A Brief Economic History of the World*. Princeton, NJ: Princeton University Press.

Coase, R. 1937. The nature of the firm. *Economica*, 4(16): 386–405.

Coase, R. 1960. The problem of social cost. *Journal of Law and Economics*, 3(1): 1–44.

Coase, R. 1988. *The Firm, the Market, and the Law*. Chicago, IL: University of Chicago Press.

Coleman, T. 2019. Milton Friedman, Anna Schwartz, and *A Monetary History of the US*. Working Paper, Harris School of Public Policy, University of Chicago.

Davidson, B., and D. Stevens. 2013. Can a code of ethics improve manager behavior and investor confidence? An experimental study. *The Accounting Review*, 88(1): 51–74.

Dierksmeier, C. 2020. From Jensen to Jensen: Mechanistic management education or humanistic management learning? *Journal of Business Ethics*, 166(1): 73–87.

Dodd, J., and S. Stern-Gillet. 1995. The is/ought gap, the fact/value distinction and the naturalistic fallacy. *Dialogue: Canadian Philosophical Review/Revue Canadienne de philosophie*, 34(4): 727–746.

Douthit, J., and D. Stevens. 2015. The robustness of honesty concerns on budget proposals when the superior has rejection authority. *The Accounting Review*, 90(2): 467–493.

Ege, M., W. R. Knechel, P. Lamoreaux, and E. Maksymov. 2020. A multi-method analysis of the PCAOB's relationship with the audit profession. *Accounting, Organizations and Society*, 84(4): 101131.

Ekelund, R., and R. Hébert. 2014. *A History of Economic Theory & Method, Sixth Edition*. Long Grove, IL: Waveland Press.

Elster, J. 1989. Social norms and economic theory. *Journal of Economic Perspectives*, 3(4): 99–117.

Emerson, R. 2003. The contexts of the Scottish Enlightenment. In *The Cambridge Companion to the Scottish Enlightenment*. Alexander Broadie (Ed.). Cambridge, UK: Cambridge University Press, 9–30.

Emmett, R. 2010. Frank H. Knight. In *The Elgar Companion to the Chicago School of Economics*. Ross B. Emmett (Ed.). Northampton, MA: Edward Elgar, 280–286.

Emmons, W., and G. Sierra. 2004. Incentives askew? *Regulation*, 27(4): 22–28.

Erhard, W., M. Jensen, and S. Zaffron. 2008. *Integrity: A Positive Model that Incorporates the Normative Phenomena of Morality, Ethics and Legality*. Harvard Business School NOM Working Paper No. 06-11.

Fama, E. 1970. Efficient capital markets: A review of theory and empirical work. *Journal of Finance*, 25(2): 383–417.

Fannie Uncovered. September 23, 2004. *Wall Street Journal*, Review and Outlook. Retrieved from: www.wsj.com.

Feser, E. 2006. Introduction. In *The Cambridge Companion to Hayek*. Edward Feser (Ed.). Cambridge, UK: Cambridge University Press, 1–12.

Financial Crisis Inquiry Commission (FCIC). 2011. *The Financial Crisis Report: Final Report of the National Commission on the Causes of the Financial and Economic Crisis in the United States*. New York, NY: PublicAffairs.

Foley, S. January 1, 2023. Record fines on audit profession recycled to help new generation. *The Financial Times*. www.ft.com/content/3381482a-e6d1-4d6d-95b9-4fe8ef082189.

Force, P. 2003. *Self-Interest before Adam Smith: A Genealogy of Economic Science*. Cambridge, UK: Cambridge University Press.

Freeman, R. E. 1984. *Strategic Management: A Stakeholder Approach*. Boston, MA: Pitman Publishing.

Friedman, D., and S. Sunder. 1994. *Experimental Methods: A Primer for Economists*. Cambridge, UK: Cambridge University Press.

Friedman, M. 1953. *Essays in Positive Economics*. Chicago, IL: University of Chicago Press.

Friedman, M. 1962. *Capitalism and Freedom*. Chicago, IL: University of Chicago Press.

Friedman, M. September 13, 1970. The social responsibility of business is to increase its profits. *New York Times Magazine*.

Friedman, M., and R. Friedman. 1980. *Free to Choose: A Personal Statement*. New York, NY: Harcourt Brace Jovanovich.

Friedman, M., and R. Friedman. 1998. *Two Lucky People: Memoirs*. Chicago, IL: University of Chicago Press.

Friedman, M., and A. Schwartz. 1963. *A Monetary History of the United States, 1857–1960*. Princeton, NJ: Princeton University Press.

Fusaro, P., and R. Miller. 2002. *What Went Wrong at Enron: Everyone's Guide to the Largest Bankruptcy in U.S. History*. Hoboken, NJ: John Wiley & Sons.

Galbraith, J. K. 1952. *American Capitalism: The Concept of Countervailing Power*. Boston, MA: Houghton Mifflin Company.

Gillette, A., D. Stevens, S. Watts, and A. Williams. 1999. Price and volume reactions to public information releases: An experimental approach incorporating traders' subjective beliefs. *Contemporary Accounting Research*, 16(3): 437–479.

Gjerstad, S., and V. Smith. 2014. *Rethinking Housing Bubbles: The Role of Household and Bank Balance Sheets in Modeling Economic Cycles*. Cambridge, UK: Cambridge University Press.

Gode, D., and S. Sunder. 1993. Allocative efficiency of markets with zero intelligence traders: Markets as a partial substitute for individual rationality. *Journal of Political Economy*, 101(1): 119–137.

Going Concern. December 1, 2022. *SEC Enforcement Released Its Greatest Hits for FY 2022*. www.goingconcern.com/sec-enforcement-greatest-hits-2022.

Goldman, L. 2014. *The Life of R. H. Tawney: Socialism and History*. London, UK: Bloomsbury Publishing.

Gordon, R., and J. Howell. 1959. *Higher Education for Business*. New York, NY: Columbia University Press.

Graafland, J., and T. Wells. 2021. In Adam Smith's own words: The role of virtues in the relationship between free market economies and societal flourishing, a semantic network data-mining approach. *Journal of Business Ethics*, 172(1): 31–42.

Graham, B., and D. Dodd. 1934. *Security Analysis*. New York, NY: Whittlesey House (McGraw-Hill).

Graham, G. 2003. The nineteenth-century aftermath. In *The Cambridge Companion to the Scottish Enlightenment*. Alexander Broadie (Ed.). Cambridge, UK: Cambridge University Press, 338–350.

Griswold, C. Jr. 1999. *Adam Smith and the Virtues of Enlightenment*. New York, NY: Cambridge University Press.

Haakonssen, K., and D. Winch. 2006. The legacy of Adam Smith. In *The Cambridge Companion to Adam Smith*. Knud Haakonssen (Ed.). New York, NY: Cambridge University Press, 366–394.

Hammond, J. D. 2010. The development of post-war Chicago price theory. In *The Elgar Companion to the Chicago School of Economics*. Ross B. Emmett (Ed.). Northampton, MA: Edward Elgar, 7–24.

Hammond, J. D. 2011. Markets, politics, and democracy at Chicago: Taking economics seriously. In *Building Chicago Economics: New Perspectives on the*

History of America's Most Powerful Economics Program. Robert Van Horn, Philip Mirowski, and Thomas Stapleford (Eds.). Cambridge, UK: Cambridge University Press, 36–63.

Hands, D. 2009. Did Milton Friedman's positive methodology license the formalist revolution? In *The Methodology of Positive Economics: Reflections on the Milton Friedman Legacy*. Uskali Mäki (Ed.). Cambridge, UK: Cambridge University Press, 143–164.

Hayek, F. 1944 (4th edition in 2007). *The Road to Serfdom: Text and Documents – The Definitive Edition*. Bruce Caldwell (Ed.). London: Routledge.

Hirsch, F. E. 1946. The end of the Junker class. *Current History*, 10(54): 146–151.

Hirsch, F. 1977. *Social Limits to Growth*. Abington, Oxon: Routledge.

Hirschman, A. 1977 (1997). *The Passions and the Interests: Political Arguments for Capitalism before Its Triumph*, 20th Anniversary Edition. Princeton, NJ: Princeton University Press.

Hirschman, A. 1982. Rival interpretations of market society: Civilizing, destructive, or feeble? *Journal of Economic Literature*, 20(4): 1463–1484.

Holiday, R., and S. Hanselman. 2020. *Lives of the Stoics: The Art of Living from Zeno to Marcus Aurelius*. New York, NY: Portfolio/Penguin.

Holmstrom, B., and S. Kaplan. 2001. Corporate governance and merger activity in the United States: Making sense of the 1980s and 1990s. *Journal of Economic Perspectives*, 15(2): 121–144.

Hühn, M., and C. Dierksmeier. 2016. Will the real A. Smith please stand up! *Journal of Business Ethics*, 136(1): 119–132.

Hume, D. 1739 (Edition 1975). *A Treatise of Human Nature, Being an Attempt to Introduce the Experimental Method of Reasoning into Moral Subjects*. Oxford, UK: Clarendon Press.

Isaacson, W. 2003. *Benjamin Franklin: An American Life*. New York, NY: Simon & Schuster.

Jellinek, G. 1895. *Erklärung der Menschen und Bürgerrechte*. Translated by Max Farrand as *The Declaration of the Rights of Man and of Citizens: A Contribution to Modern Constitutional History*. New York, NY: Henry Holt, 1901.

Jensen, M. 1978. Some anomalous evidence regarding market efficiency. *Journal of Financial Economics*, 6(2/3): 95–101.

Jensen, M. 1983. Organization theory and methodology. *The Accounting Review*, 58(2): 319–339.

Jensen, M. 2000. *A Theory of the Firm: Governance, Residual Claims, and Organizational Forms*. Cambridge, MA: Harvard University Press.

Jensen, M. 2001. Corporate budgeting is broken – Let's fix it. *Harvard Business Review* (November): 94–101.

Jensen, M. 2002. Value maximization, stakeholder theory, and the corporate objective function. *Business Ethics Quarterly*, 12(2): 235–256.

Jensen, M. 2008. Foreword. In *Moral Markets: The Critical Role of Values in the Economy*. Paul J. Zak (Ed.). Princeton, NJ: Princeton University Press, ix–x.

Jensen, M., and W. Erhard. 2011. A "Value-Free" approach to values (PDF file of PowerPoint slides). *SSRN Electronic Journal*. https://doi.org/10.2139/ssrn.1640302.

Jensen, M., and K. Murphy. 1990. Performance pay and top management incentives. *Journal of Political Economy*, 98(2): 225–263.

Jensen, M., and W. Meckling. 1976. Theory of the firm: Managerial behavior, agency costs and ownership structure. *Journal of Financial Economics*, 3(4): 305–360.

Johnson, H., and R. Kaplan. 1987. *Relevance Lost: The Rise and Fall of Management Accounting*. Boston, MA: Harvard Business School Press.

Kaplan, R., and D. Norton. 1996. *The Balanced Scorecard: Translating Strategy into Action*. Boston, MA: Harvard Business School Press.

Kaufman, B. 2010. Chicago and the development of twentieth-century labor economics. In *The Elgar Companion to the Chicago School of Economics*. Ross B. Emmett (Ed.). Northampton, MA: Edward Elgar, 128–151.

Keynes, J. M. 1919. *The Economic Consequences of the Peace*. London, UK: Macmillan & Co.

Keynes, J. M. 1926. *The End of Laissez-faire*. London, UK: The Hogarth Press.

Keynes, J. M. 1930a. Economic possibilities for our grandchildren. In *Essays in Persuasion*. New York, NY: Harcourt, Brace and Co. (1932), 358–373.

Keynes, J. M. 1930b. *A Treatise on Money*. New York, NY: Harcourt, Brace and Co.

Keynes, J. M. 1936. *The General Theory of Employment, Interest and Money*. London, UK: Macmillan.

Keynes, J. M. 1938. My early beliefs. In *The Collected Writings of John Maynard Keynes*. London, UK: Macmillan & Co (1938), 433–451.

Keynes, J. M. 2015. *The Essential Keynes*. Edited and with an Introduction by Robert Skidelsky. London, UK: Penguin Books.

Khurana, R. 2007. *From Higher Aims to Hired Hands: The Social Transformation of American Business Schools and the Unfulfilled Promise of Management as a Profession*. Princeton, NJ: Princeton University Press.

Knight, F. 1935 (1976 edition). *The Ethics of Competition/Frank Hyneman Knight*. With a new introduction by Richard Boyd (Ed.). Chicago, IL: University of Chicago Press.

Koch, C. 2007. *The Science of Success: How Market-Based Management Built the World's Largest Private Company*. Hoboken, NJ: John Wiley & Sons.

Koch, C. 2015. *Good Profit: How Creating Value for Others Built One of the World's Most Successful Companies*. New York, NY: Crown Business.

Koch, C., and B. Hooks. 2020. *Believe in People: Bottom-Up Solutions for a Top-Down World*. New York, NY: St. Martin's Press.

Kuhn, T. 1962 (3rd Edition 1996). *The Structure of Scientific Revolutions*. Chicago, IL: University of Chicago Press.

Lambert, R. 2001. Contracting theory and accounting. *Journal of Accounting and Economics*, 32(1–3): 3–87.

Leonard, C. 2019. *Kochland: The Secret History of Koch Industries and Corporate Power in America*. New York, NY: Simon & Schuster.

Lester, R. 1946. Shortcomings of marginal analysis for wage-employment problems. *American Economic Review*, 36(1): 63–82.

Lowenstein, R. 2000. *When Genius Failed: The Rise and Fall of Long-Term Capital Management*. New York, NY: Random House.

Löwith, K. 1993. *Max Weber and Karl Marx*. With a new preface by Bryan S. Turner. New York, NY: Routledge.

Machlup, F. 1946. Marginal analysis and empirical research. *American Economic Review*, 36(4): 519–554.

Maddison, A. 1995. *Explaining the Economic Performance of Nations*. Cheltenham, UK: Edward Elgar Publishing.

Mäki, U. 2009. Reading the methodological essay in twentieth-century economics: Map of multiple perspectives. In *The Methodology of Positive Economics: Reflections on the Milton Friedman Legacy*. Uskali Mäki (Ed.). Cambridge, UK: Cambridge University Press, 47–67.

Mallaby, S. 2010. *More Money than God: Hedge Funds and the Making of a New Elite*. New York, NY: Penguin Press.

Mandeville, B. 1732 (1954 edited by F. B. Kaye). *The Fable of the Bees*. Oxford, UK: Clarendon Press.

Marchand, R. 1998. *Creating the Corporate Soul: The Rise of Public Relations and Corporate Imagery in American Big Business*. Berkeley and Los Angeles: University of California Press.

Marshall, A. 1890 (8th edition 1920). *Principles of Economics*. London, UK: Macmillan.

Marx, K. 1867 (1990 translation by Ben Fowkes). *Capital, Volume I*. London, UK: Penguin Books.

Maskin, E. 2019. The economics of Kenneth J. Arrow: A selective review. *Annual Review of Economics*, 11: 1–26.

Mayer, C. 2013. *Firm Commitment: Why the Corporation Is Failing Us and How to Restore Trust in It*. Oxford, UK: Oxford University Press.

McCabe, K., S. Rassenti, and V. Smith. 1996. Game theory and reciprocity in some extensive form experimental games. *Proceedings of the National Academy of Sciences*, 93: 13421–13428.

McCloskey, D. 2006. *The Bourgeois Virtues: Ethics for an Age of Commerce*. Chicago, IL: University of Chicago Press.

McCosh, J. 1875 (1990 reprint). *The Scottish Philosophy, Biographical, Expository, Critical, from Hutcheson to Hamilton*. Bristol, UK: Thoemmes.

McDonald, L., and P. Robinson. 2009. *A Colossal Failure of Common Sense: The Inside Story of the Collapse of Lehman Brothers*. New York, NY: Crown Business.

McKitterick, R. 2008. *Charlemagne: The Formation of a European Identity*. Cambridge, UK: Cambridge University Press.

McLean, B., and P. Elkind. 2003. *The Smartest Guys in the Room: The Amazing Rise and Scandalous Fall of Enron*. New York, NY: The Penguin Group.

Medema, S. 2011. Chicago price theory and Chicago law and economics: A tale of two transitions. In *Building Chicago Economics: New Perspectives on the History of America's Most Powerful Economics Program*. Robert Van Horn, Philip Mirowski, and Thomas Stapleford (Eds.). Cambridge, UK: Cambridge University Press, 151–179.

Miles, E. 2016. *The Past, Present, and Future of the Business School*. Basingstoke, UK: Palgrave Macmillan.

Milgate, M., and S. Stimson. 2009. *After Adam Smith: A Century of Transformation in Politics and Political Economy*. Princeton and Oxford: Princeton University Press.

Milgrom, P., and N. Stokey. 1982. Information, trade and common knowledge. *Journal of Economic Theory*, 26(1): 17–27.

Mill, J. S. 1836 (collected works edition 1967). On the definition of political economy. In *Collected Works of John Stuart Mill: Essays on Economics and Society*. J. M. Robson (Ed.). Toronto, ON: University of Toronto Press, 309–339.

Mirowski, P. 2011. On the origins (at Chicago) of some species of neoliberal evolutionary economics. In *Building Chicago Economics: New Perspectives on the History of America's Most Powerful Economics Program*. Robert Van Horn, Philip Mirowski, and Thomas Stapleford (Eds.). Cambridge, UK: Cambridge University Press, 237–275.

Mitch, D. 2010. Chicago and economic history. In *The Elgar Companion to the Chicago School of Economics*. Ross B. Emmett (Ed.). Northampton, MA: Edward Elgar, 114–127.

Mitnick, B. 1974. *The theory of agency: The concept of fiduciary rationality and some consequences*. Unpublished PhD dissertation, Department of Political Science, University of Pennsylvania. University Microfilms No. 74-22,881.

Modigliani, F., and M. Miller. 1958. The costs of capital, corporate finance, and the theory of investment. *American Economic Review*, 48(3): 261–297.

Montes, L. 2003. *Das Adam Smith Problem*: Its origins, the stages of the current debate, and one implication for our understanding of sympathy. *Journal of the History of Economic Thought*, 25(1): 63–90.

Moore, G. E. 1903. *Principia Ethica*. Cambridge, UK: Cambridge University Press.

Moore, T. 1986. Introduction. In *The Essence of Stigler*. Kurt Leube and Thomas Moore (Eds.). Stanford, CA: Hoover Institution Press, xxi–xxviii.

Morgan, M. 2006. Economic man as model man: Ideal types, idealization and caricatures. *Journal of the History of Economic Thought*, 28(1): 1–27.

Mulligan, T. 1986. A critique of Milton Friedman's essay 'The Social Responsibility of Business Is to Increase Its Profits'. *Journal of Business Ethics*, 5(4): 265–269.

Nik-Khah, E. 2011. George Stigler, the Graduate School of Business, and the Pillars of the Chicago School. In *Building Chicago Economics: New Perspectives on the History of America's Most Powerful Economics Program*. Robert Van Horn, Philip Mirowski, and Thomas Stapleford (Eds.). Cambridge, UK: Cambridge University Press, 116–147.

Noreen, E. 1988. The economics of ethics: A new perspective on agency theory. *Accounting, Organizations and Society*, 13(4): 359–369.

North, D. 1991. Institutions. *Journal of Economic Perspectives*, 5(1): 97–112.

Peikoff, L. 1991. *Objectivism: The Philosophy of Ayn Rand*. New York, NY: Penguin.

Phillipson, N. 2010. *Adam Smith: An Enlightened Life*. New Haven, CT and London: Yale University Press.

Pierson, F. 1959. *The Education of American Businessmen: A Study of University-College Programs in Business Administration*. New York, NY: McGraw-Hill.

Pigou, A. C. 1920. *The Economics of Welfare*. London, UK: Macmillan and Co.

Pincus, S. 2009. *1688: The First Modern Revolution*. New Haven, CT: Yale University Press.

Polanyi, K. 1944 (2001 edition). *The Great Transformation: The Political and Economic Origins of Our Time*. Foreword by Joseph E. Stiglitz with a New Introduction by Fred Block. Boston, MA: Beacon Press.

Polanyi, K. 1947 (2014 English edition). Economics and the freedom to shape our social destiny. In *Karl Polanyi for a New West: Essays, 1919–1958*. Giorgio Resta and Mariavittoria Catanzariti (Eds.). Cambridge, UK: Polity Press.

Polanyi-Levitt, K., and M. Mendell. 1987. Karl Polanyi: His life and times. *Studies in Political Economy*, 22(1): 7–39.

Popper, K. 1934. *The Logic of Scientific Discovery*. New York, NY: Routledge Classics, 2002.

Posner, E. 2000. *Law and Social Norms*. Cambridge, MA: Harvard University Press.

Posner, R. 2009. *A Failure of Capitalism: The Crisis of '08 and the Descent into Depression*. Cambridge, MA: Harvard University Press.

Pratt, J., and R. Zeckhauser. 1985. Principals and agents: An overview. In *Principals and Agents: The Structure of Business*. J. W. Pratt and R. J. Zeckhauser (Eds.). Cambridge, MA: Harvard University Press, 1–35.

Public Company Accounting Oversight Board. October 18, 2022. *PCAOB Imposes Highest Individual Penalty Ever and Bars Audit Partner for Misleading Inspector and Investigators*. https://pcaobus.org/news-events/news-releases/news-release-detail/pcaob-imposes-highest-individual-penalty-ever-and-bars-audit-partner-for-misleading-inspectors-and-investigators.

Ramanna, K. 2020. Friedman at 50: Is it still the social responsibility of business to increase profits? *California Management Review*, 62(3): 28–41.

Rand, A. 1957. *Atlas Shrugged, 50th Anniversary Edition*. New York, NY: Signet.

Rand, A. 1964. The objectivist ethics. In *The Virtue of Selfishness: A New Concept of Egoism*. Ayn Rand (Ed.). New York, NY: Signet.

Raphael, D., and A. Macfie. 1982. Introduction. In *The Theory of Moral Sentiments*, 6th edition. D. D. Raphael and A. L. Macfie (Eds.). Indianapolis, IN: Liberty Fund, Inc., 1–52.

Reeder, J. 1997. Introduction. In *On Moral Sentiments: Contemporary Responses to Adam Smith*. J. Reeder (Ed.). Bristol, UK: Thoemmes Press, vii–xxi.

Reiss, S. 2015. *The 16 Strivings for God: The New Psychology of Religious Experiences*. Macon, GA: Mercer University Press.

Revell, J. 2003. Mo' money, fewer problems: Is it a good idea to get rid of the $1 million CEO pay ceiling? *Fortune*, March 31: 34.

Robinson, J. 1933. *The Economics of Imperfect Competition*. New York, NY: St. Martin's Press.

Robinson, J. 1956. *The Accumulation of Capital*. London, UK: Palgrave Macmillan.

Rogan, T. 2017. *The Moral Economists: R. H. Tawney, Karl Polanyi, E. P. Thomson, and the Critique of Capitalism*. Princeton, NJ: Princeton University Press.

Roscher, W. 1854 (1877 English translation). *Principles of Political Economy*, Vol. 1, J. J. Lalor (Trans.). New York, NY: Henry Holt.

Ross, S. 1973. The economic theory of agency: The principal's problem. *American Economic Review*, 63(2): 134–139.

Rothschild, E., and A. Sen. 2006. Adam Smith's economics. In *The Cambridge Companion to Adam Smith*. Knud Haakonssen (Ed.). Cambridge, UK: Cambridge University Press, 319–365.

Rutherford, M. 2010. Chicago economics and institutionalism. In *The Elgar Companion to the Chicago School of Economics*. Ross B. Emmett (Ed.). Northampton, MA: Edward Elgar, 25–39.

Sass, S. 1982. *The Pragmatic Imagination: A History of the Wharton School, 1881–1981*. Philadelphia, PA: University of Pennsylvania Press.

Scaff, L. 1989. *Fleeing the Iron Cage: Culture, Politics, and Modernity in the Thought of Max Weber*. Berkeley, CA: University of California Press.

Scaff, L. 2011. *Max Weber in America*. Princeton, NJ: Princeton University Press.

Schindler, J. 2015. *Fall of the Double Eagle: The Battle for Galicia and the Demise of Austria-Hungary*. Lincoln, NE: Potomac Books.

Schmotter, J. 1998. An interview with Robert H. Frank. *Selections*, 15(1): 15.

Schumpeter, J. 1942 (3rd edition 1950). *Capitalism, Socialism, and Democracy*. New York, NY: Harper & Bothers.

Scitovsky, T. 1976 (2nd edition 1992). *The Joyless Economy: The Psychology of Human Satisfaction*. Oxford, UK: Oxford University Press.

Scott, R. 1995. *Institutions and Organizations*. Thousand Oaks, CA: SAGE Publications.

Security and Exchange Commission. June 28, 2022. *Ernst & Young to Pay $100 Million Penalty for Employees Cheating on CPA Ethics Exams and Misleading Investigation* [Press release]. www.sec.gov/news/press-release/2022-114.

Sen, A. 1970 (Expanded edition 2017). *Collective Choice and Social Welfare*. London, UK: Penguin Random House.

Sen, A. 1987. *On Ethics and Economics*. Malden, MA: Blackwell Publishing.

Sen, A. 2022 (First American Edition). *Home in the World: A Memoir*. New York, NY: Liveright Publishing Corporation.

Sen, A., A. Deaton, and T. Besley. 2020. Economics with a moral compass? Welfare economics: Past, present, and future. *Annual Review of Economics*, 12: 1–21.

Sen, S. 2019. *Ganges: The Many Pasts of an Indian River*. New Haven, CT: Yale University Press.

Sidgwick, H. 1874 (1907 reprint). *The Methods of Ethics*. London, UK: Macmillan and Co.

Siegel, S., and L. Fouraker. 1960. *Bargaining and Group Decision Making*. New York, NY: McGraw-Hill.

Simons, R. 2019. *Self-Interest, The Economist's Straightjacket*. Harvard Business School Working Paper 16-045.

Skidelsky, R. 1986. *John Maynard Keynes: Hopes Betrayed 1883–1920*. New York, NY: Elizabeth Sifton Books, Viking.

Skidelsky, R. 1994. *John Maynard Keynes: The Economist as Savior 1920–1937*. New York, NY: Allen Lane. The Penguin Press.

Skidelsky, R. 2001. *John Maynard Keynes: Fighting for Freedom 1937–1946*. New York, NY: Allen Lane. The Penguin Press.

Skinner, A. 2003. Economic theory. In *The Cambridge Companion to the Scottish Enlightenment*. Alexander Broadie (Ed.). Cambridge, UK: Cambridge University Press, 178–204.

Smith, A. 1759 (6th edition 1790). *The Theory of Moral Sentiments*, the Glasgow Edition. D. D. Raphael and A. L. Macfie (Eds.). Indianapolis, IN: Liberty Fund, Inc., 1981.

Smith, A. 1776 (6th edition 1791). *An Inquiry into the Nature and Causes of the Wealth of Nations*, the Glasgow Edition. R. H. Cambell and A. S. Skinner (Eds.). Indianapolis, IN: Liberty Fund, Inc., 1981.

Smith, T. 2006. *Ayn Rand's Normative Ethics: The Virtuous Egoist*. New York, NY: Cambridge University Press.

Smith, V. 1976. Experimental economics: Induced value theory. *American Economic Review*, 66(2): 274–279.

Smith, V. 2003. Constructivist and ecological rationality in economics. *Les Prix Nobel*, Stockholm, SE: Nobel Foundation. Reprinted in *American Economic Review*, 93(3): 465–508.

Smith, V. 2008. *Rationality in Economics: Constructivist and Ecological Forms*. Cambridge, UK: Cambridge University Press.

Smith, V. 2018a. *A Life of Experimental Economics, Vol I: Forty Years of Discovery*. Cham, Switzerland: Palgrave Macmillan.

Smith, V. 2018b. *A Life of Experimental Economics, Vol II: The Next Fifty Years*. Cham, Switzerland: Palgrave Macmillan.

Smith, V., G. Suchanek, and A. Williams. 1988. Bubbles, crashes, and endogenous expectations in experimental spot asset markets. *Econometrica*, 56(5): 1119–1151.

Smith, V., and B. Wilson. 2019. *Humanomics: Moral Sentiments and the Wealth of Nations for the Twenty-First Century*. Cambridge, UK: Cambridge University Press.

Soll, J. 2014. *The Reckoning: Financial Accountability and the Rise and Fall of Nations*. New York, NY: Basic Books.

Soros, G. 1995. *Soros on Soros: Staying Ahead of the Curve*. New York, NY: John Wiley & Sons.

Soros, G. 2009. *The Crash of 2008 and What It Means: The New Paradigm for Financial Markets*. New York, NY: PublicAffairs.

Stevens, D. 2002. The effects of reputation and ethics on budgetary slack. *Journal of Management Accounting Research*, 14: 153–171.

Stevens, D. 2019. *Social Norms and the Theory of the Firm: A Foundational Approach*. Cambridge, UK: Cambridge University Press.

Stevens, D. 2022. *In Search of a New Chicago School: Revising the Theory behind Corporate Governance and Management Control*. Georgia State University Working Paper.

Stevens, D., and A. Thevaranjan. 2010. A moral solution to the moral hazard problem. *Accounting, Organizations and Society*, 35(1): 125–139.

Stigler, G. 1942. *The Theory of Competitive Price*. New York, NY: Macmillan.

Stigler, G. 1946. *The Theory of Price*. New York, NY: Macmillan.

Stigler, G. 1965. *Essays in the History of Economics*. Chicago, IL: University of Chicago Press.

Stigler, G. 1971a. Smith's travels on the ship of the state. *History of Political Economy*, 3(2): 265–277.

Stigler, G. 1971b. The theory of economic regulation. *The Bell Journal of Economics and Management Science*, 2(1): 3–21.

Stigler, G. 1988. *Memoirs of an Unregulated Economist*. Chicago, IL: University of Chicago Press.

Tawney, R. H. 1926 (Edition 2017). *Religion and the Rise of Capitalism: With a New Introduction by Adam B. Seligman*. New York, NY: Routledge.

Teichgraeber, R. III. 1981. Rethinking das Adam Smith Problem. *Journal of British Studies*, 20(2): 106–123.

Teixeira, P. 2010. Gary S. Becker. In *The Elgar Companion to the Chicago School of Economics*. Ross B. Emmett (Ed.). Northampton, MA: Edward Elgar, 253–258.

Thaler, R. 1992. *The Winners Curse: Paradoxes and Anomalies of Economic Life*. New York, NY: The Free Press.

Thomas, C. 2002. The rise and fall of Enron: When a company looks too good to be true, it usually is. *Journal of Accountancy*, 193(4): 41–48.

Townsend, J. 1786. *A Dissertation on the Poor Laws: By a Well-Wisher to Mankind*. London, UK: C. Dilly.

Turco, L. 2003. Moral sense and the foundations of morals. In *The Cambridge Companion to the Scottish Enlightenment*. Alexander Broadie (Ed.). Cambridge, UK: Cambridge University Press, 136–156.

Van Horn, R. 2010. Aaron Director. In *The Elgar Companion to the Chicago School of Economics*. Ross B. Emmett (Ed.). Northampton, MA: Edward Elgar, 265–269.

Van Horn, R., and P. Mirowski. 2015. The rise of the Chicago School of Economics and the Birth of Neoliberalism. In *The Road from Mont Pélerin: The Making of the Neoliberal Thought Collective*. Philip Mirowski and Dieter Plehwe (Eds.). Cambridge, MA: Harvard University Press, 139–178.

Vromen, J. 2011. Allusions to evolution. In *Building Chicago Economics: New Perspectives on the History of America's Most Powerful Economics Program*. Robert Van Horn, Philip Mirowski, and Thomas Stapleford (Eds.). Cambridge, UK: Cambridge University Press, 208–236.

Watts, R., and J. Zimmerman. 1986. *Positive Accounting Theory*. Englewood Cliffs, NJ: Prentice Hall, Inc.

Weber, M. 1975. *Max Weber: A Biography*. H. Zohn (Trans.). New York, NY: Wiley.

Weber, M. 1905 (2002 English translation). *The Protestant Ethic and the "Spirit" of Capitalism and Other Writings*. Edited, translated, and with an introduction by Peter Baehr and Gordon C. Wells. New York, NY: Penguin Books.

Wightman, W. 1982. Introduction. In *Essays on Philosophical Subjects*, the Glasgow Edition. W. P. D. Wightman (Ed.). Indianapolis, IN: Liberty Fund, Inc., 5–27.

Williamson, O. 1975. *Markets and Hierarchies: Analysis and Antitrust Implications: A Study in the Economics of Internal Organization*. New York, NY: The Free Press.

Williamson, O. 1985. *The Economic Institutions of Capitalism*. New York, NY: The Free Press.

Williamson, O. 2009. Friedman (1953) and the theory of the firm. In *The Methodology of Positive Economics: Reflections on the Milton Friedman Legacy.* Uskali Maki (Ed.). Cambridge, UK: Cambridge University Press, 241–256.

Wilson, E. 1975. *Sociobiology: The New Synthesis.* Cambridge, MA: The Belknap Press of Harvard University Press.

Young, M. 1985. Participative budgeting: The effects of risk-aversion and asymmetric information on budgetary slack. *Journal of Accounting Research*, 23(2): 829–842.

Index